'The book illuminates, with commendable scope political and philosophical dimensions of Natu stop course companion to the subject.'
— **Chris Megson**, *Royal Ho*

'Pickering and Thompson have crafted a rich and supremely organized text. Students will be both engaged and challenged by this creative and critical approach to the study of theatre history.'
— **Margaret Araneo-Reddy**, *Brooklyn College, City University of New York, USA*

Naturalism in Theatre provides a comprehensive introduction to one of the most enduring and integral movements in theatre history. Accessibly written and assuming no prior knowledge, this complete resource explores the theory and practice of Naturalist theatre. Beginning with the meaning of Naturalism, it goes on to examine the major Naturalist plays, players and playhouses, considering the influences of visual art, music, philosophy and psychology throughout. Setting the movement within its nineteenth-century European context, the text ultimately asks how Naturalism has come to be such a dominant mode of contemporary performance.

Kenneth Pickering is founder/director of the Institute for Arts in Therapy and Education in London and is Honorary Professor of Drama and Theatre at the University of Kent, UK.

Jayne Thompson is Lecturer in Drama and Theatre Studies at the University of Kent, UK.

Also by Kenneth Pickering

KEY CONCEPTS IN DRAMA AND PERFORMANCE
STUDYING MODERN DRAMA
THEATRE STUDIES (with M. Woolgar)

Kenneth Pickering and Jayne Thompson

NATURALISM IN THEATRE

Its Development and Legacy

palgrave
macmillan

First published 2013 by
PALGRAVE MACMILLAN

Palgrave Macmillan in the UK is an imprint of Macmillan Publishers Limited,
registered in England, company number 785998, of Houndmills, Basingstoke,
Hampshire RG21 6XS.

Palgrave Macmillan in the US is a division of St Martin's Press LLC,
175 Fifth Avenue, New York, NY 10010.

Palgrave Macmillan is the global academic imprint of the above companies
and has companies and representatives throughout the world.

Palgrave® and Macmillan® are registered trademarks in the United States,
the United Kingdom, Europe and other countries

ISBN: 978–0–230–36107–2   hardback
ISBN: 978–0–230–36108–9   paperback

This book is printed on paper suitable for recycling and made from fully
managed and sustained forest sources. Logging, pulping and manufacturing
processes are expected to conform to the environmental regulations of the
country of origin.

A catalogue record for this book is available from the British Library.

A catalog record for this book is available from the Library of Congress.

10 9 8 7 6 5 4 3 2 1
22 21 20 19 18 17 16 15 14 13

Printed and bound in Great Britain by
CPI Antony Rowe, Chippenham and Eastbourne

Contents

List of Illustrations

List of Boxes

Acknowledgements

The authors wish to express their sincere thanks to the following: The University of Miami Press for permission to include extracts from Antoine's *Memories of the Théâtre Libre*; David Griffiths for introducing us to Richard Holmes as a biographer; Irene Pickering for sharing her knowledge of Mahler; Jill Davis for her patience and support; Patrice Pavis, Cheryl Yates, Park Yung Hee, Hedwig Müller and Ruth O'Dowd for their help with the illustrations; Charlotte Emmett for her work on the MS; Jane Gallagher, Special Collections, Templeman Library, University of Kent; colleagues in the Drama Department at the University of Kent for their encouragement; and our editor at Palgrave, Jenni Burnell, for her constant support and guidance.

Timeline for Naturalism

	EVENTS	THEATRE
1850	Invention of wet-collodion photographic plate to enable portrait photography.	
1852	Felix Nadar begins his series of portrait photos in Paris. Zola one of his subjects.	
1858	Launch of revolutionary steamship *Great Eastern*.	
1859	Darwin's *Origin of Species*. John Stuart Mill's *On Liberty*.	
1861–5	American Civil War.	
1862	William Powell Frith's painting *Paddington Station* indicates massive expansion of rail network across Europe	
1863	Manet's painting *Déjeuner sur L'herbe* exhibited in Paris.	
1865		First Variety theatre opened in New York.
1869	John Stuart Mill's *The Subjection of Women*.	
1870–1	Franco-Prussian War.	
1871	German unification complete. The Paris Commune.	Verdi's *Aida*. Irving opens *The Bells*.
1872		Strindberg's first play *Master Olaf*.
1873		Zola's dramatization of *Thérèse Raquin*.

1874	First Impressionist Exhibition in Paris.	
1876	Bell patents the telephone.	Wagner opens Bayreuth Festival with *The Rheingold*.
1878		Irving is manager at the Lyceum Theatre.
1879		Ibsen's *A Doll's House*, Copenhagen.
1880	Edison develops the light .bulb	First Ibsen play seen in England: *The Pillars of Society*.
1881		Zola's essay *Naturalism in the Theatre*. Savoy theatre opens with electric lighting for Gilbert and Sullivan's operettas. Ibsen's *Ghosts* rejected for production.
1882		Ibsen's *An Enemy of the People*. *Ghosts* opens in Chicago.
1884	Invention of Turbine.	Ibsen's *The Wild Duck*.
1886	Daimler produces first motor car.	Ibsen's *Rosmersholm*.
1887		Antoine's Théâtre Libre established in Paris with Zola's *Jacques Damour*. Strindberg's *The Father*.
1888	Kodak portable camera produced.	Strindberg's *Miss Julie* with its *Preface*. Antoine's production of Tolstoy's *The Power of Darkness*.
1889	Eifel Tower built. Rodin's 'The Thinker'	'Freie Bühne' established by Brahm in Berlin. Opens with *Ghosts*. Hauptmann's *Before Sunrise* creates furore at Freie Bühne. Antoine's production of *Ghosts*. Strindberg establishes an experimental Theatre in Denmark (a failure).

	EVENTS	THEATRE
1890		Ibsen's *Hedda Gabler* in Munich seen by Annie Horniman.
1891		Grein's 'Independent Theatre' established in London. Opens with *Ghosts*. Shaw's *The Quintessence of Ibsenism*. Hamlin Garland's proposal for an Independent theatre in the US. Herne's *Margaret Fleming*.
1892		Ibsen's *The MasterBuilder*. Shaw's *Widowers' Houses*. Antoine produces Brieux's first play. Hauptmann's *The Weavers*.
1895	Marconi's first wireless message.	Tchaikovsky's *Swan Lake*. Irving knighted.
1896		First production of Chekhov's *The Sea Gull*.
1897		Herne's article 'Art for Truth's Sake'.
1898	Spanish Civil War.	Moscow Art Theatre established with Stanislavsky's iconic production of *The Sea Gull*. Strindberg's *To Damascus* and 35 plays in the following 11 years.
1899	Boer War begins and is recorded on movie camera.	Chekhov's *Uncle Vanya* at MAT.
1900	Freud's *On the Interpretation of Dreams*.	
1901		Chekhov's *Three Sisters* at MAT.
1902		Antoine's production of Zola's *The Earth* with real chickens on stage. Brieux's *Damaged Goods*. Gorky's *The Lower Depths* at MAT.
1903	First powered flight by the Wright brothers.	

1904	Russo-Japanese War begins.	Chekhov's *The Cherry Orchard* at MAT.
1904–7		Vedrenne-Barker season at the Court.
1905	First Russian Revolution (Gorky much involved). Destruction of Russian Fleet. Norway separates itself from Sweden.	
1906	Discovery of Vitamins.	Galsworthy's *The Silver Box* at Court.
1906–12		Several 'Little Theaters' established in Chicago (USA).
1907		Strindberg founds Intimate Theatre in Stockholm. Elizabeth Robins's *Votes for Women* at Court.
1908		Annie Horniman opens the Gaiety in Manchester as a home for 'New Drama'. Programme includes *Candida, The Return of The Prodigal* and *Women's Rights*.
1909		Galsworthy's *Strife* at Court. First *The Sea Gull* in England. Lawrence writes *A Collier's Friday Night*.
1910		J. M. Barrie's *The Twelve Pound Look*. Lawrence writes *The Widowing of Mrs. Holroyd*.
1911		Elizabeth Robins's *Votes for Women* and Monkhouse's *Mary Broome* at Gaiety
1912	Titanic sinks.	D. H. Lawrence writes *The Daughter-in-Law*. Houghton's *Hindle Wakes* in Manchester.

	EVENTS	THEATRE
1914–18	First World War.	
1915	Einstein's Theory of Relativity.	Kafka's *Metamorphosis*. Washington Square Players established (USA). Brighouse's *Hobson's Choice* in Manchester.
1916		Provincetown Playhouse established on Cape Cod (USA). Susan Glaspell's *Trifles* (USA).

PART ONE

Introducing Naturalism

CHAPTER 1

Initial Definitions

Naturalism is one of the most intriguing and enduring developments in the history of the theatre. Like so many of the ideas and 'isms' helping to shape the creation, description, discussion and analysis of works of art during the last 150 years or so, Naturalism had its origins in France. It was the French novelist and dramatist Émile Zola (1840–1902) who first articulated the concept of Naturalism as it is understood today in relation to theatre and we shall be investigating his ideas in detail at a later stage.

That 'Naturalism' is a problematic term is something acknowledged in the majority of texts dealing with the subject. The immediate problem facing most people is how to distinguish between 'Naturalism' and 'Realism', a situation not made any easier by the confusion the Naturalists and commentators of the mid-nineteenth century also appear to have had in this respect. Furst and Skrine in their book *Naturalism* (1971) provide an interesting analysis of the usage of these terms in the nineteenth century which tended, even then, to be used interchangeably, not least by Émile Zola from whom we would expect to find some degree of clarity. For some critics writing about 'Naturalism' the terms were synonymous, 'merely one and the same thing', and to illustrate this point Furst and Skrine cite the critic Brunetiere who, in his book *Le Roman Naturaliste* (The Naturalist Novel), refers to Flaubert's *Madame Bovary* as both a 'masterpiece of the realistic novel' and later in the text as 'the true harbinger of naturalism' (1971: 6). Since then, of course, scholars and critics have attempted to make these distinctions a great deal clearer for the individual, and one of the most useful explanations of the term 'Naturalism' is one provided by Raymond Williams in his book *Keywords: A Vocabulary of Culture and Society*. Williams's writing on Naturalism, and his reflections on the development of the form into the twentieth century are extremely enlightening and we will return to consider them at various stages throughout the book.

Raymond Williams (1921–1988) novelist, literary critic, cultural historian and academic produced an extensive body of work during his lifetime. The range of his work is as 'unclassifiable' as the range of titles we might confer upon him. A founder member of the Socialist Society, and regarded as a 'leftist intellectual' his work has had an important influence on the ideas and work of many key figures. Stuart Hall in his obituary for *The New Statesman* (1988) acknowledges that the field of 'cultural studies' as we know it today 'would have been impossible without his path-breaking work'. In terms of his contribution to the study of drama,

Williams, who was a Professor of Drama at Cambridge in the mid-seventies, produced a number of essays and books on the subject, amongst which the following essays are of particular value in the study of Naturalism, 'Theatre as a Political Form', 'The Case of English Naturalism', and 'Strindberg and Modern Tragedy'. Williams's books on drama include *Modern Tragedy, Drama in Performance* and *Drama from Ibsen to Brecht*.

Williams, in his introduction to *Keywords* (1976), describes for the reader the 'new' and 'strange' world in which he found himself upon his return to England in 1945 at the end of the Second World War. This was a world in which attitudes had clearly changed, but more significantly for Williams, he felt he was in a world where 'they just don't speak the same language' (1976: 11). He increasingly became preoccupied with what he perceived to be more regular use of the word 'culture'. At the time it seemed to him that he was now hearing the word used in two distinct and more developed senses. Where previously it had been an active word concerned with writing, making and working in the arts, and also in a different sense the 'preferred' word to indicate a social superiority in relation to behaviour, he was struck by its new use to 'indicate, powerfully, but not explicitly some central formation of values' and in more general discussion it was used to indicate 'society: a particular way of life – American culture, Japanese culture' (1976: 12). From our own perspective this may seem rather curious because we have, of course, assimilated these senses into our own usage of the word but, within the specific conditions and context of the time, Williams was not alone in his preoccupation with the word 'culture'. The term was to become central to post-war discourse, and as we see later in the book, becomes a key concern in relation to post-war drama. Williams's preoccupation with the word eventually resulted in the publication of his book *Culture and Society* which he completed in 1956. *Keywords*, published 20 years later, is in fact the appendix he was forced to omit from *Culture and Society* prior to publication. As he says, it is not a dictionary or glossary, but rather 'the record of an inquiry into a *vocabulary*: a shared body of words and meanings in our most general discussions, in English, of the practices and institutions which we group as *culture* and *society*' (1976: 15).

For our purposes Williams provides an extremely useful account of his enquiry into the word 'Naturalism', contextualising the emergence and usage of the word before going on to situate it in relation to the form of theatre representation we are exploring in this book. As Williams points out, 'Naturalism' is a 'more complex word' than is generally recognized and the tendency to regard it as simply 'a style of accurate external representation' is to neglect the 'philosophical and scientific' sense of the word which is fundamental to our understanding of 'Naturalism' as a form of theatre representation.

Williams traces the first appearance of the words 'naturalist' and 'naturalism' in English from the late sixteenth century and early seventeeth century respectively. In both cases, the words were used as a 'term in religious and philosophical arguments' which, as Williams notes:

> followed a particular sense of NATURE (q.v.) in which there was a contrast with *God* or *Spirit*. To study the **natural causes** of events, or to explain or justify morality from *nature* or *human nature*, was to be a **naturalist** and to propound **naturalism**, although the actual terms seem to have been conferred by their opponents. (1976: 216)

It seems that the word 'Naturalist' becomes a 'common C17 term for **natural philosopher**', those individuals who, as Williams points out, we would more readily recognize as '*physicists* or *biologists*': 'As late as mC19 these senses of **naturalism** and **naturalist** (either (i) opposition to **supernaturalism** or (ii) the study of **natural history** – now mainly biology) were predominant'.

Williams identifies three specific effects of the prevailing senses of **natural, natural history and naturalism**, which have a bearing on the development of art and literature. The first of these effects relates to the sense of 'natural' to imply a 'simple and natural manner of writing'. The second 'effect' is of the sense of natural history, specifically 'in its special characteristic of close and detailed observation'. What Williams argues tends to be omitted in the history and critical discussion, and thus our understanding, of 'Naturalism' is:

> [...] the third effect, from **naturalism** in the general philosophical and scientific sense, itself much influenced by the new and controversial developments in geology and biology and especially by Darwin's theory of **natural selection** in EVOLUTION (q.v.). (217)

As we will discover the Naturalists were particularly influenced by this sense of 'Naturalism':

> [...] by the idea of the application of scientific method in literature: specifically the study of heredity in the story of a family, but also, more generally, in the sense of describing and interpreting human behaviour in strictly natural terms, excluding the hypothesis of some controlling or directing force outside human nature.
>
> This **naturalism** was the basis of a major new kind of writing, and the philosophical position was explicitly argued: cf. Strindberg: 'the naturalist has abolished guilt by abolishing God'; 'the summary judgments on men given by authors [...] should be challenged by naturalists, who know the richness of the soul-complex and recognize that "vice" has a reverse side very much like virtue' (*Preface to Lady Julie,* 1888). A new importance was given to the *environment* of characters and actions. (*Environment* in its special and

now primary sense of the conditions, including the physical conditions, within which someone or something lives and develops, was an associated eC19 development from the earlier general sense of surroundings.) Character and action were seen as affected or determined by *environment*, which especially in a social and social-physical sense had then to be accurately described as an essential element of any account of a life. This connected with the sense of careful and detailed observation, from natural history, but it was not (as was later supposed) detailed description for its own sake, or from some conventional plausibility; rather it rested on the new and properly **naturalist** sense of the determining or decisive or influential effect of an environment on a life (in the variations between *determining* and *influential* much of the subsequent development can be understood) [...] (218–19)

Williams, in his essay 'Social Environment and Theatrical Environment – The Case of English Naturalism' provides a more concise overview: 'there are three relevant senses of Naturalism and the associated "naturalist" and "naturalistic"' (1980: 125). The first and probably most commonly used relates to: 'a method of "accurate" or "lifelike" reproduction' which we might more usefully consider as technical Naturalism. The second relates to 'a philosophical position allied to science, natural history and materialism' (125). These then are individuals or groups of individuals whose understanding and view of the world is inextricably linked to the 'material substance' of this world, its natural and physical laws. The third sense 'indicates a movement in which the method of accurate production and the specific philosophical position are intended to be organically fused' (125) and it is this third sense which is 'the most significant in the history of drama' (125), and which distinguishes realism from Naturalism. It is this 'third sense [that], in specific application to a particular kind of novel or play, and thence to a literary movement, appeared in French in the late 1860s and is common in English from the 1880s' (125).

Williams notes that aspects of 'naturalism' start to become 'habitual', certainly in English bourgeois drama, from the middle of the eighteenth century. In his chapter 'Theatre as a Political Forum' in *The Politics of Modernism* he identifies five influential factors which emerge, and become increasingly more evident in the different stages of the 'long and slow lines of development through' to the twentieth century:

First, there was the radical admission of the *contemporary* as legitimate material for drama. In the major periods of Greek and Renaissance drama the inherent choice of material was overwhelmingly legendary or historical, with at most some insertions of the contemporary at the margins of these distanced events. Second, there was an admission of the *indigenous* as part of the same movement; the widespread convention of an at least nominally exotic site for drama began to be loosened, and the ground for the now equally widespread convention of the *contemporary indigenous* began to be prepared. Third, there was an increasing emphasis on *everyday speech forms* as the basis for dramatic language: in practice, at first a reduction from the extraordinary linguistic range, including the colloquial, which had marked the English Renaissance, but eventually a decisive point of reference for the nature of all dramatic speech, formal rhetorical, choral and monological types being steadily abandoned. Fourth there was an emphasis on *social extension*: a deliberate breach of the convention that at least the principal personages of drama should be of elevated social rank. As in the novel, this process of extension moved in stages from the court to the bourgeois home and then, first in melodrama, to the poor. Fifth, there was the completion of a decisive *secularism*: not, in its early stages, necessarily a rejection of, or indifference to, religious belief, but a steady exclusion *from the dramatic action* of all supernatural or metaphysical agencies. Drama was now, explicitly, to be a human action played in exclusively human terms.(1989: 183–4)

What we find, increasingly, in the development of bourgeois drama is an attempt towards 'positive interventions in its own images, sentimental and conformist as these undoubtedly were' (183). What we have yet to find in the development of this earlier drama is the 'production' of character and action determined by the physical and social environment. For Williams, late nineteenth-century Naturalism is a 'shocking intensification' of these five factors and, 'in practice', the first phase of a Modernist theatre (183).

Scribe and the well-made play

As we shall see, the drama produced by the Naturalists in the late nineteenth century was both a response to the 'spirit' of the time and a determined attempt to break with existing theatre conventions. In order to fully comprehend and interrogate the work of the Naturalist playwrights, it is important to understand the drama against which they were reacting. We will briefly consider the work of Eugène Scribe (1791–1861), the dramatist who developed the 'pièce bien faite' (well-made play), and whose plays not only dominated the French stage in the first half of the nineteenth century but were regularly translated for the European stage where they, similarly, enjoyed enormous popularity. Scribe's influence is evident not only in the drama of his immediate successors, the French playwrights Sardou, Augier and Dumas fils, but also in the work of successive foreign playwrights.

Orphaned at the age of 15 Scribe inherited enough money on his mother's death to permit him a degree of freedom in life, he was thus in the enviable position of being able to choose the path of his career. Scribe's passion for theatre was such that the only career he had in mind was to be a dramatist and whilst his early attempts at playwriting were not entirely successful, someone with less determination and commitment might well have abandoned the profession. He persevered, and these formative years clearly served him well in relation to the development of his dramatic skills when at the age of only 24, he finally achieved success with *Une nuit de la Garde Nationale* at the Vaudeville theatre (Koon and Switzer, 1980:14).

Although never his intention, Scribe was, in his own way, affecting a 'transformation' in the conventional theatre of the time. As Koon and Switzer note, the play proved to be:

> an innovation in his own work and on the boulevard stage. Scribe had applied his 'theatrical technique' in a manner that was quite distinct from the fanciful pastorals: the subject was contemporary, the treatment realistic and the language colloquial. (1980: 15)

We should note here that the play was the result of a collaboration, which at the time was common practice and, indeed, a practice Scribe, for the most part, continued throughout his career. This probably accounts for the prodigious number of plays he was able to produce in his lifetime, which number some four hundred. The range of work he produced is, similarly, quite extraordinary, and alongside the comedies for which he is best known, we find operas, historical plays and tragedies. As Cardwell notes in his article 'The Well Made Play of Eugene Scribe' in *The French Review*, Scribe also produced a melodrama and 'a pre-naturalist play that traces in dismal detail the decline and death of a woman who falls under the influence of wrong friends' (1983: 877).

Scribe's rise to fame was speedy and within five years of his initial success at the Vaudeville in 1815, he had become the most popular dramatist in Paris. An acute business man, he was a millionaire before he reached the age of 40 and 'the first Frenchman to get rich by writing plays' (Cardwell, 1983: 876) For John Russell Taylor, author of *The Rise and Fall of the Well Made Play*, Scribe's unique abilities lay both in his realization that 'the most reliable formula for holding an audience's attention was a well-told story' and his recognition that 'performance, is an experience in time, and that therefore the first essential is to keep one's audience attentive from one minute to the next' (1967: 11–12). This was precisely what Scribe expertly achieved in his *pièce bien fait* – the well-made play.

Whilst Scribe's plays very much depend on the basic structure of exposition, action, denouement and resolution, it is important to recognize that within this structure his dramatic approach varies from work to work. Critics have attempted to ascribe a formula seeking out the key features that recur in Scribe's plays but, for Douglas Cardwell, 'the search for a formula that will explain the structure of the well made play is doomed to failure' (1983: 877) Cardwell goes on to argue that whilst common practices and tendencies can be found in Scribe's work there is 'no general structure that is common to all such plays' (877). The term 'well-made play' has come to have rather negative associations; contrived, formulaic and favouring 'form over substance', with the result that Scribe is a much misunderstood dramatist.

Scribe's play *Le Puff – ou Mensonge et Verité* (The Puff – or Falsehood and Truth), written in 1848 and translated into English by Ranjit Bolt with the title *Believe it or Not* (2004), provides us with a fine example of Scribe's work. As Nicholas Dromgoole notes in his introduction to the play, 'to puff' meant in both English and French '"to praise unduly" and "to bring to the public's attention"' (2004: 7). As Dromgoole notes, the significance of the title relates to the increasing 'power of the press' in which 'reputations were boosted or blasted' (7), something akin to what we are familiar with as 'spin'.

DESGAUDETS: […] You seem to be the only person who hasn't found out that in this whole, gigantic metropolis, there isn't a word of truth to be had. Puff is kind, my boy. Puff and publicity.
ALBERT: Puff?
DESGAUDETS: Puff, or 'peuff', as our friends across the Channel would say – the art of promulgating, for financial gain, that which … erm … isn't exactly so. It's lying carried to the level of speculation, for the greater good of society and the capitalist system. The rhapsodising of poets; the posturing of politicians; the fashionable lady, feigning a headache so her lover gives her diamonds; the merchant, hawking his wares; the minister threatening to resign; the industrialist touting his latest venture; the stockbroker peddling his new share offering; the connoisseur; the philanthropist – they're all just different types of puff. (Scribe, 2004: 22)

What we find in the play is a representation of reality to the degree that Scribe is dealing with contemporary matters, and setting up for his characters situations in which he primarily exposes the 'manipulation of the press' for both personal success and financial gain. Generally, Scribe avoided exploring ideas that might potentially 'displease' the audience but we find in this play a number of aspects which the middle-class audience would recognize if not identify with, these were as Dromgoole notes: 'well aimed and serious truths, admittedly wrapped around with the appropriate humour that made them palatable, but only just' (Scribe, 2004: 15).

The play centres on the character of Albert d'Angremont, a cavalry captain, who has returned to Paris after five years' service in Algeria to seek justice for the widow of his commander. The exposition in the first act occurs within the setting of a bookshop, which facilitates the coming and going of the characters as they are introduced to the audience. Whilst Scribe's characters grew increasingly more 'realistic', they remain undeveloped, serving primarily to further the action. Although, as Koon and Switzer point out, it is a mistake to judge them by the page alone because: 'in the theatre they come to life in a remarkably rich and distinctive manner' (1980: 38). Information relating to the characters' situation, background events and the two female characters, who have yet to be introduced, emerges through the dialogue, which is carefully constructed to ensure that there are no exchanges of information which are already known to the characters. As Cardwell notes, one of the Scribean principles of the exposition is that it 'must be complete' to the extent that there is an 'allusion to every previous event' (1983: 877). Scribe, of course, uses a range of dramatic devices and in the first act, Albert unexpectedly meets his old friend Maxence who is entering the shop just as he is leaving it which, of course, is entirely plausible given the setting. It transpires from their conversation that Albert is in love with Maxence's sister. The subsequent action of the play largely revolves around Albert's attempts to overcome the obstacles which prevent him from marrying Antonia. The various twists in the plot are executed with ingenuity, and whilst Scribe is drawing on a number of recognizable techniques, secrets, misunderstandings and so on, these are carefully orchestrated within the overall structure of the play. The obstacles increase in complexity, and although tantalizingly near to resolution at times, finally reach the 'climax', the *scene a faire* which paves the way to the denouement. As Dromgoole notes, this is 'stock stuff', where the innovation lies is in Scribe's ability to integrate his formulaic 'tendencies' with a degree of criticism and thus 'every twist of the plot seems to depend, not on the interaction of one character with another, but on the ability or failure of the main personages to manipulate the media or stock exchange effectively enough' (Scribe, 2004: 16). The denouement which completes the action and resolves the situation is problematic in that Albert's integrity is compromised when he must choose whether to expose the Count's historical writings as a piece of fiction or keep quiet to ensure the 'happy ending' which he agrees to: 'alright then. But the moral of all this ... because there has to be a moral ... ' (124).

We should not underestimate the importance of Scribe's contribution and influence on drama both in France and elsewhere in Europe. Despite the protestations of the newly emerging Naturalist playwrights that they were responding to the plot-driven drama of the well-made play, they were to a large degree reliant upon it. If we consider Zola's first attempt to produce a Naturalist drama we find *Thérèse Raquin* bears the hallmark of the well-made play as much as any of the innovations we might also detect. Ibsen, who had spent his formative years producing and directing Scribe's plays in Norway, drew on the conventions of the well-made play for his Naturalistic drama. Interestingly, George Bernard Shaw in *The Quintessence of Ibsenism* notes:

This, then, is the extension of the old dramatic form effected by Ibsen. Up to a certain point in the last act, *A Doll's House* is a play that might be turned into a very ordinary French drama by the excision of a few lines, and the substitution of a sentimental happy ending for the famous last scene: indeed the very first thing the theatrical wiseacres did with it was to effect exactly this transformation with the result that the play thus pithed had no success and attracted no notice worth mentioning. But at just that point in the act the heroine very unexpectedly (by the wiseacres) stops her emotional acting and say: 'We must sit down and discuss all this that has been happening between us.' And it was by this new technical feature: this addition of a new movement, as musicians would say, to the dramatic form, that *A Doll's House* conquered Europe and founded a new school of dramatic art. (1913: 192)

T. W. Robertson

One of the most accomplished and successful exponents of the well-made play was the dramatist T. W. (Tom) Robertson (1829–1871) who, through a series of plays depicting ordinary people in recognizable domestic situations, established important foundations for the development of Naturalism in the English theatre. Robertson was steeped in the theatre practice of his day; he was, at one time, stage manager for Madame Vestris (see p. 66) and a sympathetic portrait of him is provided in the character of Tom Wrench in Arthur Pinero's play *Trelawney of the 'Wells'* (1898). Robertson was responsible for encouraging the young W. S. Gilbert (see p. 69) to turn to writing plays and libretti, but it is his nickname 'doorknobs Robertson' and the labelling of his plays as 'cup and saucer dramas' that provide clues to his innovative nature. Robertson was passionate about the physical detail of his plays; their setting and actions. His stage directions provide the most precise instructions for the construction and décor for the domestic interiors, including the nature of the door handles and the way in which the setting could be accommodated on a stage still utilizing grooves and shutters (see p. 63). Furthermore, he draws on his work as an actor and stage director to specify stage business, the use of properties (props), gestures, facial expressions and mime. Many of his plays do, indeed, require homely activities like drinking tea, all of which contribute to the reality of the situations. The single-word titles of his most famous plays are significant: *Society* (1865), *Ours* (1866), *Caste* (1867; see Illustration 1), *Play* (1868), *School* (1869) and *The M.P.* (1870). These are a far cry from the elaborate titles of the popular melodramas of his day and suggest an engagement in the problems of the contemporary world. Robertson's plays are, by no means, profound and retain some of the characteristics of gentle comedy and melodrama, but they mark a considerable progression towards a less escapist and more relevant form of drama of ideas. This is best exemplified in his most enduringly popular play: *Caste*.

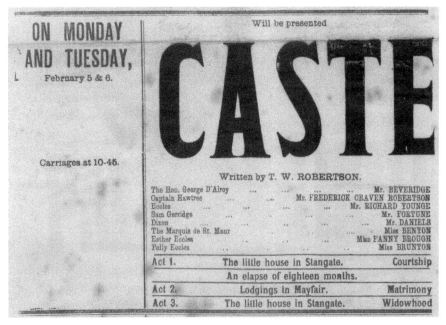

ILLUSTRATION 1
Play bill for a performance of T. W. Robertson's *Caste* (1872), courtesy of University of Kent, Special Collections

This play was first staged by the Bancrofts, who, in partnership with Robertson brought new standards of realistic production to London through their management of the Prince of Wales' theatre between 1860 and 1880. The production of *Caste* was notable for its understatement and the way in which emotions were revealed through the representation of the detail of everyday, domestic life. The play is set in the world of the theatre and, importantly, its most powerful and spirited characters are the two young women, both actresses, around whom the action revolves. The theme is snobbery: described as recently as 2012 by the British Deputy Prime minister as 'our national pastime'! Esther Eccles, who works in the theatre (regarded then as very low status) has captivated the Hon. George d'Alroy, an army officer and they embark on a marriage which breaks all the 'rules' of relationships across the social classes and provokes the fury of d'Alroy's mother. We shall encounter this play again when we discuss the development of the railways, but at this point it is worth noting that the juxtaposition of a number of characters from varying social strata is the main source of the play's interest. The real climax comes when George is reported missing in action in India and his mother appears in Esther's humble home, to demand that she relieves her of the responsibility of bringing up her infant son in an 'appropriate' way. Esther's rebuttal of her mother-in-law's attitudes and the warm support of her actress sister, Polly, demonstrate some of that strength and independence that was to typify the women in subsequent naturalistic plays. When George makes an unexpected re-appearance at the end of the play and Esther's and Polly's infuriating and devious drunken father is eventually packed off to Jersey, the play shows its melodramatic legacy but there is no doubt that those who saw it realized that a new kind of play drama was invading the English theatre in the 1860s.

CHAPTER SUMMARY

- In general terms there is a tendency to view 'Naturalism' as simply a belief that works of art should reproduce the reality of the natural world as accurately as possible.
- As Williams notes, the term 'Naturalism' is more complex when applied to theatre representation.
- A 'Naturalist' play must represent on stage the factors that determine the behaviour of the characters and provide a detailed picture of the environment they inhabit, not simply as a 'backdrop' but rather, as Williams notes, because 'it is a causal or symptomatic feature' (1980: 127).
- When applied to drama this means that a play must show all the factors that determine the behaviour of the characters and provide a detailed picture of the world they inhabit as objectively as possible.
- Raymond Williams, a major figure in the development of Cultural Studies, provides an extensive survey of the apparently conflicting definitions of Naturalism and Realism.
- Naturalistic plays usually employed the structure of the 'well-made play' which was popularized by the playwright Eugene Scribe in the mid-nineteenth century.
- Scribe's formula was: exposition; action; denouement; and resolution.
- Through the use of colloquial language and other techniques he achieved a representation of reality that laid the foundation for Naturalism.

SEMINAR AND WORKSHOP TOPICS

1 Consider the definitions offered by Raymond Williams and arrive at your own, initial understanding of the term Naturalism when applied to the theatre.
2 In order to achieve Naturalism a play might involve a great deal of realistic detail: how does this affect your understanding of the difference between Naturalism and Realism? Give examples of plays that appear to depend on presenting substantial realistic detail.

3 Identify plays that seem to you to be naturalistic and state why this is the case.
4 Provide an example of a 'well-made play' and present scenes from it that illustrate the features of exposition; action; denouement; and resolution.
5 Identify plays which contain scenes that depend on building to a climax and/or deliberately concealed information.

FURTHER READING

Cardwell, D. (1983) 'The Well Made Play of Eugene Scribe', *The French Review*, 56:6 (May), pp. 876–84.

Koon, H. and Switzer, R. (1980) *Eugene Scribe*, Boston, MA: Twayne Publishers. A helpful introduction to this influential dramatist.

Russell Taylor, J. (1967) *The Rise and Fall of the Well Made Play*, London: Methuen. An extremely useful book charting Scribe's influence on the work of a number of British dramatists.

Scribe, E. (2004) *Believe it or Not*, trans. Ranjit Bolt, London: Oberon. This new version of Scribe's *Le Puff* demonstrates his skills and characteristics admirably.

Williams, R. (1976), *Keywords : A Vocabulary of Culture and Society*, London: Fontana. This remains an invaluable guide to students of drama and the arts.

CHAPTER 2

Manifestos

Émile Zola

Émile Zola is generally regarded as the 'father' of Naturalism and whilst, as we have seen, he cannot be credited for inventing the term, he is responsible for producing what have come to be regarded as the key theories of Naturalism in relation to literature and drama. The key sources which make up this body of theory are Zola's Preface to the second edition of his novel *Thérèse Raquin* (1867), written in 1868, the Preface to his stage adaptation of the novel (1873), his essay 'Le Roman Experimental' ('The experimental novel') (1880), his manifesto 'Le Naturalism au théâtre' (Naturalism in the Theatre) (1881) and his book *Nos Auteurs Dramatique* (Our Dramatists) (1881). For obvious reasons, greater attention tends to be paid to Zola's manifesto 'Naturalism in the Theatre', but in fact the Prefaces to his novel and play provide us with a clearer understanding of his earliest views on the 'human subject' and his obsession with the 'scientific methodology' which underpin his concept of 'Naturalism'.

Zola was as much a product of the time in which he was writing as the characters and environments he describes in his novels and represents in his plays. In this respect he, along with other Naturalists, was influenced by the scientific discoveries and subsequent theories and ideas being espoused at the time. Of course, Darwin's theory of evolution presented in *On the Origin of Species by means of Natural Selection* (1859), and discussed elsewhere in this book, was the most significant of these new theories, and as Furst and Skrine note: 'it is no exaggeration to call it *the* crucial landmark of the nineteenth-century science and thought' (1971: 16). Indeed, it provided the basis for a number of subsequent ideas developed by key Naturalist figures. As most accounts of Zola and Naturalism will testify, Hippolyte Taine, a French historian and critic, was one such influential figure. His contribution to Naturalist theory is most commonly associated with his concept of 'race, milieu et moment' presented in his *Essais de critique et d'histoire* written in 1866 but several other of his ideas were also very influential in determining the creative approach adopted by the Naturalists. As Furst and Skrine note his: 'function was virtually that of go-between between science and literature'; clearly drawing on Darwin's theory of evolution, Taine takes the concept of 'heredity' and the importance of the 'environment' and situates them 'within the human realm' (1971: 17). Furst and Skrine provide a useful translation of Taine's three key principles:

In the preface to the second edition of his *Essais de critique et d'histoire* (1866) he popularized Darwin's ideas. 'L'animal humain continue l'animal brut' ('the human animal is a continuation of the primitive animal'); in both 'la molécule originelle est héréditaire et la forme acquise se transmet en partie et lentement par l'hérédité' ('the primary molecule is inherited and its acquired shape is passed on partially and gradually by heredity'); in both 'la molécule organisée ne se développe que sous l'influence du milieu' ('the molecule as it is develops only under the influence of its environment'). To these purely biological factors Taine adds 'le moment', immediate circumstances, to complete the explanation of human behaviour. So to the Naturalists man is an animal whose course is determined by his heredity, by the effect of his environment and by the pressures of the moment.   (1971: 17–18)

Claude Bernard, an eminent French physiologist and scientist, similarly exercised a significant influence on Zola's concept of Naturalism. It was Bernard's *Introduction à l'étude de la médicine expérimentale* (1865) (*Introduction to the Scientific Study of Medicine*), in which he formulates a number of theories establishing medicine firmly within the 'domain' of experimental science, which proved particularly important to Zola's notion of a scientific methodology. The basic premise of Bernard's paper was that the methodologies of investigation and experiment used on 'inanimate objects' in chemistry and physics should similarly be adopted on 'the living body' in physiology and medicine. Claude Schumacher suggests that in Bernard's thesis 'Zola found only confirmation that what he was attempting to achieve in literature had a scientific basis thus legitimizing and giving it greater respectability' (1990: 2).

Indeed, Zola devotes his essay 'Le Roman Experimental', written in 1880, to contextualizing the importance of Bernard's scientific methodology of observation and experiment in relation to his own experimental method:

> I have said before that I chose 'L'Introduction' because medicine is still looked upon by many as an art. Claude Bernard proves that it ought to be a science, and in his book we see the birth of a science, a very instructive spectacle in itself, and which shows us that the scientific domain is extending and conquering all the manifestations of human intelligence. Since medicine, which was an art, is becoming a science, why should not literature also become a science by means of the experimental method?   (1893: 32)

Zola's essay is lengthy, repetitive and lacks any detailed explanation of how a scientific methodology might actually be applied to form and style. None the less, for all these disadvantages, it does provide for the reader willing to persevere some insight into what Zola was attempting, particularly in the light of some of Bernard's examples which Zola includes to illustrate his own argument. In Zola's introduction to the essay, we find the ubiquitous statement: 'It will often be but necessary for me to replace the word 'doctor' by the word 'novelist' to make my meaning clear and to give it the rigidity of a scientific truth' (1). This is the source of much misunderstanding, and it is reductive to resort to the analogy between doctor and scientist as a summary of his purpose, to do so undermines the essence of what Zola was attempting to articulate.

What we might more fruitfully consider are Zola's efforts to develop a 'modern' method of writing which could more authentically represent the complex reality of the late nineteenth century. In this he was inspired by the methods of scientific inquiry to the extent that the writer was like a scientist, 'an observer' who collects 'the facts as he has observed them'. These facts provide: 'the point of departure, the solid earth on which his characters are to tread and the phenomena to develop' (1893: 8).

In the manner of the experimental scientist who, acting on what he observes, embarks on an experiment to verify the hypotheses, so too the novelist sets up his own experiment: 'that is to say, sets his characters going in a certain story so as to show that the succession of facts will be such as the requirements of the determinism of the phenomena under examination call for' (Zola, 1893: 8). Inspired by Bernard's example of the 'experimental method' conducted by the ordinary observer:

> if we wish to judge of the acts of another man, and know the motives which make him act, that is altogether a different thing. Without doubt we have before our eyes the movements of this man and his different acts, which are, we are sure, the modes of expression of his sensibility and his will. Further, we even admit that there is a necessary connection between the acts and their causes; but what is this cause? We do not feel it, we are not conscious of it, as we are when it acts in ourselves; we are therefore obliged to interpret it, and to guess at it, from the movements which we see and the words which we hear. We are obliged to check off this man's actions one by the other; we consider how he acted in such a circumstances, and in a word, we have recourse to the experimental method. (10)

Zola maintained that the novelist has a responsibility to do likewise, which meant that rather than relying on personal sentiment, inspiration and imagination to account for the behaviour of characters and the development of the narrative, the writer should connect: 'the natural phenomena to their conditions of existence or to their nearest causes' (15). For Zola, 'determinism dominated everything' and the novelist needed: 'to possess a knowledge of the mechanism of the phenomena inherent in man, to show the machinery of his intellectual and sensory manifestations, under the influences of heredity and environment, such as physiology shall give them to us, and then finally to exhibit man living in social conditions' (20).

The Experimental Novel was, in fact, written seven years after the publication of Zola's novel *Thérèse Raquin* (1867) which is generally regarded as his first attempt to produce a 'Naturalist' piece of writing using the experimental method. Zola felt compelled to include a preface to the second edition in 1868 largely in response to what he perceived to be 'hypocrisy' on the part of critics who had not appreciated or fully understood his objectives in presenting what was a very detailed account of two individuals who, driven by their passion for each other, commit adultery and subsequently murder. Responding to accusations of 'depravity', 'immorality' and 'pornography', he set out to put the record straight outlining his intentions in the form of a preface.

What then were Zola's intentions? Seemingly inspired by a newspaper article, Zola set himself the task of analysing and explaining how two individuals are driven to murder and suicide: 'While I was writing *Thérèse Raquin* I was lost to the world, completely engrossed in my exact and meticulous copying of real life and my analysis of the human mechanism [...]' (1992: 2). In this novel he identifies himself as 'an analyst' and clearly situates his endeavours within the realms of scientific enquiry: 'I wrote every scene, even the most torrid ones, with the sole curiosity of the scientists' (3). Zola views the novel as a 'study in physiology' convinced that anyone from the Naturalist school would recognize his: 'starting point, the study of temperaments and the profound modifications brought about in the human organism by the pressure of surroundings and circumstances' (5). It is in these terms that he sets out to: 'study, not characters, but temperaments. Therein lies the essence of the book. I chose to portray individuals existing under the sovereign dominion of their nerves and their blood, devoid of free will and drawn into every act of their lives by the inescapable prompting of their flesh' (1). Thérèse and Laurent are 'human beasts' driven by their instincts, their behaviour is determined by their heredity, the environment and the pressure of the circumstances they find themselves in:

> Love, for my two heroes is the satisfaction of a physical need; the murder they commit is a consequence of their adultery, a consequence they accept as wolves accept the slaughter of sheep; and last, what I have been obliged to call their remorse consists simply in an organic disorder, the revolt of a nervous system stretched beyond breaking-point. There is a total absence of soul, as I will readily admit, for such was my intention. (2)

In spite of the criticisms levelled at Zola's approach, not least his attempt to represent guilt as an organic disorder, the novel remains a powerful and compelling read and the preface provides us with an important document articulating the Naturalist principles and experimental methodology he was attempting to explore in the novel.

Zola, for whom *Thérèse Raquin* provided 'an excellent subject for a play', produced an adaptation of the novel in 1873. In his Preface to the play, written two years later, Zola reflects on what had motivated him. He provides a brief outline of his approach together with a review of the actors' interpretation of the characters in the 1873 production at the Théâtre de la Renaissance which ran for nine performances. Adaptations from novels were not unusual at the time but for Zola this attempt was, in many respects, an experiment in which his overarching aim was to further 'Naturalism' as a form of theatre representation the 'murmurings' of which were 'beginning to be heard in the theatre' (1969: 2).

Zola was of the view that the moment had arrived when the public 'unknowingly' had reached a point of exhaustion with all that conventional theatre offered, desiring instead a modern form in line with the 'new spirit in the air' (1969: 1). In order for drama to survive it needed to become modern, and the future as Zola saw it lay in the representation of 'the human problem studied in the setting of reality' (2). It was, he says: 'under the influence of such ideas that I turned *Thérèse Raquin* into a play. As I have said, there was a subject, characters and an environment which provided, in my view, excellent material for the attempt I had dreamed about' (2).

The dream was not without problems and for Zola these were two-fold. As he readily acknowledged: 'The theatre and the novel have conventions so completely different that the writer is obliged to amputate his own thought, exposing longeurs and gaps and to coarsen and deface the work in forcing it into a new mould' (1969: 1). The adaptation of the novel into a drama presented one set of difficulties, as he suggests, but these were compounded by the fact he was at the same time attempting to develop this 'new mould' or theatre form as we would call it. As Furst and Skrine note: 'If the human being, his actions and reactions, are only comprehensible in the light of his environment and heredity, his mental and physical state at any given moment, and the social pressures being exerted on him, the Naturalist dramatist must devise ways and means of illustrating these conditioning factors' (1971: 54).

Of these 'conditioning factors', Zola chose to represent the environment by setting the action in a lower middle-class domestic interior for which he provided very detailed instructions:

> A large bedroom which also serves as dining room and parlour. The room is in the Pont-Neuf Passage. It is high, dark, in a state of decay, hung with faded grey wallpaper, furnished with threadbare poor furniture, littered with haberdashery cardboard boxes.
> (Zola, 1989: 8)

Zola goes on to describe doors leading to the kitchen, passage and exterior, the top of the staircase leading to the shop and to the left of the stage: 'on a slant, a bed in an alcove with a window looking onto a bare wall' (8). Zola describes the furniture and props in detail, setting them precisely to convey the oppressively cluttered, 'multi-purpose' environment. As Williams notes: 'A real environment had to be reproduced on the stage because within this perspective an actual environment – a particular kind of room, particular furnishing, a particular relation to street or office or landscape – was in effect one of the actors: one of the true agencies of the action' (1989: 85). The set took on a new significance, it was no longer a 'backdrop' to the action, it contributed to the action. It is within this environment that the characters' behaviour and progressive degeneration become 'comprehensible'.

As Zola mentions in his Preface, the staging was intended to: 'reflect at all times the ordinary occupations of my characters, in such a way that they do not 'act' but 'live' for the audience' (1989: 2). It is worth considering Zola's opening scene which immediately draws the audience into the life of the Raquin family:

ACT ONE

Eight o'clock on Thursday summer evening, after dinner. The table has not yet been cleared; the window is half open. There is a feeling of peace, of a sense of middle-class calm.

SCENE ONE

Laurent, Thérèse, Madame Raquin, Camille
Camille is sitting in an armchair stage-right, stiffly posing for his portrait, wearing his Sunday best. Laurent is painting, standing at his easel in front of the window. Next to Laurent sits Thérèse, in a day-dream, her chin in her hand. Madame Raquin is finishing clearing the table.

CAMILLE:	(*After a long pause.*) All right if I talk? Won't disturb you, will it?
LAURENT:	Not in the least, so long as you don't move.
CAMILLE:	I fall asleep after dinner if I don't talk … You're lucky, you're healthy. You can eat anything … I shouldn't have had that second helping of syllabub, it always makes me ill. My stomach is so delicate … You like syllabub don't you?
LAURENT:	Oh yes. It's delicious – so sweet
CAMILLE:	We know what you like here. Mother spoils you – she makes syllabub specially for you, even though she knows what it does to me … That's true, isn't it, Thérèse, that Mother spoils Laurent?
THÉRÈSE:	(*Without raising her head*) Yes
MADAME R:	(*Carrying a pile of plates*) Don't listen to them, Laurent […]

(Zola, 1989: 9)

Throughout the remainder of the first scene Madame Raquin continues with her domestic activities, exiting with plates and re-entering to continue clearing the table. Thérèse sits daydreaming and Laurent continues to paint Camille who remains seated.

For a modern audience there is nothing unusual about the way in which Zola has chosen to open the play, but for an audience attending the performance in 1873 this would have been a different matter. Not only does the curtain open to reveal a dingy apartment, a shocking contrast to the elaborate, and often spectacular, settings they were used to, it reveals a scene in which the action has already commenced. The audience are confronted with silent, ordinary domestic action, and a long pause before Camille speaks. We see in this short extract from the opening scene Zola's attempt to make his characters 'live' for the audience. What we discover in the play as a whole is a dramatist determined to bring a more authentic representation of contemporary life to the stage. We find in Zola's dialogue and his respective stage instructions an attempt to reproduce natural speech on stage both in general conversation that is at times rather banal and ordinary, and in the more heightened scenes between Thérèse and Laurent. For the most part Zola keeps the dialogue short, longer sentences are broken with pauses or remain unfinished and he is unafraid to use silences.

Compared to other playwrights of the time, Zola makes significant use of stage directions throughout the play to achieve the naturalistic quality he sought in performance. His directions are frequent and detailed to ensure a convincing physical representation of the individual characters within the staged environment. Not only must the natural behaviour of all characters on stage appear believable, but in the case of Thérèse and Laurent, their physical degeneration must be apparent and equally authentic. Zola was impressed by the standard of acting achieved in the performance, noting in his Preface to the play that he was: 'delighted to see them realize so fully what I had in my mind' (1989: 3). He goes on to praise the interpretation and portrayal of complex characters and the quality of 'ensemble' acting which had resulted in even the 'minor roles' taking on a depth which he had not anticipated.

In an attempt to move beyond the plot-driven drama dominating the contemporary French stage, Zola is at pains to point out in his Preface to the play that: 'the action no longer resided in a story as such, but in the interior struggles of the characters. There was no longer a logic of events but a logic of sensations and feelings. And the ending became the mathematical solution of the problem posed' (1989: 2). The two key events, Camille's murder and the wedding of Thérèse and Laurent, occur off stage with the result that the spectator is witness only to the effect these events have on the characters' 'mental and physical' state. A year passes between Act I and Act II, but this is not immediately evident to the audience. The opening scene of Act II replicates the closing scene of the previous act, and the curtain opens to reveal everyone seated exactly as they had been at the end of Act I. Once again, Zola uses silent domestic action to open the scene: 'A silence during which Madame R. And Suzanne serve tea, exactly repeating their motions of Act

One' (35). It is only after some thirteen lines of dialogue, when Madame Raquin suddenly bursts into tears, that we discover Camille is dead.

The 'logic of sensations and feelings' Zola is attempting is the progressive degeneration of two characters who will ultimately commit suicide. This is set against the: 'foolish and useless secondary characters in order to underpin the terrible anguish of my principal characters with the banality of everyday life' (1989: 2).

Zola's ambition was to bring to the stage 'a purely human study, free from all extraneous material, going straight to the point' (2). Furst and Skrine note: 'In a play there is no room for commentary and explanation; yet it must provide the audience with all the relevant data, with the case histories of characters who must be left to speak for themselves without using the improbable conventions of monologue and aside' (1971: 55).

For those who have read the novel, it is evident that when the play opens Thérèse and Laurent are already lovers. Zola must therefore find a way to inform the audience of the necessary background detail to account for the circumstances which originally drew these two 'human beasts' together. The naturalness of dialogue that Zola attempts at some points in the play is often undermined by the lengthy exposition he must resort to in order to provide the 'relevant data' for the audience. Thus we find the powerful dramatic action Zola sets up in the scene where Laurent joins Thérèse alone on stage in Act I

SCENE FIVE

Thérèse, later joined by Laurent.
Thérèse, left alone, stays still a moment, looking around, then at last she lets out a sigh. Silently she moves downstage and stretches with lassitude and boredom. Then she hears Laurent enter by the small side door and she smiles, shaking with joy. During this scene it gets darker and darker as night falls.

(1989: 16)

interrupted by the lengthy exposition intended to provide the audience with the background detail to their affair and, more importantly, to situate their immediate and future behaviour in relation to the 'conditioning factors' of heredity and pressure of circumstances.

THÉRÈSE: [...] They told me my mother was the daughter of a nomadic African chief. It must be true; so often I dreamt of escaping; roaming the roads and running barefoot in the dust, begging like a gypsy ... you see I preferred starving in the wild to their hospitality.   (18)

Throughout the play we find examples where Zola is forced to use the dialogue to provide essential information to the audience and whether this is simply to draw attention to elements of setting, 'They've got the haberdashery shop down-stairs' (10) or report on action, the overall result is that conversations between the characters become less plausible and therefore less natural as they impart details to each other which, presumably, they would already have been aware of. Zola must, similarly, use the dialogue to reinforce the physiological factors associated with the characters:

> MADAME R: I watch her every day, the rings under her eyes, her hands that suddenly start shaking feverishly. (44)

The adaptation required Zola to condense the action he does retain in the play, with the consequence that Madame Raquin's paralysis occurs speedily and suddenly at the end of the third act in a manner reminiscent of gothic melodrama:

> MADAME R: (*Advancing, staggering.*) Oh just God! They killed my child! (*Thérèse, desperate, cries out in terror; Laurent bewildered, throws the portrait onto the bed, and falls back in front of Madame R, who stammers.*) Murders, murders! (67)

In the further stage directions she goes on to have an 'attack of spasms' which Zola, in his inimitable way, describes very precisely. It is worth noting the following line of dialogue:

> LAURENT: It's the attack they warned her of. The paralysis is rising to her throat.

Here Zola is clearly attempting to counter the melodramatic element by providing a more scientific account for what has just occurred. In spite of this he confesses 'I relied, with some calculation, on the gripping element of the play to make the audience accept the lack of plot and the minutiae of detail' (1989: 2). In the final analysis it is clear that the play does draw on existing conventions and Zola himself was aware of this 'Indeed, I have no ambition to wave the flag for my play. It has many faults, and I am a harsher judge of it than anyone' (1).

As Zola acknowledged in the opening lines of his Preface to the play, 'One of the two is bound to be inferior to the other and often both are diminished in the process' (1). Unfortunately, of the two, it is the play that has tended to be regarded in this light. In reviewing one of the rare productions of *Thérèse Raquin* which ran at the National Theatre in London in Autumn 2006, critic Michael Billington commented in the *Guardian*: 'The play, in short, is nothing like as powerful as the novel'. In common with other critics Billington is right, there is a great deal that is lost in the adaptation but in drawing comparisons between them we are in danger of overlooking the importance of the play in terms of what Zola achieved for theatre. If, on the other hand, we compare *Thérèse Raquin* to plays being produced at the time, we gain a clearer picture of the innovations Zola brought to the stage in his attempt to create a 'new mould'. Seen in these terms, Zola felt : 'The attempt has been successful, and I am happier for my future plays than for *Thérèse Raquin*, because I am publishing the latter with a vague regret and a crazing longing to alter entire scenes' (2).

In his manifesto 'Naturalism in the Theatre', written some seven years after his own attempt to bring Naturalism to the stage with *Thérèse Raquin*, Zola is still looking for 'a dramatist of genius' who will revolutionize theatre. Zola provides a lengthy, and at times repetitive, account of theatre as he sees it at the time of writing. He describes the evolution of French drama from the neo-classical tragedy and comedy of the seventeenth-century dramatists Corneille, Molière and Racine through to the eighteenth-century plays produced by Beaumarchais and Voltaire in which: 'romantic drama was already stirring inside tragedy' (1893: 352). He goes on to discuss the early nineteenth century when the romantic drama of Victor Hugo emerged after the revolution. Zola is not dismissive of the earlier drama forms which he recognizes produced artists of genius: 'each within his differing civilization and formula' (355). Indeed, he acknowledges romantic drama as:

> the first step in the direction of the Naturalistic drama towards which we are now advancing. The romantic drama cleared the ground, proclaimed the freedom of art. Its love of action, its mixture of laughter and tears, its research into accuracy of costume and setting show the movement's impulse towards real life. (354)

The drama form, Zola argues, evolves in relation to the specific social conditions and spirit of the time and if we consider the history of drama more extensively we can trace these distinct periods and their respective forms. Romantic drama, a necessary response to the conditions of the time, was, for Zola, now outdated: 'Naturalism alone corresponds to our social needs; it alone has deep roots in the spirit of our times [...]' (359). Zola insightfully reminds the reader: 'one can never tell quite when a movement is getting under way; generally its source is remote and lost in the earlier movement from which it emerged' (357).

In this respect he acknowledges: 'the great naturalist evolution, which comes down directly from the fifteenth century to ours has everything to do with the gradual substitution of physiological man for metaphysical man' (1893: 367). For Zola then, the 'physiological man' has emerged with greater clarity in succeeding dramatic forms. The nineteenth-century dramatists have similarly contributed to the increasing: 'reality of our corpus of drama, to progress towards truth, to sift out more and more the natural man and impose him on the public' (368).

Indeed, Zola suggests that some excellent work has been produced by the contemporary playwrights Alexander Dumas fils and Émile Augier, and whilst critical of their style, acknowledges they have produced: 'characters in them who are ingeniously examined and bold truths taken right on to the stage' (1893: 357). For Zola, drama was evolving to the degree that realist tendencies were becoming more evident: 'Can we believe that *L'Ami Fritz* would have been applauded at the Comédie-Française twenty years ago? Definitely not! This play, in which people eat all the time and the lover talks in such homely language, would have disgusted both the classicists and the romantics. To explain its success we must concede that as the years have gone by a secret fermentation has been at work' (357). Clearly, Zola felt that whilst there had been various attempts and experiments at a Naturalist formula, of which he, of course, had first-hand experience, in the final analysis none of these attempts had any 'decisive' impact.

Convinced that the future lay in Naturalism and that a formula would be found, Zola believed that this meant a return to the 'tragic framework', not the rhetoric or declamation of tragedy but rather the: 'simplicity of action and its unique psychological and physiological study of the characters [...] one deed unwinds in all its reality, and moves the characters to passions and feelings, the exact analysis of which constitutes the sole interest of the play – and in a contemporary environment, with the people who surround us' (1893: 366).

In the final pages of the manifesto Zola sets out his views on costume, stage, design and speech, producing what is, in effect, a guide to playwrights. He urges playwrights to explore the possibilities of a range of settings for their drama suggesting factories, mines, stations, markets, where they will find 'the activities of modern life' (369). A visit to observe the different classes and different occupations within the setting is all that is required for inspiration. Zola hopes that the playwright will represent real people and: 'not those whining members of the working class who play such strange roles in the boulevard melodrama' (369).

In terms of the staging, costume must be authentic, and the set must be a detailed and accurate reproduction of the environment, not simply for the 'picturesque quality' but rather for dramatic utility: 'The environment must determine character' (369). For Zola 'everything is interdependent' if the set and costume are accurate, then so too will be the character. Each character is an individual and it is incumbent upon the playwright to represent them as such with: 'individual ways of thinking and expressing themselves' (371). Critical of the conventions of 'theatre language' and 'theatre voice', Zola maintains that each character should have their own language. Playwrights should avoid the temptation to use conventional theatre language which is then imposed on all characters irrespective of age and gender. Instead, dialogue should be simple: 'the exact word spoken without emphasis, quite naturally' (370). If the theatre language is natural, the actors' voice and diction will similarly be natural: 'he will speak on stage as he does at home' (371). What remained to be found, however, were the new playwrights: 'men of genius who can fix the naturalistic formula' (359). As we shall see, new actors would be required to interpret the work and new theatres to produce the work.

Without doubt Zola is the most important figure associated with the development of Naturalism. His writing, both literary and theoretical, had an enormous influence on the development of the Naturalist form of representation in drama and his theories provided the basis on which other dramatists would go on to produce their own manifestos on Naturalism.

August Strindberg

In 1887 the Swedish writer August Strindberg sent a copy of his play *The Father*, which had earlier been rejected by theatres in Stockholm, to Émile Zola. In a letter to Zola, he described the play as: 'a drama composed with an eye to the experimental formula' (Strindberg quoted in Schumacher, 1996: 302). Strindberg was extremely disappointed to find that, whilst Zola saw some merits in the work, he was largely critical and:

> somewhat uncomfortable with the shortcuts in your analysis. You know perhaps that I am not fond of abstraction. I like it when characters have a complete social identity, when one can rub shoulders with them, when they breathe the same air as we do. And your Captain who does not even have a name, and your other characters, who are almost reasonable beings, do not give me the complete sense of life which I demand.
>
> (Zola quoted in Schumacher, 1996: 303)

As Evert Sprinchorn notes in his article 'Strindberg and the Greater Naturalism' in *The Drama Review* (1968), Zola's criticisms of *The Father* were to have a significant influence on his next play, *Miss Julie: A Naturalistic Tragedy*, written the following year. Strindberg had stood trial for blasphemy in 1884 and, although acquitted, understandably: 'felt that his whole career as an original writer depended on attracting a European following' (Sprinchorn, 1968: 120). Eager to please both Zola and Antoine (whose work at the Théâtre Libre was by now widely acknowledged) and perhaps concerned that the play would not be naturalistic enough, Strindberg produced a Preface in an attempt to give the work a 'proper façade' (120). This view is echoed to a greater or lesser extent by most critics and the general consensus seems to be that *Miss Julie* is rather less naturalistic than the Preface, written shortly after the play was completed, would suggest. Consequently, a number of Strindberg's claims are a little confusing, if not somewhat misleading. None the less, it is considered to be one of the most important manifestos on Naturalist theatre, and given the popularity of the play and the frequency of productions today it is probably the most well known of Naturalist manifestos.

Strindberg's Preface is, in many respects, remarkably similar to Zola's manifesto 'Naturalism in the Theatre'. He, similarly, regards European theatre as being in a state of crisis, a 'dying art form' which will continue to die all the while dramatists simply pour 'new ideas into old forms'. Where Zola, in his manifesto, is calling for someone to revitalize theatre, Strindberg in his Preface appears to have taken on this role, and *Miss Julie* is his attempt to 'modernize the form' both in terms of subject matter and style. In an essay 'On Modern Theatre and Modern Drama' (1889) written for the monthly journal *Ny Jor,* Strindberg discusses in greater detail the state of European contemporary theatre. He acknowledges 1873 as the first milestone of Naturalist representation 'With *Thérèse Raquin,* the great style, the deep excavation into the human mind, had for a moment attracted attention, but no successors seem to have the courage to appear' (Strindberg quoted in Schumacher, 1996: 300). Interestingly, Strindberg chose to overlook the plays of Henrik Ibsen but rather focus on the drama of Henry Becque. Becque (1837–1899), a French playwright whose work was produced at Théâtre Libre, was, as Schumacher notes, 'the model of the new Naturalist school, but he refused steadfastly to ally himself to Zola and kept aloof of the exciting theatrical ventures of the late 1880s and 1890s' (1996: 17). Strindberg is dismissive of Becque's play *Corbeaux* and it is in relation to Becque's notion of Naturalism that Strindberg most clearly articulates his own view:

> This is photography which includes everything, even the grain of dust on the lens of a camera: this is realism, a working method elevated to a form of art, or the small art which does not see the wood for the trees; this is mistaken naturalism which believes that it is merely a matter of copying a corner of nature in a natural manner, but it is not the great naturalism which seeks those points where the great battles take place, which loves seeing what you don't see every day, which rejoices in the struggle of the natural forces, whether those forces are called love and hatred, the spirit of revolt or social instincts, which is indifferent to whether something is ugly or beautiful, as long as it is great. (Strindberg quoted in Schumacher, 1996: 300)

Strindberg, for whom 'the joy of living' is to be found in the 'hard ruthless battles of life' (1992: xiii), chose in *Miss Julie* an 'unusual but instructive case'(xiii) based on a story he had heard. Strindberg, a prodigious writer known also for his novels, poetry and political essays, very often drew on events and experiences that had shaped his own life. The 'case' he presents in *Miss Julie* is one Ross Shideler in the *Cambridge Companion to Strindberg* suggests has its origins in Strindberg's own experience: 'the son of an upper-middle-class merchant and a serving woman' (2009: 61). He similarly draws on: 'his own love affair with the upper-class Siri von Essen, who was married when their affair began […]' (61). It would seem that additional material might also derive from a period of time he spent living in Denmark and his acquaintance with a countess and her half-sibling brother, the product of his father's relationship with a servant. It seems Strindberg also had a relationship with the young man's 17-year-old sister (61). Clearly, the subject matter for *Miss Julie* is informed by Strindberg's own experience: 'of these various class conflicts based on sexual relationships [...]' (61). We should note, as Shideler points out: 'that Strindberg identified with both of his main characters; thus their battle offers an insight into the struggle within himself between his own sense of a lower- and upper-class split identity' (62).

The subject of class conflict situates the play within the prevailing milieu, the social and cultural environment in which the aristocracy was falling apart under the weight of the rising middle classes. Strindberg views Jean and Julie as: 'modern characters, living in an age of transition, an age more restless and hysterical at any rate than the preceding one, I have portrayed them as unstable and split, as a mixture of the old and new!' (1992: xv). His 'souls' are 'conglomerations' of the past and the present and Strindberg draws on the language of the Naturalists to explain this split: 'Jean, belches up certain modern ideas alongside his hereditary ideas of a slave soul' (xv). Julie, the product of a mixed heritage, is the modern version of: 'the half woman, the man-hater who will inflict vengeance on herself, as she does here, out of that innate or acquired sense of honour, which the upper classes inherit' (xvii).

Strindberg articulates the struggle of the social classes in what we would now regard as more dubious terms drawing on Darwin's concept of 'survival of the fittest' to account for: 'the fall of one family means the rise of another' (1992: xii). In similar terms: 'The servant Jean is the founder of a new species. He is the son of a farm labourer working his way up to becoming a gentleman' (xviii). It is Jean who will emerge unscathed: 'from the conflict and will very likely end up as a hotel keeper, and even if he does not become a Romanian count, his son will probably go to university and perhaps even reach a position of power' (xviii). In a similar manner, his misogynistic and somewhat uncomfortable account of the 'half-woman' is couched in terms of evolutionary theory for which the 'law of genetics' will determine the outcome: 'the breed is degenerate and unhealthy. They don't last' (xvi). Strindberg here is discussing the characters as representations of different classes, and in Julie's case, a type of female.

Of more interest is his discussion of the individual characters in the play. Drawing on the Naturalist view of determinism, Strindberg builds on these ideas to demonstrate the complexity of human behaviour, Julie's 'tragic' fate is therefore determined by what Strindberg calls a 'multiplicity of motives':

> The mother's 'bad' basic instincts; the father's wrong way of bringing up the girl; her own nature and the influence of her fiancé's suggestions on her weak, degenerate brain. More specifically: the festive atmosphere of Midsummer's Eve; her father's absence; her menstruation; her preoccupation with the animals; the exhilarating effect of the dance; the nocturnal twilight; the strong aphrodisiac influence of the flowers and finally, chance, which

brings these two people together in a private room – plus, of course, the confidence of the aroused man. (1992: xiii)

In this respect his approach is as 'modern' as he boasts. There is no opportunity for the spectator to simply 'select' the motive 'that is easiest for him to grasp' (xii). What is played out in performance is a complex psychological process between two individuals that not only draws them into a sexual encounter, but leads to a destructive struggle for which the outcome can only be tragic. Julie's suicide is problematic, particularly if we consider it solely in terms of class or gender as Strindberg sets out in the Preface. If we focus more on Julie as a complex individual she 'kills herself not because she is an aristocrat but because she is Julie' (Sprinchorn cited in Shideler, 2009: 68).

Strindberg, in fact, has little to say on this and yet it is in this psychological process that he exerts his power as a dramatist most fully: 'I have done this because today people are mostly interested in the psychological process. Our inquisitive minds are not satisfied with seeing something happen, without finding out how it happens' (1992: xx). In this respect Strindberg has attempted to produce a more authentic dialogue which 'meanders', as 'one brain randomly connects with another brain' (xx). It is the psychological drama at the core of the play which accounts for its continuing popularity.

It is worth noting Strindberg's reference to: '"waking suggestion", a kind of hypnosis' (xvi). Later in the Preface he refers to the 'suggestive influence of the author-hypnotist' (xxi). These references are significant both to the relationship between Jean and Julie and to the relationship between performance and audience. Strindberg had, two years earlier, written a series of essays focusing on psychic phenomena. In one essay, 'Psychic Murder (Apropos 'Romersholm')', reproduced in *The Drama Review*, Strindberg explains his view that the struggle for power between individuals which once was a physical one: 'has developed into something more psychic but no less cruel' (1968: 115). In this essay, as Rolfe Fjelde notes, Strindberg suggests that human relationships centre on a 'contest of and for power' (1978: 113). This is a psychological contest in which the cultivation of suspicion, the power of suggestion, and self-deception have a role to play. Among the examples Strindberg provides to support his ideas, he cites Ibsen, who, in his character Rebecca: 'has unconsciously, it seems, touched on the psychic murder phenomenon in *Romersholm*' (1968: 115). Sprinchorn (1968) points out that in another of Strindberg's essays 'The Battle of the Brains' he elaborates further on psychic struggle and the power of suggestion. Drawing on the ideas of Hippolyte Bernheim, a French neurologist whose work on hypnotism and suggestion Strindberg was familiar with, Strindberg argues: 'suggestion is only the strong brain's struggle with and victory over the weaker, and that this procedure is applied unconsciously in everyday life' (Sprinchorn, 1968: 123). As the earlier Naturalists had been influenced by the natural and biological theories emerging in the middle of the century, Strindberg was similarly influenced by new theories in neurology and psychology. As Sprinchorn notes: 'The bedrock of his philosophy lay in the conviction that life was to be viewed less as a struggle against heredity and environment, as the Naturalists insisted, than as the struggle of minds, each seeking to impose its will on other minds' (122).

The Preface not only provides the opportunity for Strindberg to contextualize the play within the realms of Naturalism it also serves to document his ideas for modernizing the form. Sprinchorn is of the view that: 'The *Julie* preface shows very clearly how alert Strindberg was to what was going on in the French capital; there is scarcely a thought in it that is original with him' (1968: 121). This is, perhaps, a little harsh because the originality of some of his ideas arguably outweigh those aspects he refers to which had already become practice elsewhere in Europe.

Strindberg is most innovatory in his experiment with the 'concentrated form'. The play runs as one 'single continuous act' which at 90 minutes plausibly becomes 'real' time in which the spectator sees the action unfold. For Strindberg it was important to maintain the audience's 'susceptibility' to both the illusion and the: 'suggestive influence of the author-hypnotist' (1992: xxi). In pragmatic terms, if people were capable of concentrating for this length of time in other circumstances, they would be able to do so for the duration of the performance. Jean and Julie leave the stage on two occasions, early in the play when Julie has persuaded Jean to return to the barn to dance with her and later when, as the revelling servants approach the kitchen, they retreat to Jean's room to escape. For these moments Strindberg introduces what he terms the Pantomime and Ballet to maintain the quality of the illusion and plausibility of what is occurring off stage. In the first instance, Strindberg provides detailed instructions for Christine's stage business but the overall effectiveness of the scene relies on the skills of the actor: 'to create and win acclaim in his own right' (xxii). The 'silent' ordinary action that we find in the opening scene of *Thérèse Raquin* is in Strindberg's play a complete scene. Acknowledging that this breaks with convention Strindberg has the music from the barn in the background in case this ordinary silent action: 'might put too much strain on the audience' (xxii).

> JEAN *offers his arm and leads* MISS JULIE *out.*
> *Pantomime*
> *This is played as if the actress really were alone in a kitchen; when necessary she turns her back to the audience; she never looks out into the auditorium; she never hurries, she's never afraid the audience may become impatient.*
> CHRISTINE *alone. Faint violin music at a distance in schottische time.*
> CHRISTINE *humming to the music: she clears the table after* JEAN, *washes the plate in the sink, dries it and puts it in a cupboard. Then she takes off the*

kitchen apron, takes out a small mirror from a table drawer, places it against
the lilac jar on the table; she lights a candle and heats a hair-pin with which
she curls her hair on her forehead.
She goes to the doorway and listens, then she returns to the table. She finds
MISS JULIE's *handkerchief, which was left behind, she picks it up and smells it;*
then she lays it out, as if in thought. She stretches it, smoothes it and folds it
into four parts.

JEAN: (*enters alone*) She really is wild. The way she dances! And the people
        stand there sneering at her behind her back. Can you believe it,
        Christine?   (1992: 7–8)

Strindberg is emphatic that The Ballet scene, in which the servants enter the
kitchen, drink, sing and dance, is played seriously: 'no coarse sniggers at a situation that puts the lid on the coffin' (xxii). There is to be no suggestion or hint of
what is taking place off stage which might 'put the lid' on what is subsequently
revealed to the audience.

Strindberg, in common with other Naturalist playwrights, chose to use the
single interior setting, relocating the action from the conventional living room
space to the working kitchen area: 'to allow the characters to merge into the
surroundings and to break with the practice of extravagant décor' (1992: xxiii).
In a similar break with convention, he rejects the box set normally associated with
Naturalist drama and instead specifies the following:

A large kitchen, the ceiling and side walls are hidden by drapes and borders.
The back wall stands at an angle. On it are two shelves with copper iron and
pewter pots and pans. The shelves are trimmed with embossed paper. Over to
the right we can see three-quarters of the high, arched exit with two glass doors.
Through these we can see a fountain with a cupid, lilac bushes in bloom and
the tops of poplars.
On the left of the stage we see only the corner of a large tiled stove.
On the right we see one end of the white pinewood kitchen table sticking out,
with a few chairs around it.
The stove is decorated with leafy birch branches. Juniper twigs are scattered
all over the floor and on the table there's a large Japanese spice-jar with flow-
ering lilacs.
An icebox, a washing-up table, a sink.
Above the door there is a large old-fashioned bell, and to the left of the door
there is a speaking tube.
CHRISTINE *stands at the stove, frying.* JEAN *comes in wearing livery, he's*
carrying a pair of large riding boots with spurs, which he puts down where
they can be seen.   (1992: 3)

Strindberg explains his decision for the set:

> As far as the design is concerned, I have borrowed asymmetry and sugges-
> tion (showing part of an object rather than the whole) from the impressionist
> painters, hoping that this might add to the illusion. By not seeing the entire
> room and all the furniture, the audience is given room for speculation, in
> other words the imagination is set in motion and completes the picture.
>
> (xxiii)

The angle of the backcloth and table are sited to enable the actors to talk to each
other across the table, providing a more convincing stage picture and stage environment for the actors.

In many respects the final section of the Preface describes Strindberg's ideal of
a new theatre. Inspired by the intimacy of Antoine's Théâtre Libre, Strindberg
similarly calls for a small stage with a small auditorium where footlights distorting
the face of the actors would be abolished, and instead side lights would be used
to enhance the actors facial expressions and subtle expressions of the eyes. In this
theatre there would be no orchestra and no boxes with distracting occupants, and
the auditorium would be kept in darkness for the duration of the performance.
Indeed, in November 1888 Strindberg attempted to set up an experimental theatre
'modelled' on Antoine's Théâtre Libre, but this was never realized and it would
not be until 1907 that his Intimate Theatre opened. Strindberg produced one
further Naturalist play *Creditors* (1888).

CHAPTER SUMMARY

- Émile Zola articulated his ideas on Naturalism in a number of publications that
  were often written in relation to his plays and novels.
- Zola's concept of Naturalism was influenced by such ideas as evolution,
  heredity and determinism.
- Zola's scientific approach to Naturalism was a product of his age with its
  advances in scientific investigation.
- Zola saw the modern writer as an observer of human behaviour and he demonstrated this in his novel *Thérèse Raquin*, which he subsequently adapted for the
  stage.
- Strindberg and Zola believed that the contemporary theatre was in crisis and in
  great need of reform.
- Strindberg set out his ideas on the modern naturalistic theatre in his preface to
  his play *Miss Julie*.

- His concerns for class struggle, determinism and the rise of the middle classes reflect the spirit of his age and his interest in human motives as causes of behaviour.
- Strindberg advocated a more intimate and less protracted form of theatre.

SEMINAR AND WORKSHOP TOPICS

1 Select scenes from *Thérèse Raquin* and act them out following the stage directions precisely. Then discuss the results and the reasons for the prescribed actions and moves.
2 Why did Zola and Strindberg consider that the contemporary stage needed reform?
3 Read the section in Chapter 3 which expands on the subject of evolution and then reread this chapter. To what extent were Zola and Strindberg influenced by Darwin?
4 Which plays were most popular in the European and American theatre of the 1880s? How do the plays of Zola and Strindberg differ from them?
5 Demonstrate how the stage version of *Thérèse Raquin* is a 'well-made play'.
6 What impression of contemporary acting practice do you gain from Strindberg's preface to *Miss Julie*?
7 What are the motives that drive the characters in *Thérèse Raquin* or *Miss Julie*?

FURTHER READING

Cole, T., ed. (1961) *Playwrights on Playwriting*, New York: Hill & Wang. This excellent collection contains both Zola's *Naturalism in the Theatre* and Strindberg's *Preface*.

Pavis, P. (1998) *Dictionary of the Theatre: Terms, Concepts and Analysis*, Buffalo: University of Toronto Press. Although never easy reading, Patrice Pavis's exposition on Naturalistic Staging is particularly useful at this point in our exploration.

Schumacher, C., ed. (1996), *Naturalism and Symbolism in European Theatre 1850–1918*, Cambridge: Cambridge University Press. This provides an excellent overview of Naturalism, reproducing important evidence and correspondence.

Strindberg, A. (1962) *The Chamber Plays*, trans. E. Sprinchorn and S. Quinn, New York: Dutton. This edition includes some fascinating pamphlets that Strindberg wrote for his own small theatre company, including his summary of the development of Naturalism.

Zola, E. (1992) *Thérèse Raquin*, trans. A. Rothwell, Oxford: Oxford University Press. The Introduction to this edition provides one of the most helpful explorations of Naturalism available.

Naturalism in Its Context

CHAPTER 3

The European Scene

A world in flux

The period which saw the development of the concept of Naturalism also experienced huge and often disturbing changes to the intellectual, social, political and physical landscape of Europe. Old certainties were swept away in the name of science, industrialization and progress, and new inventions in transport and communications created a world of bewildering and ever-increasing speed. The poet Matthew Arnold spoke of 'this strange disease of modern life/with its sick hurry, its heads o'er taxed, its divided aims, its palsied hearts' (*The Scholar Gypsy*). Writing about the experience that must have confronted the mid-nineteenth-century author Nerval, the brilliant biographer Richard Holmes captures the *Zeit-geist* of the period:

> The rootlessness of his condition in many ways represents the larger transformation that was painfully coming over the whole of Europe since the Revolution and the Napoleonic Wars. France was changing from a traditional to a modern, industrial society with its popular press, its railways and steamships, its banking and commerce and its increasingly materialistic values. The spirit of Romanticism was being overcome by Realism like a candle being carried into a room fitted with electric lights. One is tempted to say that had Nerval been born earlier he would have been saved by religion; had he been born later he would have been saved by psychology.
>
> (1985: 262)

In this short paragraph Holmes highlights many of the key issues which we shall explore in this chapter. The steady and unnerving shift from a predominantly rural to an industrial, urban society can be seen in records of population changes in Britain. The census of 1830 showed that the population had doubled in 30 years. During the second half of the century cities like London and Paris also doubled in size and this, very often, resulted in chronic overcrowding. The Naturalist Charles Darwin, whose writing was to make such a profound impact on Europe and America, observed that London had become 'the modern Babylon' and so overwhelming in size that 'a pedestrian could not encompass it in a day's time' and that one found oneself engulfed in 'great waves of people silently surging through the gloom' (Desmond and More, 1992: 197). By contrast, English villages showed a steady decline in population. For example, records for the Sussex village of Ringmer show a loss of 100 inhabitants every ten years, many of the young women going into service or joining men in factories, mechanized mills or dock-yards.

Industrialization demanded enormous resources in energy and power: initially it was water power, but increasingly it was coal that provided steam, gas and, even-tually, electricity. The constant demand for coal to fire the steam engines shaped the physical landscape and the lives of generations of miners and their dependants and there was a heavy price to pay. Reliance on coal impinged on everyday life in many cities. When Charles Darwin spoke of the dark clouds of 'a soft black drizzle, with flakes of soot in it as big and full-grown as snow flakes – gone into mourning, one might imagine, for the death of the sun', he could have been describing life in any one of the great industrial cities and the effect produced by a large population burning coal: 'hell's own fuel, torn from the bowels of the earth' (quoted in Desmond and More, 1992: 206). In London, he said, 'one draws gloom with every breath: it is in the air; it enters every pore, One's head is heavy and aching, one's stomach has trouble functioning, breathing becomes difficult for the lack of pure air' (206). But, regardless of health hazards, the factories manufacturing goods for the new consumerism required the energy that coal provided and so did the railways that transported both that coal and an increasingly mobile population.

The railways were a great catalyst for change: from the 1840s onwards over 100,000 people in London were forcibly displaced from their homes to make way for new railways and, as a result, were obliged to live even closer to the centre of the city in order to find work. Most parts of the country were rapidly joined together by a network of railways; in 1844 there were just 2000 miles of track and by 1890 this had extended to 13,000 miles. The British invention rapidly spread and the nation was soon building or advising on the building of railways in Germany, Belgium, France, Russia, Spain and Italy, and in Africa, the Americas and Australia, where this linking together of huge territories was an instrument of control and imperialism.

In Norway, the dramatist Ibsen reflected on the human cost and impact of industrial progress, and particularly of the railways in his play *The Pillars of Society* (1877). A major strand of the play deals with the controversy surrounding a proposed building of a coastal railway line. The wealthy shipping owner (Bernick), who is behind the scheme, debates the morality of the project with a local school-master and, in so doing, identifies one of the central dilemmas of the movement for 'progress' that engulfed Europe :

BERNICK: Well, say a man is thinking of building a great factory. He knows for certain, because all his experience has taught him, that sooner or later in this factory, human life will be lost.

ROERLUND:	Yes, I fear that is only too likely.
BERNICK:	Or a man is planning to open a mine. He employs men and children, and young men with all their lives before them. It's certain, is it not, that some of these men will lose their lives in his service?
ROERLUND:	Alas, yes.
BERNICK:	Well, a man in such a position knows before he starts that the project he is launching will at some stage of its development cost human life. But this project is for the general good. For every life it takes it will equally, beyond doubt, provide the means of happiness for many hundreds of people.
ROERLUND:	Ah, you're thinking of the railway—all that dangerous quarrying and dynamiting and so on—
BERNICK:	Precisely, I'm thinking of the railway. (1980d: Act III, 89)

The awful truth that lay behind Bernick's concern was vividly demonstrated in the 1890s when the construction of the Uganda Railway in that British colony in Africa resulted in the deaths of 2498 workers.

Manufactured goods, ideas, fashions, literature, plays and theatre companies traversed the continents by rail and the seas by steamship. Ibsen's plays are littered with characters who have arrived by steamer or travelled by rail. One such journey demonstrating the impact of these new modes of transport and the way in which they linked countries and communities is described memorably in his play *When We Dead Awaken* (1899):

RUBEK:	It reminds me of that night we spent in the train coming up from the Continent—
MAJA:	You were asleep the whole time.
RUBEK:	Not the whole time. I noticed how silent it was at all those little places we stopped at. I—heard the silence-like you, Maja—And then I realised we had crossed the frontier. Now we were home. I knew it because at every one of those little roadside halts, the train stopped, and stood quite still—though nothing ever happened.
MAJA:	Why did it stop if there was no one there?
RUBEK:	Don't know. No one got off, no one got on—and yet the train stood there absolutely silent, for minute after minute—as it might have been eternity. And at every station I heard two men walking down the platform—one of them had a lantern in his hand—and they muttered to each other softly, tonelessly, meaninglessly in the night.
MAJA:	Yes, you're right. There are always two men who walk and talk together—
RUBEK:	About nothing. (*Changes his tone, and speaks more cheerfully*)

> Never mind, we only have to wait until tomorrow. Then the liner
> will put into harbour; and we shall go on board, and sail along the
> coast, northwards, as far as we can go-right up to the Arctic.
>
> (1980d: 218)

People were forced to mix together in transit, for although the railway carriages
may have been classified as First, Second or Third Class, we know from the
popular contemporary paintings of stations that the railways were busy and sometimes chaotic meeting places of all sections of society. It was no longer possible
for travellers to live in ignorance of those other people who shared the planet. In
many ways the railways were a great leveller, but this was not always a comfortable
experience: when the first major railway station in Germany was opened in
Hanover in 1846, the King, Ernst August, was said to have remarked that it was
unacceptable that 'a mere shoemaker could travel at the same speed as a king'
(quoted in the audio guide to the Historisches Museum, Hanover). However, the
early Realist British playwright Tom Robertson was quick to make reference to
the modern experience of rail travel in his play *Caste* (1867), for one of his characters supplies this metaphor for life in his insistence that people should 'know
their place':

> I mean what I say. People should stick to their own class. Life's a railway
> journey, and Mankind's a passenger—first class, second class, third class.
> Any person found riding in a superior class to that for which he has taken
> his ticket will be removed at the first station stopped at, according to the by-
> laws of the company. (1972: 359)

Scribe's play *Le Puff*, usually translated as *Believe it or Not* (1848) opens with an
omnibus incident, a reminder that it was the railways and the omnibus and tram
(both initially horse-drawn) that enabled the new middle classes to work in one
location and live and find their entertainment in another. Thus the 'suburbs' came
into being with their comfortable housing and local amenities and, to some extent,
this helped to relieve the overcrowding of cities and to intensify the squalid living
conditions of the working classes who could travel only on foot. The inhabitants
of the suburbs were the new theatre audiences who wanted to see plays that
reflected the truth of their lives, the reality of contemporary debates and of their
personal values. The energy, vision and sometimes ruthless entrepreneurship that
characterized the period in which Naturalism flourished is summed up by another
of Ibsen's characters, the former banker John Gabriel Borkman in the play of the
same name (1896):

> BORKMAN: Yes, but I could have created millions! Think of all the mines I
> could have brought under my control, the shafts I could have

sunk. I would have harnessed cataracts—hewn quarries. My ships would have covered the world, linking continent to continent. All this I would have created alone. (1980d: Act II, 159)

And at a later stage in the play, Borkman tells that he has had visions of 'being an aeronaut … in some giant balloon' (Act II, 167).

Nevertheless, it was difficult for even the most self-centred of the new middle class to ignore the fact that rapid industrialization and urbanization had resulted in many thousands of their fellow citizens living in the most appalling and unsanitary conditions which, combined with minimal provision for public health, led to a bleak and often hopeless existence for a section of society constantly surrounded by death. A visit to any nineteenth-century cemetery will reveal the extent to which middle-class families, still unaware of the true nature of infection, suffered bereavement and took comfort from their religious beliefs, but the degree of infant and adult mortality among the lower classes was shocking.

Playwrights, visual artists and novelists were among those who strove to draw attention to such social conditions and problems; attempting to confront their audiences with uncomfortable reality.

The great Naturalist

The publication of Charles Darwin's *Origin of Species* (1859) had profound implications for the development of Naturalism in drama and continues to have repercussions to this day. Darwin's theory of evolution, based on the systematic, careful and detailed observation of nature, radically changed the way in which European and North American society thought about the factors that determined human behaviour and the position of humanity in the universe.

The revolutionary idea of evolution challenged the 'truth' of the biblical account of the creation of the world as contained in the first book of *Genesis* and therefore cast doubt on the authority of any branch of Christianity that based its teaching on scripture. However, not only did it suggest that the story of the creation of the world in seven days was, at best, a myth, it also implied that human behaviour was not based on humankind's inherent wickedness and sinfulness, as taught by *Genesis*, but was, like any other animal behaviour, driven by the primal needs of survival and reproduction and by heredity or the environment. In considering the almost infinite variations of the natural world Darwin felt convinced that: 'These elaborately constructed forms, so different from each other and dependent upon each other in so complex a manner, have all been produced by laws acting around us' (*Origin of Species*).

Understanding those laws became not only the task of the naturalist but also of the dramatist. The world which playwrights set out to explore was one in

Charles Darwin 1809–1882

Charles Darwin was the son of a Shrewsbury doctor and the grandson of Erasmus Darwin, one of the most original and radical free thinkers of the eighteenth-century Enlightenment. Both Darwin's mother and his wife were descendants of the famous potter Josiah Wedgwood: a key figure in the Industrial Revolution in Britain.

In 1831, following periods at Edinburgh and Cambridge Universities, the young Darwin turned his back on possible careers in medicine or the Church in order to become Naturalist aboard the ship *HMS Beagle* that was to undertake a scientific expedition to the South American Coast and the Pacific Islands. The meticulous collections, observations and recordings of what he saw of wildlife, human life and geological features on this five-year voyage led to the publication of Darwin's *Voyage of the Beagle* on his return. This established him as a central figure in the popularization of science and his collection of plants, insects, fossils and other specimens remain in the Natural History Museum to this day.

However, Darwin's observations, deductions and creative thinking undertaken during and following his expedition resulted in his conviction that species, including the human race, *evolve* and that through *natural selection*, only those that adapt and modify will survive. In one of many publications extending the ideas of Darwin, Herbert Spencer was later to express this idea as 'the survival of the fittest'.

Darwin was acutely aware that such notions would be deeply offensive to many believers in the idea of a creator God and particularly to his wife, Emma, a committed Christian. He therefore was reticent in publishing his theory, aware of the hurt and controversy it would cause.

Darwin was, nevertheless, not alone in his deductions from what he had ▶

which there was no intervening God who shaped events and fixed the position of individuals in a hierarchy or social scale. Instead, it was a world in which conduct was affected by the physical conditions for living (as in Hauptmann's *The Weavers*), by what might have been inherited in terms of character or disease (as In Ibsen's *Ghosts* or Brieux's *Damaged Goods*) and by the need for survival (as in the plays of Zola). Darwin had already established the idea of natural selection by which the fittest and strongest species survived, often by developing behaviour and characteristics appropriate to particular living conditions.

Some of Darwin's ideas were also extended by his cousin, Francis Galton, to include the concept of 'good breeding'. In 1863 he suggested that controlled human breeding might be desirable and, in his book *Hereditary Genius* (1869), postulated the idea that the improvement of the human race could be achieved by encouraging reproduction only among the virtuous, aristocratic and observed in nature and several scientists, including Thomas H. Huxley, urged him to publish his findings. The final push came when the remarkable, almost self-educated Alfred Wallace, sent Darwin a manuscript that almost pre-empted the closely guarded Theory of Evolution and reluctantly Darwin published his revolutionary *Origin of Species* in 1859. The debates following its publication, especially the public confrontation between Huxley and the Bishop of Oxford have become almost legendary, but from that point onward, Darwin became the most translated and influential scientific thinker in Europe and America, demonstrating a passion for the *truth* in all aspects of this work. In many respects his next book, *The Descent of Man* (1871), was of even greater significance because it ranged widely over such topics as ape ancestors and sexual selection to the emergence of morality and religion. All of the many subsequent books by Darwin became immensely popular and were sold out and reprinted very quickly.

Darwin's ideas were widely drawn upon and discussed by those who argued for a fairer society and, conversely, those who justified poverty and mass emigration as aspects of the 'survival of the fittest' as well as by those who investigated and wrote about the determinants of human behaviour.

In a small pamphlet which he wrote for the actors of a small theatre in 1907, the playwright Strindberg spoke of 'the zoological age of Darwin through which we have just passed (1962: 218) and, indeed, the ghost of Darwin stalks the pages of almost every serious nineteenth- or early twentieth-century play. Yet, his ideas have remained controversial, particularly among fundamentalist Christians who adhere to the Genesis narrative. In 1925 a high school science teacher was prosecuted by a court in Tennessee for the 'crime' of teaching Darwin's theory of evolution and this became the subject of the play *Inherit the Wind* (1955) by Jerome Lawrence and Robert E. Lee and of four subsequent movies.

talented. Such ideas, in a society obsessed by class and social standing, were not seen for the danger which they contained, but all too soon the dark shadow of 'eugenics' (as Galton called his science) was to fall across Europe in the hands of the Nazis.

The doctrine of evolution also suggested a degree of inevitability in the idea of progress. Dramatists following Zola aimed to study human behaviour in the same detailed way that Darwin had done and examine those factors that determined a course of action or personality. In this way they embraced the growing concept of Determinism. In his impressive Introduction to *Playwrights on Playwriting* John Gassner (1961) speaks of 'the ambition to give dimension to a character, a degree of meaningful determinacy to behaviour and fluidity to dramatic action' as a characteristic of all of the writers aspiring to achieve Naturalism in their plays and we can see this ambition also in the aims and performance techniques proposed by Stanislavsky.

The study of the mind and the development of psychology

In his *Origin of Species* Darwin pointed to the fact that he saw 'open fields for more important researches' and cited the development of psychology by Herbert Spencer. Darwin's own *The Expression of Emotion in Man and Animals* (1872) and Tuke and Buckhill's *Psychological Medicine* (1882) demonstrated that before Freud there was considerable interest in the subconscious mind.

Even before Darwin postulated his revolutionary theory of evolution, scientists were suggesting that the brain and the mind were not separate entities and that the soul was merely a religious construct for which there was no rational evidence. These contentious ideas were put forward by a group of radical thinkers based in Edinburgh: a city which had established itself in the early nineteenth century as the intellectual capital of Europe and visited by scientists and other thinkers from all over the continent. Darwin was a medical student in Edinburgh and was a great admirer of the militant scientist William Browne who, from his investigations into madness, argued that a belief in the so called 'spiritual' dimension of life was simply a means for perpetuating the power and influence of the Church (which dominated every aspect of society) and that 'saints' were insane. The idea that humans shared with animals very similar brain functions was deeply shocking to those who maintained that in humankind God had created an entirely separate level of being. However, scientists persisted in arguing from material evidence. 'The argumentation which applies to brutes holds equally good of men' maintained Darwin's great supporter Huxley, 'our mental conditions are simply the symbols in consciousness of the changes which take place automatically in the organism' (Harvie, Martin and Scharf, 1970: 200). This materialist argument, suggesting that there are universal laws governing the physical world, was supported in a popular lecture in 1874 by W. K. Clifford, a brilliant young Professor of Mathematics. 'There is no reason', he said, 'why we should not regard the human body as merely an exceedingly complicated machine' but, he added, 'it is not *merely* a machine, because consciousness goes with it. The mind, then, is to be regarded as a stream of feelings which runs parallel to, and simultaneous with, a certain part of the action of the brain' (quoted in Harvie, Martin and Scharf, 1970: 216). Clifford went on to explore whether it was possible to conceive of the idea of mind without body, but came firmly to the conclusion that it was not.

The new work in biology and in particular the theory of evolution from about 1860 onwards enabled scientists to focus on a new range of problems including mental development in the human race and in individuals as influenced by heredity and environment. Work also began in child and animal psychology and on the differences between races and individuals, largely through the influence of Darwin and Galton. As Robert S. Woodworth put it:

Out of the physiological laboratory grew the psychological laboratory, though it was not until 1879 that the first recognized psychological laboratory was set up by Wundt in Leipzig. Soon there were many laboratories, especially in Germany and the United States, and the 'new psychology' as it was in 1900, was experimental psychology. (1931: 7)

Early attempts to popularize and extend the frontiers of the understanding of the brain and mind were initially unable to engage with ideas of emotion, imagination or the effect of experience. These areas of investigation became the prime concern of Sigmund Freud, who enrolled as a student in 1885 and who produced his seminal work *On the Interpretation of Dreams* in 1900. With Freud's work, the focus of development in psychology shifted to Vienna and it was here that the concept of the subconscious mind was developed. What Freud deduced from his many, largely female, patients was that the 'mind' was really the brain's collection of stored experiences and primal drives, many of which could only be accessed through dreams. In developing his technique of 'psychoanalysis', he perceived that human behaviour was constantly shaped by archetypal sexual and relational energies which needed to be sublimated or suppressed, but were often repressed. Society, he argued, was often the chief agent of unhealthy repression and thus, the attitudes pervading 'respectable' living were the root cause of mental disturbance. Freud, and his followers, helped to establish the idea that environment and heredity were major factors in determining human behaviour.

Two of the most striking aspects of the growth of psychology are the diversity of schools of thought that it included and the extent to which it engaged minds in Europe and America. We have, for example, *Functional Psychology*, concerned with the faculties, which had evolved quite early in Europe but was defined in America in 1898; *Structural Psychology*, investigating sensations, which emerged in Germany from 1879 onwards; *Associationism* which explored memory, learning and responses to stimuli and was popular in Britain and Russia by 1903; *Psychoanalysis*, centred on an understanding of desire, developed in Austria in 1900; and *Personalistic and Organismic Psychologies* focusing on the individual as a whole, which were defined in Germany and America from 1900 onwards. Within a few years these were joined by *Behaviourism*, which investigated motor activity in the brain, and *Gestalt* psychology, which was concerned with perception and memory.

We see the influence of the growth of psychology clearly in the work of such dramatists as Zola, Strindberg and Chekhov. We have only to consider Zola's careful observation of disturbed psychological states in his *Thérèse Raquin* to see how a scientific investigation of, and an interest in, the workings of the mind became a characteristic of naturalistic writing. Strindberg developed an interest in dreams and Chekhov, himself a medical doctor clearly aware of the developments in psychology, presents his audiences with studies of repressed, frustrated and often inarticulate characters who are unable to come to terms with inner

Sigmund Freud 1856–1939

Freud lived and practised in Vienna, the capital of the fading Austro-Hungarian Empire, from 1891 until he fled in 1938. During the closing years of the nineteenth and the early years of the twentieth centuries Vienna was in many respects the cultural and intellectual centre of Europe. Freud, for example, made the early German translation of the works of John Stuart Mill that so influenced the naturalistic dramatists and it was here too that Freud created what the novelist William Boyd calls 'one of those revolutions in human understanding and self-knowledge that ranks with [...] Copernicus and Darwin' (*The Guardian*, 04.02.12). For it was Freud who established that much of the irrational, repressed and neurotic behaviour and many of the taboos which characterize human conduct emanated from the unconscious rather than the conscious mind. Freud's model of the unconscious was developed over many years and led him to abandon traditional neurology and hypnosis and to part company with his most famous colleague, Carl Jung. (This rift is now the topic of the film *A Dangerous Method*, 2012). But the terminology and concepts he developed remain current.

In describing the makeup of what he termed 'the psyche', Freud identified the 'id': consisting of the primary drives of life and death, urges and inherited instincts. One major aspect of the id is what Freud called the 'Oedipus complex', that is, the child's craving for exclusive possession of the parent of the opposite sex. The 'ego' Freud claimed, was part of the id and works to ensure the survival of the individual and thus needs to suppress the more antisocial aspects of the id that are at variance with what might be termed 'civilized behaviour'. As a child develops it develops the 'super-ego' or conscience which determines what behaviour is acceptable to the ego and what must be repressed. If the ego is in a state of equilibrium the mental state is healthy but if the ego leans towards the id or the super-ego neuroses will result. One of Freud's most commonly employed terms is the 'libido', the primary sexual longing which ensures the survival of the species, and he maintained that much of the neurosis in society was caused by the repression of the libido because of societal taboos. Accordingly,

drives of which they are unaware. It is no coincidence that it was the characters in Chekhov's plays that became the subjects of the psychologically-based approach to acting devised by Stanislavsky.

The subjection of women

The biblical narrative in the book of *Genesis* had been accepted in Western society as an accurate account of the origins of the world and of humanity for many centuries, and in some circles it still is. Sinful Adam and Eve are ejected from he argued, these repressed desires will emerge in symbolism or slips of speech.

Freud's work is of particular interest to the student of Naturalism in drama: partly because many of the plays that strove for Naturalism employ what we would now recognize as 'Freudian symbolism' of totemic objects and qualities of light as symbols of sexual repression or other mental states . However, Freud himself turned to the analysis of a great naturalistic play, Ibsen's *Rosmersholm*, in an essay he wrote during the First World War. Many of Freud's clients were women and he had developed an intense interest in the pressures and aspirations of women living in an age of repression and attempted emancipation. The character of Rebecca West in Ibsen's play epitomized some of the issues faced by the 'new woman': educated, well-read, radical and sexually adventurous. Kroll, one of the characters, who views Rebecca with total suspicion, comments on how 'the spirit of the age has cast its shadow over my domestic as well as my official life' and laments 'These decadent, cantankerous, demoralising heresies' (Act 1, 39). In his essay *Character Types*, Freud discusses Rebecca's attitudes, her domination by the Oedipus complex and the reasons why she cannot finally agree to marry the man with whom she has been living, has clearly desired and who she has encouraged to adopt an entirely new outlook on life following the death of his wife by suicide.

Freud's words bring to mind the dilemma of the many young women who entered service (see p. 48) and which became the topic of many plays and he also hints at one of his major beliefs: that incidents in early childhood have an indelible effect on subsequent behaviour:

> The practising psycho-analytical physician knows how frequently, or how invariably, a girl entering a household as servant, companion or governess, will consciously or unconsciously weave a daydream which derives from the Oedipus complex, of the mistress of the house disappearing and the master taking the newcomer as his wife in her place. *Rosmersholm* is the greatest work of art of the class that treat of this common fantasy in girls. What makes it into a tragic drama is the extra circumstance that the heroine's daydream has been preceded in her childhood by a precisely corresponding reality (Ibsen, 1980c: 28).

Paradise because of their disobedience to God and their realization of their fall from grace is a sudden awareness of their physical nakedness. As punishment God, who has created Adam and then provided him with a companion, tells the man that he will now have to toil for his living and the woman that she will endure painful labour when she gives birth and will constantly desire, but be subservient to her husband. It is hardly surprising, therefore, that, once this narrative began to be called into question by Darwin and his followers, women began to rebel against the gloomy prospect prescribed for them in *Genesis* and that an entire edifice of attitudes began to crumble. Other changing factors in society also contributed to a shift in the role and prospects for women during the nineteenth century. In England, for example, over one million young women had gone into 'service' in the homes of the aristocracy and newly wealthy middle classes, thus bringing about an imbalance between the sexes in many rural communities. Such women would observe at first hand the behaviour and privileges of their employers and, although their employment created some form of security for them, some also began to harbour aspirations of a better and more independent life. Liaisons between servants and employers became a sometimes shocking topic for new plays: Strindberg's *Miss Julie*, Ibsen's *Ghosts* or the Manchester School's *Mary Broome* (see Illustration 2) are three striking examples. The life of servants 'below stairs' has, in fact, once again become a source of fascination through such television dramas as *Downton Abbey* and *Upstairs Downstairs*.

Those women from poorer families who did not go into service were frequently forced to undertake the role of Adam and toil long hours for their living in mines or in factories, enduring dreadful and physically draining conditions. The wretched state of such women was highlighted in the novels of Zola and Dickens, the etchings of Dore and, in Britain, through a number of Parliamentary Commissions: one such report quoted Betty Harris, a women aged 37, describing her life dragging a coal wagon in a coal pit at Little Bolton:

> I have a belt round my waist and a chain passing between my legs, and I go on my hands and feet. The road is very steep and we have to hold by a rope [...] I am not as strong as I was, and cannot stand the work so well as I used to. I have drawn till I have had the skin off me; the belt and chain is worse when we are in the family way [...]. (Harvie, Martin and Scharf, 1970: 108)

Such terrible accounts did, eventually begin to prick philanthropic consciences across industrial Europe and, slowly efforts were made to provide some more humane working conditions and some rudimentary education for the working classes. At the same time the more leisured classes of women began to seek new educational and professional opportunities and we see the emergence of what finally provided the title of Sidney Grundy's play *The New Woman* (1894).

The concept of women having rights, the entitlement to careers and a life independent of reliance on men, had been strongly advocated by the remarkable Mary Wollstonecraft in the late eighteenth century. Inspired by many of the ideals of the French Revolution, she published her *Rights of Woman with Strictures on Political and Moral Subject* (1792) and this, along with her earlier *Thoughts on the Education of Daughters* (1786), established her as a major force in emerging European feminism. When she took up residence in Paris and her seminal book was translated as *Une Défense des Droit des Femmes* her cause was espoused by the 'Girondists' group, who were determined to bring about social and educational reform, and she became influential with the emerging number of women who were pressing for change.

ILLUSTRATION 2
Mary Broome by Alan Monkhouse: one of many naturalistic plays featuring young women 'In Service'. Production at the Orange Tree Theatre, Richmond, London, 2011. Katie McGuiness as Mary and Leonard Timbrell as Jack Farthing. Directed by Sam Walters (photo by Robert Day)

By the time that the 'Naturalist' playwrights were exploring the role and character of women, a further catalyst for the new attitudes was J. Stuart Mill's *On the Subjection of Women* (1869), where the writer argues strongly that any form of legal impediment to woman's equality with man is wrong and that societal and gender attitudes together with education and marriage all inhibited women's and, indeed, humanity's progress. When this work was translated into Danish it had an immediate effect on the dramatist Ibsen and much of his subsequent work reflects this. In preparation for his play *Hedda Gabler* (1890), which tells the story of a bored, aristocratic women married to an academic, he wrote the following notes about women:

> They aren't all created to be mothers.
> They all have a leaning towards sensuality but are afraid of the scandal.
> They realize that life holds a purpose for them but cannot find that purpose.
> Women have no influence on public affairs. So they want to influence individuals spiritually. (1980b: 233)

Ibsen's rough notes for his play *Ghosts* (1881) are equally revealing:

> These modern women, misused as daughters, as sisters, as wives not educated according to their talents, barred from their vocation, robbed of their inheritance, their minds embittered – these are the women who are to provide the mothers for the new generation. What will be the consequence? (1980a: 21)

The sense of frustration and restriction felt by women was often caused by the very limited prospects they enjoyed even if they did find 'respectable' employment. For most educated women the obvious socially acceptable opportunity was to become a governess in a middle-class home, but as Jeremy Paxman has pointed out in his *Victorians* (2009), this could often be a lonely and problematic existence and was vividly depicted in a number of contemporary paintings. The most memorable portrayal of the role of governess may be in Charlotte Brontë's *Jane Eyre* but in 1841 we find the author writing of a friend, Mary Taylor, who had decided to emigrate to New Zealand because she had 'made up her mind that she cannot and will not be a governess, a teacher, a milliner, a bonnet-maker, nor housemaid. She sees no means of obtaining employment she would like in England, therefore she is leaving it' (quoted in Paxman, 2009: 141)

The 'new woman' rebelled against the theological and legal positions that made her the property of her husband and the intellectual and social inferior of men.

At the same time, educational opportunities for women slowly increased: from the 1860s onwards University places became available to women across Europe and, by the end of the nineteenth century, professions such as medicine, architecture and dentistry included women. As the century progressed an increasing proportion of musicians and performers in theatre were female and these, no doubt, particularly benefited from the dress reforms of the 1860s and 1870s which released women from the bondage of excessively tight and restricting corsets. Accordingly, as Paxman observes, female artists, of whom there was a growing and significant number, depicted women:

> playing tennis, riding bicycles and enjoying the 'intoxication that comes from unfettered liberty', walking around un-chaperoned in towns, engaging in political campaigning – and divorcing their husbands.   (2009: 147)

One such woman is found in the character of Miss Hessel in Ibsen's play *The Pillars of Society* (1877) who, finding herself at a meeting of the Society for the Redemption of Fallen Women. is asked 'Forgive my asking, madam, but what can you possibly contribute to our Society?' and responds: 'Fresh air – Reverend!'

The character of Lona Hessel appears to have been based on the activist Asta Hanseen, who had delivered a controversial and much vilified series of lectures on women's rights in Norway. But, in addition to the impact of John Stuart Mill's work, the impetus for the movement and Ibsen's championing of women's rights also included a number of publications such as Matilda Schjoett's *Conversation of a Group of Ladies about the Subjection of Women,* significantly published anonymously in 1871; the founding of a Women's Reading Society in Christiana (modern day Oslo) in 1874 and the attitudes of his own wife, Susannah.

There were, however, still many impediments to the ambitions of a growing number of educated women in the new 'middle classes'. The influential art critic John Ruskin, who reportedly failed to consummate his marriage when he discovered that his wife had pubic hair, asserted that, were women to learn Latin or Greek, valuable brain space would be taken that would otherwise be better employed in domestic tasks. Other examples of sheer ignorance and prejudice included the common belief that education might lead to sterility and that women should reserve their limited energy for child bearing. Even in the early years of the twentieth century a Victorian mother informed her prospective daughter-in-law that 'all the exercise woman needs is making the bed'! Queen Victoria herself had little time for the 'new woman' either. In response to Caroline Norton, who had scandalized respectable society by walking out on an abusive marriage, she wrote that she 'deplored this mad, wicked folly of Women's Rights', insisting that 'God created men and women different – let them remain each in their own position' (Paxman, 2009: 146). The fact remained that the majority of middle-class women who entered marriage embarked upon years of childbearing (no satisfactory form of contraceptive was widely available) and a constant duty of care for a large family and dependent husband. Families of 11 or 12 children were common and, even among the prosperous, instances of infant mortality common. Charles and Emma Darwin, for example, lost several of their children from what was by all reports, a very happy household.

It was, perhaps, the obsession with 'respectability' engulfing society across Northern Europe and America in the second half of the nineteenth century that made life for women so frequently stressful. Fuelled by the stricter Protestant churches, such as the Lutherans and Baptists, the three stigmas of infidelity, illegitimacy and divorce were heavily tilted against women. Appearances had to be maintained at all costs: the devoted and caring wife/mother living within the rules of marriage was the expected norm. In many cases, their husbands felt free to visit the vastly growing number of prostitutes in the cities provided that discretion was maintained, but any woman found to be unfaithful was marked for life. Many individuals now researching their family histories discover obvious fabrications on birth or marriage certificates designed to cover up illegitimate births or that their ancestors were hastily shipped off to Canada or Australia rather than endure the shame at home when they discovered that they were to be parents before marriage. Divorce was virtually impossible for any other reason than infidelity and in that case the wife, who was her husband's property, was considered the wrongdoer. It was rare for any man to be forced out of employment or home from shame, but all too frequent for that to be the lot of women.

Accordingly, many women were trapped in loveless marriages, a state wonderfully captured in William Quiller Orchardson's 1884 painting *Marriage de Convenance* and it is hardly surprising that when Freud published his seminal work *The Interpretation of Dreams*, which established the foundations of psychoanalysis, he attributed the majority of mental disturbances to repressed sexuality. The bulk of the clients who visited Freud in his Vienna practice were women and his painstaking observation and analysis of their experiences reveals the inner turmoil and blend of respectability and hypocrisy that women often endured.

Given the mental energy and independent spirit that motivated some women unwilling to meekly accept their restricted existence, we find that by far the most engaging and memorable characters in naturalistic drama are female. Whether it be Zola's Thérèse, Ibsen's Hedda Gabler, Nora Helmer, Rebecca West or Lona Hessel, Strindberg's Miss Julie or Chekhov's three sisters or any of his women in *The Cherry Orchard* or *The Seagull*, we see a succession of powerful individuals, often consumed by frustration and boredom, who totally dominate the stage of the late nineteenth and early twentieth centuries. Furthermore, the impetus is continued in the plays of D. H. Lawrence and Arnold Wesker.

As Michael Meyer, the translator of Ibsen's plays, points out (1980), Ibsen particularly frequently returned to the theme of loveless marriages. In *Love's Comedy, Pillars of Society, A Doll's House, The Lady from the Sea* and *Hedda Gabler* he highlights the predicament of trapped women, whereas in *Brand, An Enemy of the People, The Master Builder* and *When we Dead Awaken* he shows men sacrificing the happiness of their wife, or of a woman they love, for some other cause. It is almost as if the affection for and of a wife is expendable. Strindberg, whose own marriage was deeply unhappy, grew impatient with Ibsen's championing of the situation of women and labelled him 'the Norwegian Bluestocking'. That term, which probably originated from the early seventeenth century as a description of what Molière parodies in his play *Les Femmes Savantes* (The Intellectual Ladies) had increasingly become associated with movements for women's equality, especially in terms of suffrage and political rights which swept across Europe, the United States and the British colonies in the late nineteenth century.

Whereas the struggle for some emancipation from crippling attitudes and restrictions was prolonged and difficult, the effort to achieve any political power was even more fraught. Sweden and Bohemia (the current Czech Republic) granted limited voting rights to privileged women in the 1860s, but it was the British colony of New Zealand that was the first 'democratic' nation to permit universal women's suffrage and that was not until 1893. Norway extended the vote to middle-class women in 1907, as did Finland, but British women had to wait until 1928 for equal voting rights, German women until 1919 and, astonishingly, French women until 1944. American women fared little better than their European counterparts for all their nation's belief in democracy and equality and it was well into the early years of the twentieth century before all states granted women equal voting rights.

The move towards women's suffrage spawned a considerable body of plays, the most interesting of which is probably Elizabeth Robins's *Votes for Women* (1907). Robins, who was born in Kentucky, toured the United States as an actress and visited Norway before arriving in England in the 1890s determined to introduce the work of Ibsen to the English stage. As one of the first successful female 'actor managers' she enlisted the support of George Bernard Shaw and other leading figures in bringing *Hedda Gabler* and *The Master Builder* to London and later recounted her struggle in *Ibsen and the Actress* (1924). But she also became a prominent member of the suffragette movement and donated the profits from her play and its subsequent expansion into a novel, *The Convert*, to the purchase of a farm as a rest home for suffragettes who had been imprisoned.

We therefore see in the plays of Ibsen in Norway or John Galsworthy in England how injustices towards women, social struggle and political ferment are a constant factor in the lives of the female characters and in their relationships with men. Such contemporary issues fuelled the need for naturalistic presentation of the dilemmas of real women in real situations if they were to be addressed intelligently.

Nations, empires and revolutions

France, which saw the birth of Naturalism, was at the centre of a Europe that, rather like a game of chess, saw constantly shifting struggles for dominance and power. During the second half of the nineteenth century, the British, Russian, Ottoman and Austro-Hungarian Empires made alliances and enemies in almost equal measure and the newly emerging spirit of nationalism began to create what we now recognize as modern Italy and Germany. As these nations and empires vied for exploitation of colonial wealth and military pre-eminence, the map of Europe was redrawn, boundaries disputed and areas of land and old alliances changed hands. New technologies enabled the construction of more terrible weapons and new modes of transport enabled armies to travel swiftly. The pattern in Europe was replicated in America, where the civil war saw terrible slaughter and armies traversing a whole continent.

By 1849 there was widespread disillusion in France that the ideals of the Revolution had not been realized and street battles resumed: in Britain, politicians watched anxiously as the Chartist movement gained popularity and support for its demands of universal suffrage. As the century progressed it was as if the working people of Europe had woken up to the fact that all talk of common ancestry, rights of men and women, the folly of monarchy and social justice had been ignored by their rulers and that they must take the initiative. What we would

John Stuart Mill 1806–1873

The Victorian British Prime Minister Gladstone described John Stuart Mill, economist, philosopher and social reformer, as 'the saint of rationalism'. His legacy of open-mindedness and the need to consider all evidence before reaching a conclusion has remained a model for all subsequent generations of thinkers.

In 1867, Mill was the first member of Parliament to make a speech in the House of Commons demanding suffrage for women and throughout his life, which included a period of work with the East India Company and a time witnessing the French Revolution at first hand, he acted as the conscience of the age and promoted his ideas in a series of publications. Of these *Principles of Political Economy* (1848) set out a theoretical basis for raising the standard of living for workers through deliberate government policies, whereas *System of Logic* (1843) was the first comprehensive study of logic based entirely on experiential principles. However, it was in the field of ethics and politics that Mill made his greatest and most lasting contribution and his famous publication *On Liberty* (1859) was a seminal work in which he discussed the problems of the individual in society. Writing of the many political and economic influences that he saw as hostile to Individuality, he said : 'it is not easy to see how it can stand its ground. It will do so with increasing difficulty, unless the intelligent part of the public can be made to feel its value'. He continues, 'if the claims of Individuality are ever to be asserted, the time is now' (203).

Mill's substantial essay *Utilitarianism* (1863) firmly established this 'ism' as the mode of thinking for philosophical ▶

now recognize as socialist ideas began to spread across Europe and by the end of the century every major European nation except Russia had acquired some form of constitution guaranteeing at least limited social rights to citizens.

Meanwhile, in Germany, Darwin's most ardent admirer, Ernst Haeckel, was employing a version of what he termed *Darwinismus*, to demand the creation of a German state, with Prussia in the lead, that would guarantee both free speech and free trade. He argued that a common ape ancestry levelled society and made privilege unacceptable, but ominously declared that the concept of biological and national evolution gave hope for a new, Teutonic, 'superior' race: the *phylum*. Indeed, Desmond and Moore tell us that in 1866 when Prussia was victorious in the battle of Koniggratz against the Austrians, Haeckel in welcoming the Prussian leader Bismarck to Jena, said : 'The booming of the guns […] announced the demise of the old Federal German Diet and the beginning of a splendid period in history of the German Reich' (1992: 542).

It was some years before the complete unification of the German states but Prussia continued its aggressive stance towards is neighbours, and by 1870 had entered into a war with France that resulted in the occupation of Paris, the loss of radicals (such as some of the characters in Ibsen's *Rosmersholm*). The underlying philosophical question of 'what is good?' is answered by the assertion that the good is what promotes the greatest happiness of the greatest number of people, and 'happiness' is defined as a preponderance of pleasure and a minimum of pain.

It is hardly surprising, given his convictions, that John Stuart Mill turned his attention to the plight of nineteenth-century women for whom individuality and preponderance of pleasure were frequently suffocated by societal attitudes and conventions

His *The Subjection of Women* (1869) was in some respects an extension of his wife, Harriet Taylor Mill's publication *The Enfranchisement of Women* (1851) and both were seen as outrageous. Arguing from a utilitarian standpoint, Mill maintained that women should enjoy the same opportunities for intellectual and moral education and advancement as men and should have equal opportunities in all aspects of life. Such ideas ran counter to the nineteenth-century ideal of the woman as loyal wife, virtuous mother and homemaker who must be cared for by her husband in exchange for total security. It also questioned biblical notions of women's role and the marriage laws which, he maintained, amounted to a form of slavery. Mill argued that by emancipating women, their relationships with their husbands or other men would be greatly improved and he based all his assertions on the belief that none of the attitudes that had kept women in subjection had ever been tested using empirical methods.

John Stuart Mill's essay was widely translated and read in Europe and acted as a major catalyst to the exploration of women's lives in the plays of the great Naturalist writers.

France's territories in Alsace and Lorraine, and the demise of Napoleon III's Empire. France, humiliated and, as always, reflective, once more became a republic and, prompted by Naturalist writers and playwrights, began to address the many lingering injustices endured by working people, their lack of rights and their poor living and working conditions.

'Have you read Nietzsche?'

This question is posed by Trofimov, one of the characters in Chekhov's play *The Cherry Orchard* (1904) and the way in which it is asked suggests that the writings of the German philosopher might be considered essential reading in thinking circles in the late nineteenth and early twentieth centuries. Friedrich Nietzsche (1844–1900) had indeed made an impact on the intellectual life of the period in an almost unprecedented way and the supreme irony of his life is that he died on the threshold of a century of titanic struggles that he had foreseen. His most famous work, *Thus Spake Zarathustra* (1883), contained his much quoted statement 'God is Dead' and it was his belief that science and rational thinking had made the concept of God redundant that eventually led to his being associated with ideas of nihilism and the meaninglessness of existence. Coupled with Darwin's private conviction that his theory of evolution had also rendered a belief in a creator God unnecessary, the writings of Nietzsche shook many of the foundations of European thought and led to considerable controversy. His main contention was that Judaeo-Christian morality was stultifying , wholly negative and life-denying, and we see this graphically shown in many of the plays of the period. In its place he proposed dispensing with traditional virtues, religions, morality and beliefs in an afterlife in favour of dynamic individual freedom, positive and vigorous living, self-perfection and a 'free spirit'. He contended that the normal limits of humankind could be surpassed by the 'Overman' (or, as it is sometimes misleadingly translated, 'Superman'). Nietzsche was dismissive of human beings who simply followed the crowd, living a comfortable life of acquiescence, and insisted that in order to achieve real vitality and give birth to a 'dancing star', one must experience a sense of inner chaos. This revolutionary approach to life was to inspire many dramatists and artists as they responded to the *Zeitgeist* of the late nineteenth century.

Nietzsche had a particular interest in drama and theatre and had an early association with the composer Wagner, who was attempting to develop a new form of art work that would combine music, poetry, design, theatre technology and acting, using myth as its principal medium. Although Nietzsche later severed his connection with Wagner, his first published book was dedicated to him and was entitled *The Birth of Tragedy* (1872). This was one of a number of important works that contributed to German dramaturgy, dramatic theory and criticism. In this volume Nietzsche focuses on the drama of ancient Greece and argues that the Greeks developed tragedy as a means of avoiding pessimism and celebrating the idea of life as an adventure and struggle against the odds. Because of his constant belief in the assertive and primitive energy of existence his chosen god was Dionysus, the god of revelry and joy in action, in whose honour it is believed that early tragedies were performed. However, Nietzsche made an important distinction between the 'dionysiac' element of drama, represented by the exuberance and dynamic action of the singing and dancing chorus and the 'apollonian' element which expressed itself in what he termed the 'individuating principle' represented by the actors and scenic elements on stage. He maintained that both elements must exist in balance in order for a tragedy to be created. In identifying these two elements he explored the relationship between emotion and thought and appears to anticipate Freud's later distinction between the 'Ego' and the 'Id' (see the section on Freud, p. 46). As Hodgson observes:

> When he says that tragedy achieves a serene synthesis of profoundly contra-
> dictory elements in life and in man himself he seems to argue that tragedy

reconciles not only the visual with the musical but the conscious with the unconscious. (1988: 347)

A considerable number of dramatists were influenced by Nietzsche's writing and in our later chapter discussing the legacy of European Naturalism we examine this factor in relation to both the Irish dramatist, George Bernard Shaw and the American playwright, Eugene O' Neill.

CHAPTER SUMMARY

- The emergence of Naturalism coincided with a period of great social, political and intellectual change in Europe.
- The shift from a largely rural to an urban, industrial economy was a major factor in creating a new audience for theatre.
- New modes of transport enabled people and ideas to travel in previously unimaginable ways.
- The impact of Darwin and his theory of evolution was a key factor in the study of humans in their environment and the challenge to religious belief.
- The exploration of human behaviour in naturalistic plays was greatly influenced by the emerging science of psychology.
- One of the most significant changes in society was a new attitude towards the role of women.
- The spirit of the French Revolution and the unification of Germany and Italy into nations brought about significant changes to the political shape of Europe and contained the potential for catastrophic armed conflict.
- Many of the ideas permeating late nineteenth-century Europe had their origins in the writing of Nietzsche.

SEMINAR AND WORKSHOP TOPICS

1 What evidence do we see of the influence of the writings of Darwin, Nietzsche or John Stuart Mill in the work of any two Nineteenth Century playwrights?
2 Undertake an analysis of any female character in a play by Ibsen using Freud's work on Rebecca West as a model.
3 Devise an improvised theatre piece based on the idea of young women in service during the nineteenth century using ideas from some of the plays mentioned.

4 Discuss the impact of the coming of railways on patterns of life in Nineteenth-Century Europe.
5 Collect photographs and other visual images from the nineteenth and early twentieth centuries and discuss : a) the costumes b) the attitudes conveyed c) examples of new technology shown in the images
6 Discuss the various attitudes to marriage outlined in this chapter.

FURTHER READING

Desmond, A. and Moore, J. (1992) *Darwin*, Harmondsworth: Penguin. A rich and fascinating study of the impact of Darwinism.

Harvie, C., Martin, G. and Scharf, A. (1970) *Industrialisation and Culture 1830–1914*, London: Macmillan for the Open University. Remains an invaluable source for the study of the period.

Holmes, R. (1985) *Footsteps: Adventures of a Romantic Biographer*, London: Hodder & Stoughton. Provides a vivid picture of Europe and key figures in the arts during the second half of the nineteenth century.

Paxman, J. (2009) *The Victorians*, London: BBC Books. Explores many important social attitudes through a consideration of contemporary paintings.

Roberts, J. M. (1997) *The Penguin History of Europe*, Harmondsworth: Penguin Books. An admirable survey of the politics of Europe.

Storrs, A. (2010) *Freud: A Very Short Introduction*, Oxford: Oxford University Press. One of several invaluable and accessible books in this series, which covers many of the topics of this chapter.

CHAPTER 4

Naturalism in the Theatre: The Search for Truth

From the middle years of the nineteenth century onwards, the theatre appeared to be engaged in a constant search for a new kind of 'truth': a concern to reproduce the material and natural world in all its detail with as much accuracy as possible. Émile Zola (1881) one of the chief promoters of Naturalism, observed, however, that:

> Truth can be shown only in small, unnoticed doses. Some people even go so far as to swear that the theatre will die the moment it ceases to be an entertaining lie, destined to console the spectators in the evening for the sad realities of the day.
> (quoted in Cole, 1961: 6)

The relationship between truth, reality and the 'entertaining lie' is a complex one but its manifestation in the mid-nineteenth century depended on a number of emerging factors. Scientific methods of observation, particularly of human behaviour, and technological innovation all became important aspects of the practice of theatre. In Gilbert and Sullivan's comic opera *The Mikado* (1885), one character jokingly points out that because he is describing something that had happened in great detail, he is providing 'artistic verisimilitude' to 'an otherwise dull and boring narrative'. The playwright W. S. Gilbert, who also pioneered a more disciplined approach to stage direction, was keenly aware of the artistic movements that impinged on the theatre and, as we have seen, by bringing together the concepts of scientific enquiry, materialism and pictorial realism, Zola had articulated the movement of Naturalism some twenty years before *The Mikado* was written. So, throughout the second half of the nineteenth century, we see the idea of presenting 'the sad realities of the day', a concern for truthfulness and for an accurate reproduction of the natural world gradually permeating the theatre in Britain, mainland Europe and the United States.

From romance to realism: Irving and the elevation of melodrama

In 1871, the English actor Henry Irving persuaded the management of the Lyceum Theatre in London to allow him to stage a translation of an obscure French melodrama, *The Bells*, by Leopold Lewis. Through his previous productions and public recitations, Irving had gained something of a reputation for playing eccentric and haunted characters, and the leading role of Mathias in *The Bells* (see Illustrations 3 and 4) clearly appealed to his intense approach to character and his macabre imagination. Only a small audience attended the opening night on 25 November but, as Austin Brereton, one of Irving's biographers, reported:

> Irving's performance of Mathias electrified the audience [...] the theatre re-echoed with such applause as had not been heard within its walls for many years and by the Monday morning, all play-going London was aware that a great personality and a great actor had come into his hard-won kingdom.
>
> (1908: 113)

It was not, however, only Irving's personal performance that was a landmark in history, although this is something we can examine carefully because it has been painstakingly documented for posterity. It was the totality of the production that has caused many subsequent critics and theatre historians to date the advent in Britain of that level of realism necessary to create Naturalism from the first night of *The Bells*. Irving's complete concept ranged from his insistence on precise and accurate sound effects to pictorially realistic settings and a passion for detail in lighting. For Irving, *every* aspect of the production had to evoke the material world in detail and this was achieved through developing technology, construction and performance technique. The first audiences were certainly aware of the remarkable nature of the physical presentation of the play. Rather than the kind of scenic display that had characterized many of the cheap melodramas of the age, Irving concentrated on providing an authentic view of life in Alsace. Brereton reports that the critic Dutton Cook had found the costumes, stage fittings and scenery 'of a most liberal and costly nature. The mechanical contrivances are perfect' (1908: 120). Whereas the *Standard* wrote: 'Nothing can be better than the careful manner in which the drama has been put upon the stage. The scenery and mechanical devices are really excellent.' Irving was fortunate in having Hawes Craven, probably the most gifted scenic designer and painter of the age, creating his settings and we can sense from contemporary reports that the entire *mise en scène* of *The Bells* was regarded as remarkable and as ushering in a new era. Something of Irving's achievement in elevating melodrama can be gauged by comparing his work to that described by the despairing and unsuccessful French dramatist Gerard Nerval:

> There is only one play that ever succeeds in Paris. It's been seen for thirty years and the public wants to go on seeing it. You take a mother and her son—Act 1, the son is lost. Act V the son is found again. The mother cries: 'my son!' The son cries: 'mother!' The audience bursts into tears and the dramatist receives a cloudburst of money. (Quoted in Holmes, 1985: 252)

ILLUSTRATION 3
Henry Irving as Mathias in *The Bells* by Leopold Lewis, first performed in 1871 (photograph courtesy of The Art Archive)

ILLUSTRATION 4
Cartoon from a Dublin Newspaper (1881) showing the electric effect on the audience of Irving's realistic acting in *The Bells* and in *The Belle's Stratagem*

We are not suggesting that Irving established Naturalism on the English stage, but we are suggesting that he created the theatrical conditions and attitudes that provided an essential bridge from the escapist, romantic dramas of the past to a more serious attempt to present real life in all its material reality on stage and to show humankind shaped by powerful environmental and psychological forces.

Melodrama and the advance of theatre technology

Le Juif Polonaise by Émile Erckmann and Alexandre Chatrian, the play on which *The Bells* was based, had been presented in Paris in 1869 and was fairly typical of the melodramas (literally 'music dramas') that were the most popular form of theatrical entertainment for relatively unsophisticated and often illiterate nineteenth-century audiences in Europe, Russia and North America. Melodrama had absorbed some of the characteristics of the romantic movement from the early years of the nineteenth century: 'an emphasis on content rather than form, on emotion rather than reason; on the natural world rather than the urban and social; on the past and distant rather than the present and immediate' (Hodgson, 1988:

330). The appeal of melodrama lay in the almost formulaic presentation of a virtuous hero or heroine ruthlessly pursued by a heartless villain and finally rescued after a series of terrifying ordeals in some wild or threatening location. Accordingly, heroines crossed ice floes (as in *Uncle Tom's Cabin*) or escaped destruction by floating away on a plank (as in Pixérécourt's *Daughter of the Exile*), or the main character saw a vision of the past (as in *The Bells*) or rescued another character tied to a railway line from the approach of a train. All such events demanded a level of stage technology that was constantly developing. As early as 1822, for instance, the new Opera Theatre in Paris included gas lighting and a water system for creating realistic fountains and waterfalls. It was no longer possible to replicate the natural world of mountains, rivers or the interiors of buildings with painted perspective 'shutters' that slid into multiple positions on grooves in the stage. Instead, the new desire for spectacle demanded more solid-looking, three-dimensional staging which could be constructed from wooden and canvas 'flats' that were 'cleated' together and kept firmly upright by adjustable stage braces and weights. Some pieces of such settings could be lowered into position from a 'fly tower' above the stage. This construction technique became particularly important when a play demanded an interior setting that created the illusion of solid walls with windows and doors. Even this development was not always sufficient to satisfy the demands of the Naturalist playwrights. Strindberg, for example, wrote in his *Preface* to *Miss Julie*:

> I have also gained something by getting rid of the tiresome exits through doors, primarily because doors in a stage set are made of canvas and move at the slightest touch. They can not even give expression to an angry father's temper, when he, after an execrable dinner, gets up and leaves, slamming the door after him 'so that the whole house shakes'. On the stage, the whole house (of canvas) moves unsteadily from one side to the other.   (1974: 73)

In the melodramatic theatre various forms of trapdoor and solid structures on the stage together with types of machinery beneath the stage all contributed to the potential for spectacular effects but, perhaps more significantly, for the theatre to simulate the real world in great and impressive detail.

Hydraulic lifts, often known as 'traps', were installed in many theatres enabling heavy pieces of scenery to be raised and lowered. Madison Square Theatre in the United States, opened in 1879, incorporated two stages, one above the other, that could be interchanged by the use of counterweights. Drury Lane Theatre in London was one of a number of theatres to have a stage that could be elevated or lowered in sections and rocked to simulate a storm at sea because of a steam-powered unit beneath the stage. Union Square Theatre in New York installed a device in 1889 that enabled a horse race to apparently take place on stage through the use of electrically powered treadmills and a moving panorama.

Henry Irving 1838–1905

John Henry Brodribb made a very inauspicious start to his acting career, forgetting his lines and fleeing in confusion from the stage. However, in one of the most intriguing reversals in theatre history, he reinvented himself as Henry Irving, exploiting his rather strange voice and gait into distinctive characteristics, and finally becoming the most famous actor in the English-speaking world. He dominated the London stage for most of the second half of the nineteenth century, every production of his being a talking point in artistic circles and he was the first actor to be knighted or to make a sound recording of his voice.

The turning point in Irving's career was his taking over the management of the Lyceum Theatre in London. Employing the best designers, stage painters, composers and carpenters of his day, he revolutionized the London stage with meticulous and sumptuous productions, in which he invariably played the leading role. Working alongside the actress Ellen Terry, he created one of the most celebrated stage partnerships of all time and he specialized in spectacular productions of melodrama and Shakespeare. Even his detractors, of whom George Bernard Shaw was the fiercest, were forced to admit that Irving could transform the most unpromising material into a masterpiece simply through the power of his performances and his rich theatrical imagination. His portrayals of Hamlet, Shylock, Macbeth and King Lear, together with those of Matthias in *The Bells* and his final role as Thomas Beckett in Tennyson's play *Beckett* were all widely admired and described. He frequently took his productions to America and in one production shared the roles of Othello and Iago on alternate nights with the great American actor Edwin Booth, who was the first American actor to make an impact on the London stage.

Although Irving made extensive use of gas lighting, he never progressed into the use of electric lighting and was

Indeed, many remarkably realistic effects were achieved by the use of the moving panorama and the diorama introduced into the theatre by Daguerre. Through the manipulation of painting and lighting, these techniques (which anticipated the invention of the movie) enabled a number of pictures to appear simultaneously and subsequently change before the audience's eyes. Such effects were to enable Naturalist playwrights like Ibsen to call for such settings and effects as: '*In the snow, high up in the wilds of the mountains. Mist hangs densely. It is raining and nearly dark*' (stage directions for *Brand*, 1866, Act I).

Irving, who was aware of the pressing need for more realistic 'pictures' for his audiences, in 1881 abandoned the use of grooves, the method employed to change scenery for nearly 200 years, in favour of using lifts (mainly located upstage) to move heavy pieces of scenery into position. By the use of 'drops', that is, large curtains lowered to section off part of the stage, major scenic changes could take unable to relate to the 'new' drama of Ibsen which he found baffling. However, by replacing the rowdy pit with the stalls in his theatre and by his constant battles to have drama recognized as an art form worthy of serious attention, he created an entirely new audience for drama among the emerging middle classes and even achieved a sympathetic interest from the Church and the not-easily amused Queen Victoria. He was as well known for his recitations and lectures as for his stage appearances and established a level of production values that acted as a benchmark for all other managements.

Both Irving and Ellen Terry virtually founded theatrical dynasties but the reaction of their successors to the 'new naturalistic drama' of Ibsen and others was markedly different. Whereas Ellen Terry rejected what Shaw called 'a stream of splendid women's parts pouring from the Ibsen volcano and minor craters' (Holroyd, 2008:270), describing the roles as merely 'silly ladies', her daughter Edy was one of the rising generation who

Shaw noted had 'snapped up' these parts and appeared at the Court Theatre in Ibsen's *A Doll's House*. Ellen Terry's son, the famous designer Edward Gordon Craig, constantly urged Irving to stage Ibsen, but he simply turned away. By contrast, one of Irving's two sons, Laurence, embraced the new playwrights with enthusiasm and appeared in Ibsen's *The Wild Duck*. Another successor in the Terry line, John Gielgud, went on to create some of the most memorable performances of Chekhov in the English theatre

After Irving's death, Shaw, who had long enjoyed a private correspondence with Ellen Terry, enticed her to appear in his play *Captain Brassbound's Conversion* at the Court Theatre and it was recognized by some critics that an aspect of the play was a thinly disguised portrait of Irving and Terry.

We owe much of our detailed knowledge of Irving's performances to his grandson, Laurence, who became a leading stage designer and Sir Henry Irving's biographer.

place upstage whilst a scene was being acted downstage in front of a drop. Irving, was also the first English actor-manager to employ the front curtain to mask substantial scene changes and, in order to cover the considerable noise made by such changes, special music would be composed and performed by the pit musicians. To facilitate the frequent changes of scene that were regarded as one of the most enjoyable elements of theatre-going, Irving was known to have employed 135 scene shifters, all of whom were dressed in appropriate costumes

As the great theatre historian Oscar Brockett points out in his massive *History of the Theatre* (1995), by about 1890 there was scarcely a theatre in Britain, mainland Europe, Russia or North America that could not, through the coming together of a number of technical innovations, create some of the most spectacular effects ever witnessed on an indoor stage. But, in addition, actor-mangers like Irving paid increasing attention to the details and accuracy of costumes and props, frequently citing the archaeological and literary sources that they had used for their research.

Naturalism and staging

The demand for great realistic detail that became an integral part of the development of Naturalism can be illustrated by a consideration of some of the stage directions in Ibsen's play *The Wild Duck* (1884). For Act II the playwright specifies:

> HJALMAR *EKDAL's studio. It is quite a large room, and is evidently an attic. To the right is a sloping ceiling containing large panes of glass, which are half-covered by a blue curtain. In the corner upstage right is the front door. Downstage of this is the door to the living room. In the left-hand wall are two more doors, with an iron stove between them. In the rear wall are broad double sliding doors.* (1980a)

Obviously, this set of instructions makes extensive demands on the stage-construction techniques available at the time. Domestic interior settings, of which there were many in the naturalistic plays of the latter half of the nineteenth century, presupposed the construction of a 'box set': a system in which the entire acting area behind the proscenium arch was enclosed by solid-looking walls punctuated by doors and windows. The box set had, in fact, been introduced in an early form during the 1830s in theatres in England, France, Germany and North America. For example, in London's Olympic Theatre, the famous manager, Madame Vestris, staged several plays with interior settings in which the rooms were equipped with rugs, carpets, door knobs and other features to make them appear as realistic as possible. However, the marked preference for spectacle in melodrama meant that even interior settings were more likely to be of courts, castles or cathedrals than of small rooms. It was not until the second half of the century that the box set became widely used.

The extent to which practitioners and ideas of theatre travelled across continents during that age of dramatically improving means of transport can be exemplified by the career of Charles Fechter (1824–1880). Fechter was the son of a French mother and German father but was born in London. As an actor he had considerable success in Paris, Berlin, London and the United States, and wherever he went he pioneered a more naturalistic acting style and the use of interior settings in a more restrained form of melodrama. It was probably Fechter who first consistently replaced the practice of entering the stage from the wings with entrances through doors that were part of a more solid construction. This led him to re-introduce the box set when he took over the management of London's Lyceum Theatre in the 1860s. By the time that Irving came to mount *The Bells* in the same theatre. the process of constructing the various interior settings that the play demanded had become firmly established. André Antoine, the innovative director of the Théâtre Libre in Paris noted in 1903 that the French, though leading the way in many aspects of stage Naturalism, were relatively slow in adopting the more solid forms of stage construction:

> The Germans and the English do not hesitate to combine, cut and ingeniously break up space, so as to present in the central portion of the stage picture nothing but the fireplace, window, desk or corner they need.
>
> These settings – so picturesque, so alive, with such novel and intimate charm – are sadly neglected in France because our stage design is still influenced, in spite of everything, by the traditional heritage of our classical theatre.

Antoine had, in fact, set out his principles for 'authenticity' in stage settings in his article 'Behind the Fourth Wall':

> For a stage set to be original, striking and authentic, it should first be built in accordance with something seen – whether a landscape or an interior. If it is an interior, it should be built with its four sides, without worrying about the fourth wall which will later disappear so as to enable the audience to see what is going on. (quoted in Cole and Chinoy, 1970: 95)

As we shall see, the concept of the 'fourth wall' remained a vital ingredient in the search for stage truth, however, the naturalistic plays of the late nineteenth and early twentieth centuries made even further demands. Consider the following stage direction, taken like our earlier example from Ibsen's *The Wild Duck* (1980a):

> EKDAL *and* HJALMAR *go to the rear wall and each of them pushes back one of the sliding doors [...]. Through the open doors can be seen a long and irregularly shaped loft full of dark nooks and crannies, and with a couple of brick chimney-pipes coming through the floor. Through small skylights bright moonlight shines onto various parts of the loft while the rest lies in shadow.*
> (1980a)

Stage lighting

We see here that not only does the playwright demand very precise construction and staging, he also specifies the quality and direction of the light. This factor reflects the growing possibilities of theatre technology for, in their attempt to present the natural and human material world on stage in great detail, playwrights, actor-managers, and eventually directors, were greatly assisted by the introduction of gas and subsequently electric stage lighting. By 1903 Antoine was able to state:

> our lighting equipment is markedly improving every day. We have come a long way from the sorry-looking candles, tapers, oil lamps and gas lights – in this field we have made steady, uninterrupted progress. For light is the life of the theatre. (1977: 98)

And such developments led the American director and playwright David Belasco to write in 1919: 'Lights are to drama what music is to the lyrics of a song'.

Although some sophistication in stage lighting had been achieved through the use of coloured glass in combination with candles and oil lamps in the eighteenth and very early nineteenth centuries, it was the introduction of gas light that enabled theatre practitioners to achieve special effects and a considerable degree of control over the direction and intensity of light used on stage

The first theatre to light its stage by gas was the Chestnut Street Theatre in Philadelphia in 1816 and the first theatre to be constructed with gas as a source of general interior and stage lighting was also in the United States: the American Theatre, which opened in New Orleans in 1824. This new alternative to oil lamps had actually been introduced into England in the late eighteenth century and employed as a means of exterior lighting at Covent Garden and possibly in the auditorium of the Lyceum in 1815. However, like so many inventions, it took the energy of the United States to recognize, develop and exploit the potential of this new medium. The new Paris Opera theatre installed gas in 1828 and, reluctantly, it would seem, the Comédie-Française adopted gas in 1843 for general illumination whilst retaining oil footlights to satisfy the concerns of actresses who feared that the new, glaring source of light would damage their complexions!

It is safe to say that, by the middle years of the nineteenth century, gas had been introduced into theatres throughout Europe and the United States but it must be remembered that although this made many new effects possible, the 'spotlight' as we understand it today had not been invented and the gas 'mantle', which provided a safe and steady source of bright light in people's houses, was not developed until the 1880s. Early gas lighting was, therefore, a relatively dangerous and non-directional form of lighting. Irving, whose important production of *The Bells* was a pivotal moment in theatre, never changed from gas to electricity for, not only was he the first actor-manager to realize the potential of the new medium but he also employed developing technology to raise the level of lighting to an art form. Chief among his innovations were his use of the 'gas table': a means whereby many gas lamps could be controlled at once, and the breaking up of footlights and borders into short sections, each with their own colours and controls to achieve even distribution of light. He also set the trend for darkening the auditorium so that the audience's attention was focused towards the lit stage and he seems to have positively enjoyed the atmosphere created by the slightly shimmering miasma through which his patrons viewed the stage pictures he created. Irving also made creative use of the 'limelight' which had been invented in 1816. The technique involved heating a column of lime by use of gas, oxygen and compressed hydrogen. The incandescent light produced was confined inside a hood fitted with a lens. By the middle of the nineteenth century, limelight was being used to create illusions of moonlight, sunlight and other such effects and, of course, even if it is no longer employed in theatre, its name has remained in common use. By the time that the gas mantle had been invented, gas was already about to be replaced by electricity because the invention of the incandescent light 'bulb' by Edison in 1879 promised greater control, refinement, intensity and even distribution. Although Irving resisted the change, others were quick to embrace the new technology. In 1881, the Savoy Theatre in London, which was to be the home of the famous Gilbert and Sullivan Operas, became the first British theatre to be exclusively lit by electricity and the new medium was widely adopted throughout the United States and Europe.

By modern standards, the early means of controlling electric light in the theatre sound crude and cumbersome. For example, an apparatus for adjusting the intensity of electric stage lighting consisted of a series of large wheels which, when turned, raised or lowered electrodes into cylinders of salt water in order to vary the electrical resistance. The precursor of the modern 'dimmer board' with its digital technology, it never the less provided a safer and more precise source of control than its gas predecessor. Many of the naturalistic plays of the late nineteenth century would have benefited from the invention of the carbon arc lamp: a device in which electrical poles were attached to a carbon stick. When these were brought together a current leaped across the gap and created an incandescent source of rather harsh light. As with several other aspects of electric stage lighting, the carbon arc was refined in Germany and it still remains in use today as a 'follow spot'.

As we have seen from Antoine's comments (see p. 68) the development of electric stage lighting was rapid. The evolution of various sizes and wattages of light bulbs and their confinement in metal casings fitted with reflectors and lenses created the spot lights and floodlights of modern theatre practice. The 'fresnel' spotlight, named after the French physicist and engineer Augustin-Jean Fresnel, utilized a ridged lens originally created for use in lighthouses and provided a soft-edged beam of light; the 'profile' spotlight with a smooth lens created a hard-edged and clearly defined pool of light; the Linnebach 'projector' could throw shadowy images on to the cyclorama and the 'floodlight' could literally flood an area with light. Means of focusing and colouring all these types of lantern were quickly developed and, mounted on stands, they were suspended from bars above the stage or auditorium or stood on the stage floor. The various forms of stage lantern could send beams and washes of light from all directions to create an almost limitless series of effects and reproduce natural outdoor or indoor appearances of light.

Directors and lighting technicians began to think in terms of the 'governing light', that is, the direction from which a stage setting was lit if it were 'real', so, for example, if a room was lit by daylight coming in from windows in a certain direction, then the source of stage lighting must appear to come from that direction, even if subtly complemented by other stage lights.

All the major stage works we have defined as part of Naturalism were written just before or during the period of transition from gas to electricity. We can see how the growing sophistication in lighting led playwrights to make very specific demands in terms of light. Light became nothing less than an additional form of stage language and its varying moods, symbols and qualities permeate the theatre of Naturalism. A consideration of the two plays by Ibsen to be presented by Antoine at the Théâtre Libre is particularly revealing. In *Ghosts*, the first Ibsen play to be written after the introduction of electric lighting in theatres, we have many references to the quality of light. The play opens in gloom: '*Through the glass wall a gloomy fjord landscape is discernible, veiled by steady rain*' (1980a: 27) and Act II begins in similar fashion: '*The mist still lies heavily on the landscape*' (57). Towards the end of Act II, '*Dusk begins to gather slowly*' (71) and soon '*Regina enters with a lamp and puts it on the table*' (75). As Act III begins: '*The lamp is still burning on the table. Outside it is dark with only the faint glow of the fire in the background*' (83) and the play culminates in a lighting effect that was to become as notorious as the famous sound effect of a slammed door in Ibsen's previous play, *A Doll's House*. As Oswald sits in an armchair '*The day breaks*' (97) and soon '*The sun rises. The glacier and snow-capped peaks in the background glitter in the morning light*' and he utters his dying words '*The sun, the sun*' (98).

But it is in his play *The Wild Duck* that we see Ibsen exploiting the possibilities of electric stage lighting most fully. Between 1885 and 1894, when it was seen in London, the play was performed in Bergen, Christiana, Helsinki, Stockholm, Copenhagen, Berlin, Berne, Wiesbaden, Dresden and Paris at Antoine's Théâtre Libre. Deeply conscious of the lighting demands of the play, Ibsen wrote to the manager of the Christiana Theatre:

> This play demands absolute naturalness and truthfulness both in the ensemble work and in the staging. The lighting, too, is important; it is different for each act, and is calculated to establish the particular atmosphere of that act. (1980a:113)

The sheer scale of Ibsen's use of light is astonishing: Act One demands '*Lighted lamps with green shades throw a soft light*' but that beyond, another room is visible '*brilliantly lit by lamps and candelabra*' and that the main room contains '*a fireplace with coals glowing in it*' (117). By Act II the location has shifted to a photographer's studio lit by a single lamp and with moonlight streaming in through the loft. It ends with the snuffing out of a candle. As Act III opens '*It is morning. The daylight is streaming in through the large window'* (156) and Act IV begins with '*Afternoon light; the sun is just going down; a little later it begins to grow dark*' (178). Ibsen constantly uses both physical and verbal images of light to enhance his meanings: for example, in Act IV Gregers says:

> I felt so sure that when I walked through that door you would be standing there transfigured, and that my eyes would be dazzled by the light, and instead I see this dull heaviness and misery—

Gena replies:

> Oh, I see. (*She takes the shade off the lamp*) (184)

Towards the conclusion of the same Act Hedvig remarks:

> In the morning it's light and then there is nothing to be afraid of any more. (197)

And, indeed Act V begins in '*A cold grey morning light*' (199)
   Ibsen was not the only dramatist to reveal a concern for the lighting of his plays. In his *Preface* to *Miss Julie*, Strindberg, who specifies various kinds of sunlight in the play, wrote:

> Another, perhaps not unnecessary innovation would be the removal of footlights. This illumination from below is said to serve the purpose of making actors fatter in the face. (1976: 103)

After some discussion of the fact that footlights seem to prevent actors from looking straight ahead in a natural way, he goes on to suggest:

> Would not side-lights of sufficient power (with reflectors, or some such device) endow the actor with this new resource, enabling him to reinforce his mime with his principal weapon of expression, the movement of his eyes? (1976)

In the play *Miss Julie* itself, Strindberg employs the new lighting technology. For example, one stage direction reads:

> *The sun has now risen and is shining on the tops of the trees in the park. Its beams move gradually until they fall at an angle through the windows* (137)

and Strindberg's later play *Ghost Sonata* concludes with a song 'I saw the sun' while: '*the room becomes filled with a white light*'.

Similar concerns motivated Antoine (see p. 122) to discuss the effects of lighting on the performance of his actors, but his experience of the new technology convinced him that:

> Light alone, intelligently handled, gives atmosphere and colour to a set, depth and perspective. Light acts physically on the audience: its magic accentuates, underlines and marvellously accompanies the intimate meaning of a dramatic work. To get excellent results from light, you must not be afraid to use and spread it unevenly.   (quoted in Cole and Chinoy, 1970: 98)

And, although this was not written until 1908, by which time he had directed many plays, including Ibsen's *Ghosts* and *The Wild Duck*, it was, perhaps the indelible experience of his seeing the Irving company in 1888 and his admiration for what was achieved by their gas lighting, that had established those attitudes and principles by which he worked.

Art and photography

The desire to create an illusion of reality with totally authentic and naturalistic stage pictures was greatly influenced by the visual art of the late nineteenth century and, indeed, some stage entertainments in the earlier part of the century had consisted simply of the creation of well-known paintings as stage tableaux. However, as artists, like dramatists and novelists, increasingly sought to portray humankind in the urban environment of industrial society, the paintings of such artists as Ingres and the Impressionist Renoir in France and the more realist Ford Maddox Brown or William Powell Frith in England were virtually social documents showing the lives of working- or middle-class people rather than the exploits of characters from classical mythology or the aristocracy.

In his excellent introduction to his translation of Zola's novel *Thérèse Raquin* (1992), Andrew Rothwell maintains that the Naturalist writers took three related ideas: 'scientific enquiry, materialism and pictorial realism' to create their new doctrine and it was, perhaps, more particularly, the invention of photography which could most fulfil the third of these ideals. The ability of photography to present images of life that were more 'truthful' and accurate than had ever been seen before contributed significantly to the passion for visual realism. Much of the action of Ibsen's *The Wild Duck* (1884) is, as we have seen, set in a photographer's studio but it was in the early 1840s that the invention of the calotype photograph enabled portraits of individuals to be printed on paper. Such was the effect and rapid development of the photograph that in an article in the *Quarterly Review* entitled 'Photography' (1857) Lady Elizabeth Eastlake wrote:

> Here, therefore, the much-lauded and much-abused agent called Photography takes her legitimate stand. Her business is to give evidence of facts, as

minutely and as impartially as, to our shame, only an unreasoning machine
can give.   (quoted in Harvie, Martin and Scharf, 1970: 282)

These intentions are, of course, similar to those expressed by Zola and he was one
of the many significant figures of the mid-nineteenth century to have his image
preserved by the most celebrated and successful portrait photographer in Paris,
Felix Nadar, who had exploited the invention of the more satisfactory 'wet-collo-
dian' photographic plate in 1850. Richard Holmes sums up the impact of this
invention in relation to that group of French painters who came to be known as
'Impressionists' (who had held their first exhibition in Nadar's studio) and who
were also attempting to create images of reality and artistic truth. He suggests that
its significance was hardly realized at the time:

> The aesthetic revolution brought about by the early photographers, and
> especially Nadar, was no less far reaching that that achieved by the Impres-
> sionists. But the impact of photography on European society was too rapid
> and too widespread to be grasped at the time. The Impressionists asserted
> new standards of private, idiosyncratic vision which penetrated only slowly,
> and among the elite of the art world. *But the photographers established, in
> little more than a decade, entirely new and universal ideas about visual reality*
> and about what everyone could commonly accept and recognize as 'lifelike-
> ness'. Photography was, from the start, irretrievably popular in its appeal and
> suspiciously democratic in its tendencies. Not surprisingly it took Paris by
> storm: in 1850 there were less than a dozen professional studios in the city;
> by the 1860s something over 200 with more than 33,000 people directly or
> indirectly employed. Of these, Nadar was the doyen.
>
> (2000: 58; our emphasis)

By the conclusion of his career Nadar had left a collection of portraits of every
leading figure in the arts in France, playwrights, composers, poets, actors, philoso-
phers and writers among them, together with some early and beautiful examples
of nude portraiture.

But the opportunity to be the subject of a photographic portrait was not
confined to the famous: a technique that involved burning images on to enamel
also spawned a huge number of photographic studios in major cities throughout
Europe and the United States and this enabled large numbers of the population
to have their likenesses preserved with the possibility of multiple copies. As early
as 1858, successful photographic portrait studios were exhibiting their products
at the Brussels Exhibition

In 1888 the American company Kodak introduced a mass-produced camera
that brought the preservation of images of the natural world within reach of large
numbers of the population and by 1900 the 'Brownie' Camera became the most

common camera for mass ownership. Such was its popularity that it is estimated that, in the same year at the 'Exposition Universelle' in Paris, as many as 51,000 cameras were being used in the exhibition grounds on a single day. By 1899, the Biograph Company were also using an effective if primitive movie camera to create and preserve haunting images of the Boer War. Within a few years many international crises and state events were preserved on film and the ideas of the 'newsreel' and 'documentary' were born.

Painters had also benefited from various aspects of technology in their search to create images of the real world: for example, the invention of the paint tube in 1840 had enabled artists to take their easels outside and to paint what they could see and what was really there rather than complying with the expectations of the Academicians and paint a classical nude. The invention of the ferrule paintbrush enabled artists to achieve that layered and variable surface which captured the sense of movement, light and shadow that seemed 'natural'. Groups of people at leisure and people that one would, perhaps, hardly notice, became legitimate subjects for art. Painters such as Monet and Pissarro were able to travel by rail to multiple venues in search of subjects. The first railways appeared in France in 1842 but by 1892 there were 30,000 miles of track and, meanwhile, between 1850 and 1870 the population of Paris doubled from 1 to 2 million people. Social change became a major concern of painters and dramatists: the modern world was seen as a fitting subject for great art and, in their search for truth the Impressionist painters sought to capture impressive aspects of nature or such memorable images as modern, technological monsters belching steam.

In Britain, it was the naturalistic detail of the paintings by Elizabeth Thompson that brought the true horrors of the Crimean War to the attention of a bemused and outraged public. A similar search for truth, devoid of cloying sentiment or misleading propaganda led the artist Millais to paint an uncompromisingly naturalistic picture of the youthful Jesus at home with his family: an image which shocked the supposedly socially concerned Charles Dickens and the same quest produced the memorable paintings of desperate human hardship in industrial society by Luke Fildes, William Dyce and the German-born von Herkimer.

In his Preface to *Miss Julie*, the playwright Strindberg claimed to have 'borrowed from Impressionist painting its asymmetry and its economy', whilst new audiences, directors and playwrights developed an insatiable desire for pictorial and 'photographic' realism in the theatre.

Opera and Naturalism

What is often thought of as the highly artificial world of opera may not seem a promising source of Naturalism. However, the revolutions in the production values and content of opera that took place in the latter half of the nineteenth and early years of the twentieth centuries made a significant contribution to theatre practice. The German composer Richard Wagner (1813–1883) reacted against the over-ornamental style of opera that, in his view, detracted from the unifying qualities of a work of art. He developed a vision of a new kind of stage work: a *Gesamtkunstwerk* which was to be a seamless fusion of poetry, music, movement, costume and scenic effects. In order to achieve this ambition he built his own theatre in Bayreuth in 1876, which included the latest stage machinery and technology and a raked, fan-shaped auditorium in which every seat faced the same way, thus breaking with the conventional design of European and American theatres and opera houses. One of Wagner's most significant contributions to the development of theatre was his appointment of the young Swiss designer, Adolphe Appia (1862–1928) to help him realize his artistic vision. Wagner had determined that the proper subject matter of opera was myth and religion and Appia was unable to move him away from the accompanying painted scenery, but he did develop a deep respect for Wagner's insistence on simplicity, symbolism and unity in all the visual elements of theatre. Appia's ideas were eventually articulated in his book *Di Musik und die Inscenierung* and it is probably true to say that few, if any, subsequent designers have not, in some way, been influenced by its principles. His main contention was that since an actor is a three-dimensional being, the flatness of painted scenery will merely be accentuated by placing an actor in front of it. Instead, Appia worked to create an environment for the actor to inhabit; and this is a key concept of Naturalism. His staging consisted of solid pieces, ramps, rostra, pillars or platforms and the techniques he used for construction were replicated in the 'realistic' settings of naturalistic plays. Appia's other major contribution to Naturalism was his experimental work with electric lighting which virtually solved the previously unyielding problem of creating the illusion of 'out of door' light with all its constantly changing shades, tones and qualities. Accordingly, playwrights followed Ibsen's lead in regarding the quality of light as an element in their representation of a 'slice of life'.

Wagner's subject matter remained anti-realistic and mythical and his ideas did not easily translate into the opera houses of Europe and the United States. However, the Austrian composer Gustav Mahler (1860–1911) took some of his principles and, together with his designer Alfred Roller, developed a whole new vocabulary of performance values in his role as director of a succession of major theatres across the two continents. Mahler made extensive use of machinery, including pioneering the concept of the revolving stage, and his work focused on replacing an outmoded and contrived performance style and approach to costume and design with a new search for artistic truth and authenticity. In an interesting parallel with the playwrights of his day, Mahler invariably gave copious instructions for performance in the scores of his musical compositions: using precise and evocative German words in preference to the traditional Italian musical terms.

By the middle years of the nineteenth century, opera had become little more than a costumed concert staged against a painted backdrop and featuring spectacular vocal gymnastics by the singers. Little attempt at characterization or dramatic narrative was made: performances were a sequence of spectacular arias and duets together with some improbable sung dialogue. The reforms instituted by Mahler, particularly at the Vienna State Opera, restored a genuine sense of theatrical action. Costumes were designed for their authenticity and the characters were placed in a three-dimensional environment that looked like the natural world. The action of the opera now told a story rather than merely acting as a vehicle for the singers' virtuosity, and the action was increasingly enhanced by the new stage technology and lighting.

Mahler's reforms included a totally new attitude towards the chorus who became, under his direction, an ensemble central to and deeply involved in the action, providing a context for and commenting on the lives of the main characters. In Britain, the playwright and director W. S. Gilbert introduced a similar approach to the chorus into the comic operas he wrote with Sullivan, insisting on discipline and involvement at all times. In Hamburg, Mahler undertook a very successful early production of the opera *Manon Lescaut* by the Italian composer Giacomo Puccini based on the stark and chilling novel of the same name by the French author Abbé Prevost. This opera was one of an increasing number of stage works that rejected the symbol and myth-laden operas of Wagner or the dramas of court life in favour of the 'real' world. Under the influence of the French Naturalist writers, especially Zola and Merimee, a new movement in opera that came to be known as *verismo* (from the Italian for 'true') was born. This search for truthfulness in the action and subject matter of opera led Puccini to set what was probably his most successful work, *La Bohème* (1896), in a squalid attic room inhabited by penniless students. This is strongly reminiscent of the setting for Zola's *Thérèse Raquin* in a miserable garret. The French composer Georges Bizet set his *Carmen* (1897) in a lower-class world of soldiers, whores and workers from a cigarette factory. Audiences were initially shocked by the realism of the plots and action of these operas and, although *verismo* is often considered to have been an Italian movement best known from Mascagni's *Cavelleria Rusticana* (1875) and Leoncavalo's *Pagliacci* (1892), we can see that the whole world of opera was, in fact, moving towards the same search for truth as drama by its portrayal of ordinary, and very often poor people in everyday situations, squalid urban environments, and familiar and 'real' predicaments. Zola's claim that his work was based on 'objective truth' had initiated a movement that embraced the main forms of theatre and had particular significance for performance styles.

Terrible truthfulness

Among those theatre practitioners who greatly admired and sought to emulate what the critic of *The Courier* in 1872 had described as 'the profundity' and 'the terrible truthfulness' of Sir Henry Irving's performances and production of *The Bells*, was the young Russian amateur actor and producer Konstantin Stanislavsky. The melodrama, with its complex and necessary sound effects and opportunity for detailed and intense acting, appealed to the restless ambitions and imagination of Stanislavsky as he strove to make an impact on the stage of the Moscow Society of Art and Literature in 1890. Stanislavsky's biographer, David Magarshack, gives a vivid impression of the production, drawing on the relatively inexperienced director's reminiscences:

> The scene showed an attic with a sloping ceiling, two large windows at the back, covered by Venetian blinds through which glimpse of the dark night outside could be caught. Between the windows in the middle of the room stood a huge bed, and the rest of the furniture – a table, chairs, a chest of drawers and so on – as well as the stove, were placed along the footlights with their backs to the audience [Stanislavsky's first attempt to treat the proscenium as the fourth wall].
>
> (1950: 118–19)

Thus, well before his famous and far better known productions of plays by Chekhov, Gorky or Ibsen at the Moscow Art Theatre, which became something of a shrine for Naturalism, Stanislavsky was employing those stage devices and settings that were, as we have seen, envisaged in such plays. The remainder of the description of his production of *The Bells* reveals that it rivalled Irving's production for special and surprising effects and for the care and precision in which he undertook the leading role of Matthias.

There had been a number of significant events and trends that had influenced Stanislavsky in the direction of more naturalistic approaches to theatre. As an amateur actor he spent much of his time labouring to improve his performances and observing himself in a mirror in an attempt to eradicate what he considered to be elements of falseness in movement and gesture. In his earliest ventures as what we would now call a 'director', he encountered Gilbert and Sullivan's *The Mikado*, and the great Russian impresario Mikhail Lentovsky, who later came to admire Stanislavsky's work, had staged an adaptation of a novel by Zola for which he imported French laundresses from Paris to give a sense of truth to the production. Perhaps most importantly, there had been two visits to Moscow by the Meiningen company under their autocratic director Ludwig Chronegk and the naturalistic style of their productions seems to have made an indelible impression on Stanislavsky.

Nevertheless, the foundations of what was to become Stanislavsky's 'system': an approach to performance that has influenced actors ever since, were established by the actor Mikhail Shchepkin in the early years of the nineteenth century. Coming to the Russian stage entirely dominated by the French pseudo-classical theatre in which 'an actor was not expected to speak his lines in a natural voice – he had to declaim them, accompanying each word by some theatrical gesture' (Magarshak,

1950: 141), Shchepkin was amazed on one occasion in 1810 when he saw Prince Meshchersky give a performance of a play in his country house, and observed that: 'the prince himself was not *acting* on the stage but just *behaving* (our italics) as he would in real life (141). Witnessing this, Shchepkin was so moved that he burst into tears and recorded in his memoirs that he 'fell under the spell of real life' (141).

Acting as an art and science

Attempts to achieve that level of reality in acting persisted throughout the nine-teenth century and, like so many other aspects of Naturalism, were often based on close and scientific observation and analysis. In the early year of the century the training of actors was a haphazard affair. In many parts of Europe and America the best that an aspiring actor could hope for was to join a company and, by a combination of imitation and bold experiment, eventually graduate from a lowly 'walking gentleman or lady' status to that of 'leading man' or 'leading lady'. Others, less fortunate, were simply left to learn their art by chance and experience. Yet, by the end of the century, acting and the training of actors had become the subject of systematic study based on scientific principles.

This remarkable change was particularly evident in attitudes towards the training of an actor's voice (which Stanislavsky always considered to be the prin-cipal instrument of expression). Irving (1893) reported that he had been told: 'always pitch your voice so as to be heard by the back row of the gallery' (Brereton, 1908: 57) but was given no methodical help. All actors were expected to strengthen or perhaps ruin their voices by constant practice of a declamatory style in large and often noisy theatres. However, by the 1890s these actors could have chosen from a large number of teachers and textbooks of 'elocution' all advocating systems derived from a painstaking observation and analysis of physiological and mechanical data relating to the voice and the body in every conceivable situation. It is, perhaps, easy for us to overlook the importance of the voice to the nine-teenth-century theatre. In the concern for 'truth' and motivation which followed the spread of Naturalism, actors and producers (directors) have tended to focus on the sub-text: a powerful and euphonious rendering of the text is no longer sufficient. But even 100 years ago, elocution was an accepted and integral part of theatre. Critics on both sides of the Atlantic paid primary attention to an actor's voice and rivalled each other in graphic descriptions of vocal achievement:

> When, as Richelieu, he threatened to launch the ecclesiastical curse, Forrest's bellow made the theatre walls tremble. Lear's delirious prayer to nature reverberated like a thunder storm. (Bogard, Moody and Meserve, 1977: 92)

There are a number of factors which contributed to the development of the study of the voice. It was, firstly, a manifestation of the general desire for scientific

Konstantin Sergeievitch Alexeiev Stanislavsky (1863–1938)

Stanislavsky, who was born in Moscow, was the greatest single influence on the development of a naturalistic acting technique in the theatre of the West. His early life was saturated in theatrical activity because his family were sufficiently passionate about it to have constructed theatres in their town and country homes. After a period working in the amateur theatre both as actor and director, Stanislavsky took a key role in the 18-hour meeting with the acting teacher Nemirovitch-Danchenko that led to the foundation in 1897 of what was to become almost a shrine to Naturalism: the Moscow Art Theatre. It was here that Stanislavsky carried out his most innovative work as a result of his dissatisfaction with the status quo of actors' and audiences' expectations. He realized that no real foundation for the teaching or development of acting technique existed and initially adopted an autocratic approach to directing, before deducing that this did not enable actors to find their own characters or motivations.

His determination to discover what he called 'elementary psychophysical and psychological laws of acting' led him to take a holiday to Finland in 1906 where he reflected upon and analysed his own practice and began to write the books that have become essential reading for all modern actors. In articulating his rules and principles, Stanislavsky drew especially upon his experience of directing and acting in Shakespeare's *Othello* in 1895: a production for which he had made meticulous and detailed preparation, including a trip to Venice to explore the architecture he wished to incorporate in the setting. Another seminal production was that of Chekhov's *The Seagull* in 1898. This landmark production in naturalistic theatre introduced Chekhov as a major dramatist and established a life-long partnership between director and playwright (not always harmonious) during which Stanislavsky directed all of Chekhov's major plays. Stanislavsky's approach in directing Chekhov's plays is still studied as rich examples of theatrical realism and as the laboratory in which the director's ideas on acting were developed into a system.

Stanislavsky's thinking was documented during a long career in a substantial body of writing. Those experiences that led to his 'teaching' books on acting are set out in his autobiographical *My Life in Art* and he also left copious notes and articles relating to various productions. However, most actors look to Stanislavsky's three 'teaching' books to enable them to develop their own techniques for dealing with the demands of naturalistic theatre. These are *An Actor Prepares, Building a Character* and *Creating a Role*, and it was the system of acting expounded in these books that was taken to America in the early twentieth century by a number of Stanislavsky's colleagues and transformed into Method acting, which underpinned the writing and performance of many great naturalistic plays in the United States.

investigation which became a feature of thought in the second half of the nine-teenth century. After the publication of Darwin's *Origin of Species* in 1859, human beings, like any other animal, became the object of constant physiological and psychological study. Rationalist materialism sought a scientific explanation for every aspect of behaviour and the study of the voice and its functions was part of this movement. Close study of the structure and operation of the larynx was made easier by the invention of the laryngoscope in 1854 by the Spanish voice teacher Manuel Garcia who taught in Paris, New York and London and, as Michael R. Turner remarks: 'A new interest in the function of the vocal cords led to a stream of books by surgeons' (1972: 4). This interest in part created and was in part gener-ated by the belief that elocution in general and recitation in particular were proper and desirable accomplishments for a new middle class to whom the industrial revolution had brought increased affluence and leisure. Whereas, in many circles, the Stage itself was regarded with great suspicion as a respectable activity, espe-cially for women, the practice of elocution or recitation became, like singing, an important aspect of self-improvement. In Britain and America these subjects were also increasingly included in the school curriculum and, by 1882, London saw the establishment of a Professorship of Elocution at both the Royal College and the Royal Academy of Music, a move which pioneered the creation of drama schools as we now know them.

Another significant allied development was the increasing popularity of public readings and recitals by actors. Many young actors in the foothills of success pieced together a living by booking a public hall and staging recitals of poetry, prose and extracts from plays. The great and famous, however, were not exempt from this practice: the serialized readings of his novels by Charles Dickens or the public renderings of Shakespeare, Tennyson or lesser-known poets by Henry Irving were eagerly anticipated performance events.

However, there was unrest among actors, critics and playwrights across Europe and America because a new emphasis on Naturalism in all aspects of performance began to cast doubts on more histrionic methods with their basis in elocution. The social realism of the 1880s and 1890s demanded that actors appeared to converse and move like real, recognizable people rather than indulge in exagger-ated declamation and gesture. The problem, as always, was to be heard at the back of huge theatres and yet appear to be behaving naturally. Actors, who had satisfied the tastes for burlesque and melodrama, now found themselves bewildered by the rival claims of widely different types of drama. No wonder that Symons remarked: 'there is not even a definite bad method, but mere chaos, individual caprice' (1909: 189). In an impassioned outburst on the legacy of naturalistic approaches to acting E. J. West identifies the actors' dilemma when he states:

> Since the last decade of the nineteenth century, the integral relationship of the histrionic and the dramatic arts has been forgotten. [...] the disappear-

ance of the old-school actor, with the concurrent development of the new-school non-actor, mainly between the years from 1870 to 1890 made possible, nay, inevitable, the so-called 'dramatic renascence' of the nineties which was a floral wreath upon the grave of histrionic genius. (1942: 436)

Delsarte

It is, nevertheless, untrue to suggest that there were no systematic attempts in the nineteenth century to develop a more acceptable style of acting based on the observation of nature and 'natural' behaviour. The most successful and influential theorist of acting was the musician, teacher and inventor François Delsarte (1811– 1871), who had ruined his own voice by faulty training and usage (like F. M. Alexander, the inventor of the Alexander Technique, at a later date) and forsook the stage to devote himself to the evolution of a scientific means of training actors that would result in a more 'natural' style of performance. He hoped to achieve this by formulating rules of elocution and gesture which had mathematical precision and maintained that, because these rules were derived from exact observation of human behaviour, the end product would be an exact representation of Nature.

Delsarte aimed for unity between the body, the voice and the spirit and regarded voice as invariably linked to gesture. In *The Delsarte System of Oratory* he wrote: 'The artist should have three objects: to move, to interest, to persuade. He interests by language; he moves by thought; he moves, interests and persuades by gesture (1893: 486). Delsarte, in fact, considered gesture to be a more potent means of communication than speech:

> Language is the weakest of the three agents. In a matter of feelings language proves nothing. It has no real value, save that which is given to it by the preparation of gesture. Gesture corresponds to the soul, to the heart; language to the life, the thought, the mind [...]. Speech is an act posterior to will, itself posterior to love [...]. Inflection is the life of speech; the mind lies in the articulative values, in the distribution of these articulations and the progressions. The soul of speech is in gesture. (1893: 487)

These assertions may seem strange to us when language, text and subtext have often been seen as the principle ingredients of naturalistic theatre. Delsarte had few technical ideas on voice production, although he was insistent on the importance of breath control. He did, however, reveal a sharp awareness of the artistic possibilities of the voice:

> If you would move others, put your heart in the place of your larynx; let your voice become a mysterious hand to caress the hearer [...]. Persuade yourself that there are blind men and deaf men in your audience whom you must

move, interest and persuade. Your inflection must become pantomime to the blind, and your pantomime, inflection to the deaf.   (1893: 529)

Delsarte made a painstaking analysis of what his biographer, the dancer Ted Denishawn, called 'every little movement'. In considering gestures he identified the 'great articular centres': the shoulder, elbow and wrist. 'Passioned expression', he maintained was in an 'emotional' state in the shoulder, but presented in an 'affectional' and 'succeptive' state by the wrist and thumb. Many complex diagrams and rules for gesture were derived from these and other principles and became a common feature of early textbooks of elocution and acting. The face and partic-ularly the mouth were also the subject of Delsarte's observation:

> The mouth plays part in everything evil which we would express, by a grimace which consists of protruding lips and lowering the corners. If the grimace translates a concentric sentiment, it should be made by compressing the lips [...]. The mouth is the vital thermometer, the nose a moral ther-mometer.   (1893: 487)

A study of the illustrations on page 91 will show just how strongly many subse-quent ideas on acting and elocution were rooted in the principles of Delsarte. Illustrations of the posture of nineteenth-century actors also reveal that Delsarte's precepts on the head position and body reaction were put into effect:

> Every agreeable or disagreeable sight makes the body react backward [...]. Conscious menace – that of a master to his subordinate – is expressed by a movement of the head carried from above downward. Impotent menace requires the head to be moved from below upward.   (1893: 487)

Once a student had mastered the various physical principles he had enunciated, Delsarte recommended that he or she should progress to textual analysis, searching out the particular emotions contained in the passage and aiming to convey them in the most appropriate way possible. Accordingly, anthologies of suitable pieces for actors and reciters were arranged according to mood. In an interesting anticipation of the work of Stanislavsky, Delsarte recommended para-phrase as a means of achieving a full understanding of a passage and although his widely adopted teachings went out of fashion by the turn of the century, he had left a considerable number of influential disciples, including his most devoted student, the celebrated actress Sarah Bernhardt.

Delsarte's teachings had a considerable influence on the search for a new and more truthful approach to acting both in Britain and America and helped to estab-lish the concept and discipline of actor training. Gustave Garcia (b.1837) was the son of Manuel Garcia, the inventor of the laryngoscope and, as a teacher of singing, joined the great man on the staff of the Royal Academy of Music in 1865. Here he was particularly concerned about stage presentation and directed a large number of operettas. Although he also taught at the Royal College of Music and Guildhall School of Music, it was as the initiator of a carefully devised teaching programme at the London Academy of Music that Garcia made his most important contributions to the development of acting. At the London Academy Garcia was described as Professor of Singing and Declamation, and he detailed his methods in his book *The Actor's Art: A practical treatise of stage declamation, public speaking and deportment for the use of artists, students and amateurs* (1882). The title itself (which may seem ridiculous and intimidating to a modern reader) is indicative of a growing interest in the subject of acting as 'teachable', whilst the contents show that the author was attempting to apply scientific principles to every aspect of acting. Such a view not only complemented the views held by his father and by Delsarte but also those of Henry Wylde, the founder of the London Academy, who maintained that the arts of singing and acting could, like grammar, be taught by means of a series of rules.

To some extent *The Actor's Art* tended to reflect the increased use of elocution as a means of imparting social graces to the sons and, more especially, the daughters of the new wealthy class. The character studies were invariably of heroic or aristocratic figures and the analyses of movement and speech styles never extended to the working classes. Garcia's fist aim was to produce beauty of body movement and voice and only then to apply these to dramatic situations. The primary importance of tonal beauty in speech resulted in an emphasis on pure vowel sounds and full resonance supported by correct breathing. Garcia's method was based on observable physical phenomena: his students were required to classify every movement of the body and face according to the emotions being expressed. From this activity, he argued, it would be possible to evolve rules for conveying the passions and, once these had been established, those passions could be conveyed in the theatre with a precision and naturalism previously unknown.

Garcia's book on acting was one of a considerable number of publications, the most famous of which, *Bell's Standard Elocutionist*, had first appeared in 1860 and was still in print in modified form one hundred years later. Bell, who later went to America and established what we would now call 'speech therapy', produced over forty publications on aspects of the voice in performance, but it was his *Standard Elocutionist* that set the pattern for textbooks containing a huge selection of suggested passages for performance. Significantly, when Sir Henry Irving was asked to make the first ever recording by an actor on the newly invented phonograph, it was a piece from *Bell* that he selected. Throughout the many textbooks on acting that appeared in the 1880s and 1890s we can detect the influence of Delsarte and the insistence on art determined by scientific principles. This was particularly evident in America where Delsarte's work was more venerated than in Europe or Britain. His system was introduced by the actor Steele MacKaye (1842–1894) and, although Delsarte himself had never written a book, his various writings were translated into English and published as *Delsarte System of Oratory: Containing all the literary remains of Francois Delsarte* (1893). At around the same time Alfred Ayres's *The Essentials of Elocution* (1886) and *Acting and Actors, Elocution and Elocutionists* (1894) together with J. A. Hamerton's *The Actor's Art* (1897) catered for the growing hunger for guidance in the American theatre. Similarly, the French actor, Benoît-Constant Coquelin's *L'Art du Comédian* (1894) was eagerly read on both sides of the Atlantic even though a translation did not appear for some years: like many of the other popular self-help books of the time, this demonstrated a universal concern for a strong theoretical basis for the art of acting.

The imitation of nature

The extent to which nineteenth-century practitioners and teachers of acting thought they were copying nature is best illustrated by considering a substantial example. The book *Voice, Gesture and Speech* published in London in 1897 included a section by the actor Henry Neville entitled 'The Head, Face, Eyes, Brows and Mouth', containing careful instructions (see Illustration 5a–e) as to how a performer might achieve the appearance of various emotions by a variety of facial expressions and angles of the head, as follows:

> *The Head* – The head must be held in an erect and natural position, its movements must be suited to the character and delivery, accord with the gestures, and harmonise with the hands and motions of the body.
>
> The *according* actions of the head and hands are – when the hand seeks the head, the head bends forward to meet it; when the hand moves from the head, the head is held back or averted; in submission, when the hands are prone, it bends downward. The head, without the aid of the expressive face, performs many useful and appropriate expressions.
>
>> *When hung down*, humility, shame and grief are expressed.
>> *When turned up*, arrogance, pride, and courage are shown.
>> *When inclined to one side*, languor, mental derangement.
>> *When stiff, rigid, and thrust forward*, nobility, barbarity: all other positions indicting modesty, doubt, admirations, indignation.
>> *A Nod* [...]. Signifies assent, willingness or approbation.
>> *A Shake* [...]. Signifies disapprobation, annoyance and rejection.
>> *A Toss* [...]. Contempt, indignation.
>> *Averted* [...]. In dislike or horror.
>> *Forward* [...]. In attention, interest, apprehension.

And besides these, impressions created by position nearly all belong to significant gestures.

Neville then continues with a more emotionally charged discourse on the face:

> *The Face* – The face is, of course, the sublime fountain of complete convincing, perfect expression, and in order to accomplish the various motions we must consider the different parts separately, but the eyes, eyelids and eyebrows may be taken together under the heading of:

> *The Eye* – 'They burn, they strain, they twinkle, they swim; they are savage, fierce, flaming and serious, distorted, submissive, insinuating and sensual', and yet this wonderful assemblage is composed simply of circles of various colours, which indicate the direction from, or to which, impressions tend.

Neville gives his potential students the following instruction:

> Practice moving the eyeball in all directions slowly whilst the eyelids are raised and steady. The eye proper requires the operation of the lids to create perfect expressions.

Then the author discourses on the differences between the sexes in their use of the eyes:

> There is a difference between the eye of a man and the eye of a woman. The former possesses the epic, philosophical and intellectual; the latter is formed for its softness and brilliancy, for the exercise of tender sentiments, characteristic delicacy, intelligence and truth.

Then, in an interesting moment which may recall some of Strindberg's concerns, Neville adds:

> Women frequently destroy the distinguishing characteristics of their eyes by a thick line of paint on the under lid. This is an error; the upper lid is the striking feature upon which much of the character depends and might be strongly marked; the lower lash does not in any degree contribute to the marking of the eye, and should be kept light and tender to softly merge into the cheek.

The book contains many illustrations of positions of the eyes and eyebrows. To reinforce this Neville reminds his readers:

Form and expression depend, as I have said, on the eyelids and positions of the head, and intensity is strongly marked by the eyebrows The eyes are the 'index of the mind' the

Strong-felt passion bolts into the face –
The mind untouch'd, what is it but grimace?
The muscles of the eyes obey the will, and also act involuntarily, subject to the affections of the mind. Their complicated fibres serve no purpose but to convey impressions to the soul and give external expression to them. 'We touch each other by the sense of sight', and the *eyebrow* plays an important part, giving the form to the eyes in different degrees, and governing the forehead, more peculiarly in man than in woman. Its elevation is indicative of intellectual power; it is arched in doubt, surprise or fear, laughter or admiration; contracted towards the nose, and lowered in rage, despair, jealousy; and in grief and pain contracted and raised upwards towards the inner extremities. They can move together or separately in the different sentiments they wish to convey.

Neville continues his exposition on the communicative potential of the human face with sections on the chin, nose and mouth; each presented with the same level of detail, interspersed with (unacknowledged) quotations and with a blend of anatomical detail and exploration of the emotions.

To a modern reader, the book from which we have quoted seems more like a treatise on non-verbal communication than a source book for actors. In fact, we may well feel that this invitation to imitate nature would create a highly artificial and anything but authentic performance. To some extent, this is because more recent approaches to acting have emphasized the motivation, inner drives or relationships of characters and our concept of what is 'naturalistic' derives from that understanding.

The truth of the passions

When the National Theatre in London recently staged a 'platform performance' entitled 'Naturalism from East to West', they presented their audience of teachers and students with a demonstration of a director working with two actors on scenes from Chekhov's *The Seagull*. The discussion and exposition entirely centred on the work of Stanislavsky as if he, alone, had invented and sought to establish a 'naturalistic' approach to acting. We shall be exploring Stanislavsky's productions at the Moscow Art Theatre in a later chapter, seeking to explain why that theatre and those productions in particular have come to be seen as the embodiment of Naturalism but, for the moment, we must consider how Stanislavsky moved from the position we have already outlined to build on the work and ideas of other practitioners and create his own, distinctive 'system' of actor-training.

Looking back on his early work, Stanislavsky realized that he had tended to concentrate on external rather that internal reality. Helen Krich Chinoy, in what remains one of the finest essays on the rise of the director, records this shift in emphasis:

> Like the Meininger, Stanislavsky was intrigued by the perfection of external realism. In preparing Alexei Tolstoy's *Czar Fyodor*, for example, he insisted on visiting the actual historical locales and purchasing authentic accessories. Looking back at this early period in his career he decided: 'This artistic truth was at the time merely external; it was the truth of objects, furniture, costumes, stage properties, light and sound effects, the reproduction of the typical features of a stage character and his external, physical life.' (Cole and Chinoy, 1970: 33)

As his career progressed it was what he termed 'the verisimilitude of the passions' that became central to Stanislavsky's ideas. In his posthumously published work *System and Methods of Creative Art*, he stated: 'It is this work – the work of grasping the true nature of each emotion through one's own powers of observation, of developing one's attention for such a task, and of consciously mastering the art of entering the creative circle – that I find absolutely essential [...]' (in Stanislavsky, 1950: 92). He maintained that the stuff of theatre and the actor's necessary research into the psychological problems of the characters must focus on 'the ordinary, everyday life lived by people all over the world' (93). His challenge to actors was to 'think of yourself as some character in the play. If you *are* that man or woman in the play what ought your organic feelings to be?'(93). To this he constantly added the necessity for actors to avoid any kind of falsehood and develop qualities that embraced a 'feeling for truth'. When the playwright Strindberg compiled a series of pamphlets on aspects of theatre to give to the members of the Intimate Theatre in 1907, he expressed similar ideas in a different way:

> I suspect that the actor puts himself in a trance, forgetting himself, and finally actually becoming the person he is supposed to represent. This may sound like sleepwalking, but it isn't the same.   (1962: 210)

In this sense of total identification with a character, we can see the beginnings of what later became known as 'Method' acting (see p. 79). For Stanislavsky the truth had not only to be realistic but also artistic and it was during a period of reflection following his production of Chekhov's *The Seagull*, which did not, apparently, satisfy its writer's ambitions for a sense of natural behaviour from its characters, that Stanislavsky came to the conclusion that the feeling for truth could be developed through a number of exercises and that nothing should happen on stage unless the requisite heightened state of awareness had been achieved.

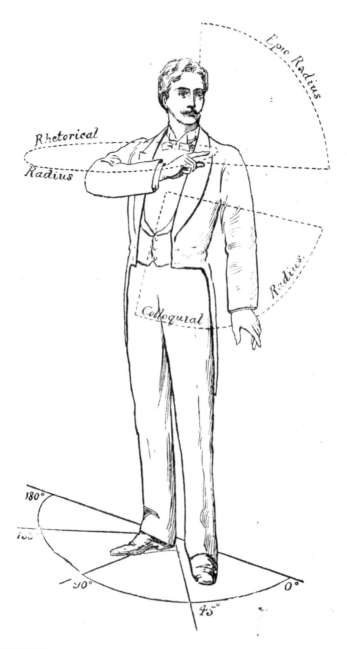

ILLUSTRATION 5a

Stage performance as an art and a science based on close observations of nature.
Illustrations by Dargavel and Ramsey from *Voice Speech and Gesture*, a nineteenth-century
textbook of performance, showing:

(a) Basic positions of the body for the declamation of a speech.

ILLUSTRATION 5b
Stage performance as an art and a science based on close observations of nature. Illustrations by Dargavel and Ramsey from *Voice Speech and Gesture*, a nineteenth-century textbook of performance, showing:

(b) Gestures and physical positions indicating emotions and mental states. L–R Terror or Dismay; Aversion or Fear; Submission or Supplication.

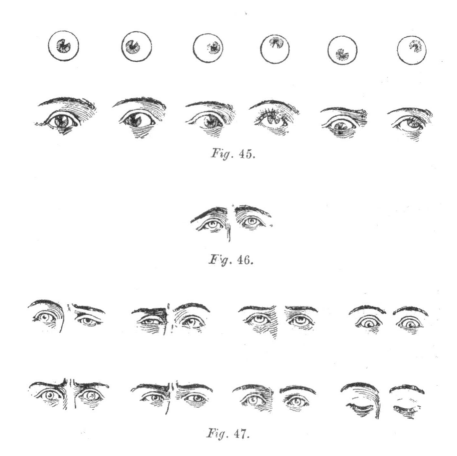

Fig. 45.

Fig. 46.

Fig. 47.

ILLUSTRATION 5c

Stage performance as an art and a science based on close observations of nature. Illustrations by Dargavel and Ramsey from *Voice Speech and Gesture*, a nineteenth-century textbook of performance, showing:

(c) Possible positions and movements of the eyes and eyebrows: the middle illustration indicates 'intelligence' and the entire set of diagrams is intended to show the eyes and eyebrows as potential 'windows of the mind'.

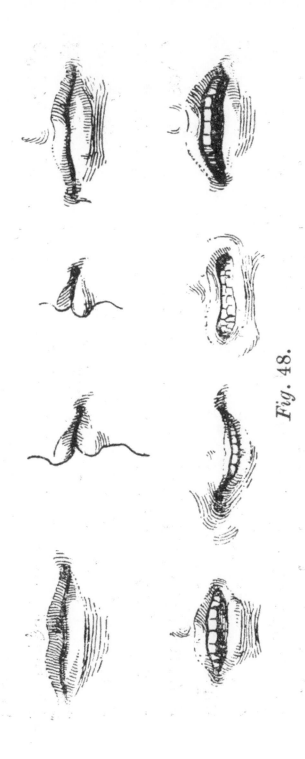

Fig. 48.

ILLUSTRATION 5d

Stage performance as an art and a science based on close observations of nature. Illustrations by Dargavel and Ramsey from *Voice Speech and Gesture*, a nineteenth-century textbook of performance, showing:

(d) The mouth as an indication of emotional states. The top row of diagrams demonstrates varieties of 'resolution or decision of character', the bottom row indicates L–R Vacancy or Idiocy; Mirth; Rage; Devotion.

ILLUSTRATION 5e

Stage performance as an art and a science based on close observations of nature. Illustrations by Dargavel and Ramsey from *Voice Speech and Gesture*, a nineteenth-century textbook of performance, showing:

(e) Attitudes of the head suggesting mental states. L–R Devotion; Surprise.

Truth in context and action

The implications of the issues discussed in this and the previous chapter can be illustrated by a close reading of the stage directions in the opening scene of Ibsen's remarkable and controversial play *Ghosts* (1980a). We use the word *reading* advisedly because, at the time of Ibsen's writing, it was the extent of sales of the published 'book' of the play rather than its first production that ensured its success or otherwise. In fact, Ibsen was deeply disappointed by the sales of his play *Ghosts*: playwrights depended on such sales, particularly around Christmas time, for much of their income, and it was many years before the play had its first stage production, not in his native Norway or Europe but in America.

The play opens with extensive and detailed stage directions describing a *'spacious garden room'*. Precise positions of the doors are specified: *'a door in the left-hand wall and two doors in the right-hand wall'* and at the rear of the stage/room there is a conservatory with *'large panes of glass'* out of which a door leads to a garden. The stage directions also specify the positions of other windows and the nature and position of the furniture: a small round table surrounded by chairs in the centre of the room and a sofa with a sewing table beside it under a window.

However, Ibsen is not content to merely describe a room, he creates the detail of an entire environment by adding that the table is covered with books, magazines and newspapers and that beyond the conservatory window, we can see a *'gloomy fjord landscape'* and that this is *'veiled by steady rain'*.

The two characters with whom the action begins are already on stage and they, their appearance and their movements, are also described in considerable detail. Engstrand, who is standing at the garden door, is, the reader is told, a carpenter and has a slightly crooked left leg which causes him to wear a boot with a block of wood under the sole to enable him to walk more easily. Regina, a housemaid whom we later discover to be Engstrand's daughter, has obviously been watering flowers because she is carrying an *'empty garden syringe'* and is clearly not pleased to see her Father as she bars his way and speaks in a low voice.

There is immediate tension as Engstrand complains that he is soaking wet from the rain and insists on limping into the room. From the dialogue and the stage directions on the first page, Ibsen provides a great deal of information. We learn that the two characters are father and daughter, that Regina is very uncomfortable about her father being there and that there is a 'young master' asleep upstairs who must not be woken. This clearly establishes her as a servant and she seems determined to contradict everything her father says. Ibsen builds the conflict in the stage directions he gives the actors: he specifies that lines are spoken *'drily'*, *'scornfully'*, *'muttered'* or *'disgusted'*, he directs that : *'he comes few steps nearer'*, *'she looks knowingly at him'*, *'her jaw drops'*, *'she mutters without looking at him'*, *'after a short silence'*, *'sniffs'*, *'stamps her foot'*, *'shrinks'* and finally as their confrontation climaxes, *'pushes him towards the garden door'*. During the course of the conversation we learn that Regina is in service to a Mrs Alving, who has brought her up and given her some education. Regina's mother, it appears, was also in service to Mrs Alving when her husband, Captain Alving, was alive and, according to Regina, her father is a drinker whose violent and inconsiderate behaviour was the cause of her own mother's death.

Regina cannot seem to get rid of her father quickly enough, but he is determined to have his say. He has been working on the building of an orphanage (which we later discover is to be dedicated to the memory of Captain Alving). Not only is there to be an opening ceremony the next day conducted by Pastor Manders, an important figure in local society, but also Engstrand has made sufficient money to contemplate opening a hostel for sailors and has come to entice Regina to join him in this venture by providing the 'bit of skirt' that sailors will appreciate. Engstrand tries to tempt his daughter to leave service with the promise of likely marriage to a ship's captain but she is adamant that her duty does not lie towards her feckless father, but to the family, especially the 'young master' who, perhaps mysteriously at this point in the play, is still asleep. Father and daughter trade insults and threats but eventually Engstrand leaves, promising to get Pastor Manders to talk some sense into her and show her duty as a child.

Thus, with very careful notes to the actors, almost telling them how to speak their lines, find their motivations and moves, Ibsen establishes the context of the play's subsequent action.

The unit of this first scene which follows in Ibsen's play shows Regina behaving in a totally different way towards Pastor Manders. The stage directions tell us that no sooner has she ejected her Father than she takes a look in the mirror to ensure that her personal appearance is immaculate. She then busies herself watering the flowers as Pastor Manders, 'in an overcoat and carrying an umbrella and a small travelling bag on a strap from his shoulder' enters 'through the garden door into the conservatory'. Regina, whose precise relationship with the Pastor Ibsen is clearly intended to be a matter of some speculation, now shows him constant attention after she has turned 'in surprise and delight' on hearing his voice. She follows him, takes his coat and umbrella, makes him sit down and puts a footstool under his feet, constantly using the word 'comfortable' and once again mentioning the 'young master' asleep upstairs. We learn from Manders that the young master is, in fact, Oswald, who has returned home, although at this point in the play no more information is given. As the Pastor relaxes, he looks carefully at Regina and then remarks on her developing figure, and this is followed by 'a short pause', perhaps a moment of awkwardness before both change the subject. After a conversation about Regina's father and her unwillingness to become part of his scheme, Regina indicates that she is looking to keep house for 'someone I could feel real affection for and look up to as a father' and she begs the Pastor to try to think of someone who would take her in on that basis. As her pleas intensify Manders 'gets up' and asks Regina to fetch Mrs Alving. The tension broken, Manders then begins to walk up and down the room until his eyes fall on the books on the table; he picks up one of them '*and glances at the title page, starts, and looks at some of the others*' saying 'Hm! I see!'

What are we to make of this incident? Obviously the audience cannot see the titles of the books, but the fact that there are books in the room establishes something about its inhabitants. Much more important, however, is the fact that the actors themselves know what the books are and this informs the naturalism of their performance. We shall return to the precise nature of these books in our suggestions for discussion.

In the small sections of the scene we have been describing, Ibsen has already established many facts and even more speculations; he has shown us an environment recognizably 'real' as a Norwegian, middle-class home near a fjord, visited by a Lutheran Pastor. Three characters have been introduced and their behaviour has been clearly specified by the playwright: we witness a domestic scene played out in a domestic setting but with many underlying tensions and unresolved questions. In such situations there is little room for the mannered acting or playing to the audience that Strindberg so vehemently opposed in his *Preface to Miss Julie* or which motivated Stanislavsky to develop his concept of truthfulness on stage.

CHAPTER SUMMARY

- Throughout the latter half of the nineteenth century, theatre practitioners and artists increasingly sought to present 'truth' in their work.
- A very significant and influential moment in the development of stage realism was Irving's production of *The Bells* in 1871.
- The spectacular and popular melodramas brought encouragement to the development of sophisticated theatre technology: especially in lighting and scenic construction.
- Stage Naturalism was greatly aided by the new technology and playwrights began to make precise demands for qualities of light and their characters' environments.
- The desire to see an accurate representation of nature on stage was greatly enhanced by developments in painting and photography.
- In the search for truth in performance, various 'systems' were devised and many textbooks appeared. The predominant trend was to encourage an exact imitation of nature and to analyse speech and movement accordingly. The Delsarte System was the most enduring and substantial.
- Innovative practitioners such as Antoine, the Duke of Saxe-Meiningen and Stanislavsky used the concept of the 'fourth-wall', the 'box set' and careful visual design to create a new kind of 'reality' on stage.

- Similar developments in search of 'truthful' performance were seen in Opera.
- Stage directions became an integral part of naturalistic plays.

SEMINAR AND WORKSHOP TOPICS

1 What is the effect on the characters and action of (a) the quality of light, (b) the weather conditions?
2 Reread all the stage directions relating to the movements of Regina and her Father. After 'walking these through', reflect upon the relationship established by these directions.
3 Now repeat the exercise with the entrance of Pastor Manders and discuss the results and differences.
4 Consult the relevant sections of our chapter on The European Scene and discuss which books you imagine to have been in Mrs Alving's house. How do you account for Pastor Manders's discomfort?
5 Find further examples in *Ghosts* where the quality of light appears to complement the mood and action.
6 Discuss the following passage in the light of the issues raised in this chapter:

> An actor entering a box set through a door must behave differently from one who walks on from the wings in front of a drop. An actor encased by a setting must relate to time and space in a different way from an actor playing on an apron in front of a painting. An actor who must pretend to be the occupant of the setting will reach an audience by different means from one whose art is partly that of the rhetorician and who can address the audience directly. An actor who moves in a setting in lights that subtly accentuate details will select different values from one who is brightly illuminated and whose wardrobe has come out of his trunk in much the same way as the scenery came out of a warehouse. (Bogard, Moody and Meserve, 1977: 38)

FURTHER READING

Baugh, C. (2005) *Theatre Performance and Technology*, Basingstoke: Palgrave Macmillan. Provides an in-depth study of the advance of lighting, scenic construction and the use of machinery in the theatre.

Brockett, O. (1995) *History of the Theatre*, Boston, MA, and London: Allyn & Bacon. Remains incomparably the best survey of many of the issues raised in this chapter.

Holmes, R. (2000) *Sidetracks – Explorations of a Romantic Biographer*, London: HarperCollins. A fascinating study of the development of literature and photography in the nineteenth century.

Holroyd, M. (2008) *A Strange Eventful History*, London: Chatto & Windus. The careers and influences of Irving and his remarkable family beautifully presented.

Latham, A., ed. (2011) *The Oxford Companion to Music*, Oxford: Oxford University Press. Contains invaluable information on the development of opera and *verismo*.

Magarshack, D. (1950) *Stanislavsky, A Life*, London: Macgibbon & Key. Remains the most accessible and helpful exploration of the influences on Stanislavsky.

Neville, H. et al. (1897) *Voice, Speech and Gesture*, London: Charles Deacon. This and similar books on elocution from the period make fascinating and illuminating reading.

PART III

Plays, Players and Playhouses

CHAPTER 5

Meiningen – A Prelude to Naturalism

The Meiningen Company

By the middle of the nineteenth century the royal courts of Europe had acquired a long history as centres for the performing arts. We may, for example, think of the composers Bach and Haydn who worked as court musicians and composers in Germany and Austria, the playwright Molière working at Versailles or of the beautifully preserved examples of lavish court theatres that we now have in Drottningholm in Sweden or at Cesky Krumlov in the Czech Republic. It was, however, in the second half of the nineteenth century at the relatively obscure German court of George Second Duke of Saxe-Meiningen that one of the most significant developments in European theatre took place.

The duke's first wife was related to the English Queen Victoria and the couple were frequent visitors to London. Here, the duke, who was clearly passionate about the theatre was greatly impressed by the moves towards pictorial realism and a more disciplined use of crowds and stage 'extras', employed by the actor manager Charles Kean. His experience inspired him to establish his own, court-based, theatre company and with the constant encouragement after 1873 of his third wife, the actress Ellen Franz, he developed a concept of theatre that was to change the approach of future generations of practitioners with particular relevance for the emergence of stage Naturalism.

Even though the duke relied heavily for the implementation of his ideas on his stage manager Ludwig Chronegk, who joined him in 1866, his creation of the idea that a production must be under the total control of an external 'director', who had what we might now term a 'governing idea' for the play, was revolutionary. He had, in fact, established the practice that was followed by all the proponents of Naturalism of having a director who was not the leading actor: a practice which has remained current to this day.

When the Meininger company had been established for some years it embarked on a number of highly influential tours of European cities and many theatre historians recognize the date of 1 May 1874, when the Meininger troupe was first seen in Berlin, as the moment when the emergence of what we may call 'director's theatre' was fully recognized. When the company visited Drury Lane in London, the great actor Henry Irving fell under its spell; when it visited Brussels, the young André Antoine was transfixed; when it visited Moscow for a second time in 1890 after having been in St Petersburg and Odessa, the virtually unknown actor Konstantin Stanislavsky was lost in admiration. What, then, were the qualities and practices that characterized the work of this extraordinary duke and his company?

From contemporary accounts of his productions and from his surviving drawings and writings we can deduce that the duke's overriding aim was to create the most truthful and accurate possible representation of reality on stage and that he sought to achieve this in three ways: innovative approaches to working with actors; a passion for historical accuracy; and new forms of stage construction.

Working with actors

Because the duke financed his own company he was able to implement reforms that ran counter to the practice of more commercial managements. He insisted that his company worked as an egalitarian ensemble and that more experienced and senior actors take more minor roles from time to time. Instead of employing extra actors for 'crowd scenes', a common practice with other companies, he used permanent members of his company and had them working in groups under the leadership of a more experienced actor. Even when the Meiningen company was touring and recruiting local actors as supers (or extras as we would now call them), they continued to use permanent members of the company as group leaders. Stage groupings were of utmost importance in the duke's concern to create a natural-looking stage picture: he forbade any form of straight line and insisted that natural groupings avoided symmetry and artificial posturing. In order to avoid a square and uninterestingly static appearance in the scenes of a play, he manipulated the grouping of actors with meticulous care and determined their movements with total precision. His method was based on his assertion that every person on stage was a character who must be fully involved in the spirit and action of the play and never be a passive spectator.

The duke aimed to remove the visual centre of interest from the physical centre of the stage and, to achieve his ends, he would not allow actors to take up positions on the centre front of the stage opposite the prompter's box (which was positioned below the stage level just in front of the stage). This avoidance of the habit of many early nineteenth-century actors of declaring their lines from the stage position we would now call 'downstage centre' was later to be recommended by Strindberg in his famous Preface to *Miss Julie* and the detailed planning and directing of the movements of every single character was later to be emulated by the English dramatist and librettist, W. S. Gilbert.

One of the duke's most important innovations and one which benefited from his personal patronage was his insistence on long and intensive periods of rehearsal. Although it appears that rehearsals were held in the evenings after the other court affairs had been attended to, the length of rehearsals frequently extended to five or six hours and, from the outset, something very close to full settings and costumes were used. After 1873, the actress Ellen Franz took responsibility for the spoken aspects of the text.

Meiningen's groupings and movement of characters, were pre-designed by him but may well have been choreographed in rehearsal by his stage manager, Chronegk, a former court comedian. The duke's explicit aim was that the staging must constitute an integrated whole in which both scenery and actors blended together to create a natural picture. One major problem he addressed in this ambition was the flimsiness of the painted scenery and the use of perspective on some of the painted pieces. He instructed that actors must not come into contact with painted flats or other stage pieces that might shake or move when touched and he forbade them to go near to painted pieces in which, in an attempt to create a sense of distance, the stage artist had made objects smaller. A full-sized actor standing near a half-sized door, for instance, was in his view, ridiculous and to be avoided. Similarly, he discontinued the practice of having child actors dressed as adults at the rear of the stage in another attempt to create artificial depth and distance.

All these concerns led the duke to adopt new and influential changes to the design and construction of the scenic pieces themselves. But before we consider these we must note another of his ideas that had repercussions both for actors and designers.

Historical truth and accuracy

The majority of the productions undertaken by the company demanded a historic setting, although Meiningen acknowledged the new drama in an early production of Ibsen's *Ghosts*. For Shakespeare and the other classic German plays that made up the bulk of the repertoire, the duke initiated a tradition of careful and extensive research into the architecture, costumes, movement styles and gestures of the appropriate period. He argued that historical accuracy was only of value if it contributed to revealing the truth of the drama. Such ideas and approaches had, by no means, been common practice. Many managements simply retained a stock of painted settings that could be made to serve almost any period and purpose and which merely attempted, at best, to convey a flavour of the period being represented. In costume, too, companies made little attempt to achieve total historical accuracy and even allowed actors to add their own embellishments to a costume taken from stock. Such aspects as hairstyles, beards or footwear were rarely adapted to take account of the historical period in which the play was set.

By contrast, Meiningen sought to recreate a truthful stage image of the precise period in which his productions were set and in order to do this, he not only undertook meticulous research but also created sketches, stage drawings and detailed designs for costumes and properties. He acquired historically accurate fabrics, armour and weapons and was therefore indirectly responsible for the growth of specialist theatrical costumiers. In the process, he created the idea of a total design concept that, to some extent, developed Wagner's ambitions for a *Gesamtkunstwerk*: a work of art that integrated all aspects of theatre.

Working within this total performance ideal, the Meininger company found that the common modes of largely two-dimensional scenic construction were proving inadequate and that the creation of a natural picture on stage required a variety of floor levels, entrances, exits and apparent sources of light. This led to some important developments in staging that were to become the stable feature of many naturalistic plays in the future.

Scenic structures

The duke's sketches for stage settings show three-dimensional interior and exterior locations. They appear to suggest solid walls, stone archways, rigid window frames, substantial doors, classical columns, flights of steps and a variety of different levels. The construction of such settings demanded considerable skill, especially as the settings were increasingly required to be portable and able to fit a number of theatre spaces. Although the duke designed all the costumes, properties and settings himself, the scenery was painted by the Bruckner brothers. These skilled artists, who had also painted scenery for Wagner, employed very strong and bold colours, whereas previous stage painters had bowed to the habit of allowing actors to stand out against pastel colours. They also, with the duke's prompting, abolished the use of fabric 'sky borders' and implemented the use of foliage, banners, beams and other similar features to create a more believable environment. The detail also extended downwards to the floor of the stage and Meiningen is usually credited with having been the first to incorporate the stage floor into his total design concept. Maintaining correct proportions, he varied the floor levels and textures with steps, rostra, rocky terrain, tree stumps and other such features.

When he had completed the outline design for the settings and costumes the duke turned his attention to the furniture which, he insisted, was to be perfectly harmonious with the rest of the design, and for which he was prepared to extend the rehearsal period so that the actors could familiarize themselves with the stage environment created for them.

With the ever-increasing solidity of the scenic structures, Meiningen reached the point where he was able to create an accurate representation of a room with rigid walls and practical doors and windows. He was one of the first practitioners to use what became known as the 'box set': an interior filling the entire stage but suggesting the existence of other rooms or outside locations beyond. Many of the plays by the Naturalist playwrights required such a setting although the idea may well have originated in England.

ILLUSTRATION 6

Sketches by the Duke of Saxe-Meiningen:

(a) Set design for *Macbeth* indicating the use of three-dimensional scenery.

(b) Typical Norwegian interior as a setting for *Ghosts* (1886) based on information supplied by Ibsen. Sketched by the duke on the reverse of the letter sent by the playwright (illustrations courtesy of Theaterwissenschaftliche Sammlung, University of Cologne)

In all his productions Meiningen aspired to respond to the needs and demands posed by the text. By abolishing anything that resembled a 'star' system, insisting on ensemble playing and a scrupulous attention to detail he laid the foundations for a new approach to theatre that sought truth of character, performance, physical appearance and context. His legacy inspired some of the key figures in the future development of Naturalism in the theatre.

Meiningen and the new drama

With his innovative approaches to play production and unhindered by laws governing public performance, the duke was able to make a unique contribution to the development of contemporary drama. It was, for instance, the Meininger company that was able to introduce Ibsen's controversial play *Ghosts* to European audiences when all avenues for its public production seemed closed.

Ann Marie Koller (1965) tells us that the duke made a visit to the rarely visited Norway early in his directing career and returned with a series of paintings and sketches that were to be the sources of the stage designs for his production of the one-act play *Between the Battles*, by the Norwegian playwright, poet and author Bjørnstjerne Bjørnson. The duke had lodged with the playwright's father and had undertaken extensive research into the customs, landscapes and history of Norway and was able to draw on that experience to re-create the spirit of medieval Nordic life and the forbidding Norwegian vistas in his production of the play for a tour to Berlin in 1874. Even though the strange and gloomy production of *Between the Battles* was not one of the Meiningen's most popular achievements it appears that Bjørnson remained one of the Duke's favourite authors and that it was he who introduced the duke to the work of Ibsen.

Given the duke's propensity for historical drama, it is hardly surprising that he was initially drawn to Ibsen's prose play about thirteenth-century Norway, *The Pretenders*, and he lavished all his pictorial skill and passion for accurate sound effects and battles scenes on his production. By his use of 'massive grey scenery and […] blues, greys, and dark reds in the heavy costumes' (Koller, 1965: 101), Meiningen created memorable stage images that impressed audiences when he took the play to Berlin in 1876.

However, by 1877, *The Pillars of Society*, the first of Ibsen's 12 great plays dealing with contemporary issues, became available in German translation and was soon to be widely read and performed there. This was followed in 1879 by his explosive play *A Doll's House*, which was eventually to be Ibsen's most performed play. Just how far Ibsen's plays challenged the values and attitudes of respectable, middle-class society in Europe can be illustrated by the event surrounding the early productions of *A Doll's House* in Germany. Michael Meyer (1965) explains in an Introduction to his English translation of the play that when it was due to open at Flensburg, the actress who was to play the leading role of Nora (a woman who finally walks out of an unsatisfactory marriage and slams the door) refused to perform unless the play was rewritten with a less contentious ending (Ibsen, 1980b: 18). Reluctantly, Ibsen agreed to this, preferring his own modified version in which the ending is left ambiguous to the possibility of its being re-written by some theatre hack. This new version that enabled disturbed audiences to imagine that perhaps Nora would remember her 'responsibilities' and 'duties' remained in the repertoire for some years but the original version was privately widely read and was eventually performed in Munich in 1880 with Ibsen in the audience. Wherever the play was performed it provoked outrage, but there was a greater threat to conventional respectability to come and it was George, Duke of Saxe-Meiningen, who was to embrace it with the greatest effect. Meyer, in his Introduction to Ibsen's *Ghosts* (1962) tells how the Danish novelist Herman Bang had reported attending a production of *A Doll's House* in Germany and noticing that the theatre was full of students. However, instead of paying close attention to the performance, they were surreptitiously reading copies of a published version of *Ghosts* because they dare not be seen reading it at home! (Ibsen, 1980a: 16–17). Bang added that students were now frequently using extracts from the play for auditions and mounting productions of this contentious and banned play in private halls. *Ghosts*, a play that was eventually to send a shaft of light across the hypocritical darkness of denial in Europe, had been rejected by theatres in Ibsen's native Norway and elsewhere, and had become a shocking book to be read in secret by the young and progressive. It was eventually to become one of the most significant plays in the establishment of the small-scale experimental theatres that contributed most to the development of stage Naturalism. The first Scandinavian production eventually took place in 1883, but it was some time before it was presented in Germany.

The duke, having heard of an unsatisfactory production of the play at the Stadtheater in Augsburg in 1886, and with a new translation becoming available was determined to mount a better performance to which he would invite the author and a substantial number of leading critics. In his very informative article, 'From Political to Cultural Despotism: The nature of the Saxe Meiningen aesthetic', John Osborne records that the duke wrote to Ibsen asking him for information about the interior of a typical middle-class Norwegian home and that it was on the reverse side of Ibsen's reply that he made his initial sketches for the set design (1965: 42).

This typical act of concern for truth was undertaken in defiance of much advice for, as Koller points out in her *The Theatre Duke: George 11 of Saxe Meiningen and the German Stage*, the critic Karl Frenzel had told the duke that 'Ibsen's *Ghosts* is a sticky piece and likely to end in failure' (1984: 176). Nevertheless and even though many of the public refused to buy tickets for 'a play so indecent and immoral', the performance went ahead at Meiningen in the period just before

Christmas. The very notoriety of the play ensured a large and intrigued audience and, because of its small cast and interior settings, the production achieved an intimacy and power that were in sharp contrast to the usual spectacular pieces. Ibsen himself described the production as 'unsurpassable' and, as Koller also tells us, the critic Isadore Landau writing 30 years after the event said:

> Everyone who saw the Ibsen drama on that evening has agreed that never again on any stage has this dreadful yet beautiful work so approached what we mean when say Ibsenism. (1984: 176)

Ghosts continued to have a mixed, and often hostile, reception in the theatres of Europe. Meiningen's production was taken to Dresden, but the second performance was cancelled because of police pressure. The duke had, however, lit a flame that refused to be extinguished and had established new standards of production that were to be emulated and developed in the ensuing years by such practitioners as Antoine, Irving, Brahm, Grein and Stanislavsky.

CHAPTER SUMMARY

- Many European courts maintained their own theatres in the nineteenth century and the drama was usually supplied by visiting companies of actors.
- The Duke of Saxe-Meiningen established the idea of a resident company who met and rehearsed frequently.
- The duke created an 'ensemble' with no 'star' actors and all actors were expected to take both small and larger roles.
- He and his colleague Chronegk worked autocratically as 'directors' and choreographed the movement and actions of the 'crowd' with great precision.
- The duke was influenced by what he had seen in London and insisted on total accuracy in period costumes and settings.
- He used three-dimensional settings and the 'box-set' to create illusions of reality.
- He was initially devoted to historical drama, but was introduced to the work of Ibsen and mounted a controversial production of *Ghosts*.
- The Meininger company undertook a number of highly influential tours and among those who were greatly impressed were Antoine, Stanislavsky, Grein and Brahm: all of whom were important figures in the development of stage Naturalism.
- The Duke of Saxe-Meiningen is usually credited with having established the modern concept of 'director'.

SEMINAR AND WORKSHOP TOPICS

1 What are the advantages of having a play directed by a 'director' rather than by the leading actor?
2 How important is historical accuracy in plays either written in or set in the past?
3 Select a 'crowd scene' from a play and work on directing the movements and action of the characters, ensuring that they are all providing a convincing 'stage picture'.
4 Experiment with finding the most powerful and effective positions on a 'proscenium' stage by avoiding the physical centre.
5 What sources did Meiningen use for his researches? Select a play and determine what sources you should use to achieve a 'realistic' and accurate production.
6 Search the library and web for illustrations of Meiningen's designs for staging and costumes. What qualities do they represent?
7 What are the advantages and qualities associated with an 'ensemble'?

FURTHER READING

Braun, E. (1982) *The Director and the Stage*, London: Methuen.
Cole, T. and Chinoy, H. (1953/70) *Directors on Directing*, New York: Crown. This and the previous title provide a good introduction to the work of the duke in the context of directing.
Koller, A. M. (1984) *The Theatre Duke: Georg II of Saxe-Meiningen and the German Stage*, Stanford, CA: Stanford University Press. The most comprehensive survey of his work.
See also the article by Osborne (1975) cited in this chapter and the appropriate entry in Brockett's *History of the Theatre* (1995).

CHAPTER 6

André Antoine and the Théâtre Libre

The intention in this section is to consider the importance of André Antoine's contribution to Naturalism. It is, perhaps, Antoine to whom we are most indebted. Not only did he initiate a new enterprise in the form of the Théâtre Libre, which was to have such a decisive influence on the development of modern theatre, he was responsible for bringing to the stage the Naturalist form of theatre representation. Antoine introduced and developed new methods of interpretation in staging, directing and acting which, as news spread of the Théâtre Libre, were quickly appropriated by other like-minded experimentalists.

André Antoine's *Mes souvenirs sur le Théâtre Libre*, first published in 1921, provides the reader with a very accessible account of his role in establishing the Théâtre Libre in 1887 and the experimental nature of his project through to 1894 when, finally, lacking the stamina to continue with his venture and facing bankruptcy, he relinquished control of the theatre. Marvin Carlson, in his translator's Preface to *Memories of The Théâtre Libre* (Antoine, 1977), advises the reader to exercise a degree of caution, pointing out that the work is not quite the accurate journal the format would suggest, but rather that it was written retrospectively, drawn from Antoine's memories of events and largely reliant on the volumes of newspaper clippings he kept. Whilst there are a number of inconsistencies in the content which Carlson duly draws attention to in his notes, the reader benefits enormously from Antoine's approach by virtue of the fact that he quotes extensively from the clippings, very often including the full text of published letters and articles in his entries. Given that much of the discussion surrounding the state of contemporary theatre and the newly emerging Naturalist drama takes the form of correspondence and articles written for publication in the leading newspapers and journals of the period, these extracts provide an invaluable source of information. It is worth bearing in mind that, having been at the centre of these debates, Antoine would have been very aware of what his memoirs might evoke and at the time of writing he would, as Carlson reminds us, have been extremely judicious in his recollections. Nevertheless, these extracts not only contextualize the theatre traditions Antoine was rebelling against, they are a key source of his ideas and early practice (1977: xii).

For all the cautionary advice, the book does, as Carlson suggests, provide us with 'a picture of Antoine the man' and momentarily allows us to inhabit the literary and artistic environment of the period, the salons and circles to which he was invited, eventually attending some of the 'most exclusive' in Paris frequented by 'celebrities' of the moment. We form an impression of what was, in fact, a rather close community of critics, novelists, dramatists and artists, with whom he gradually became acquainted and upon whose connections he relied in pursuit of his venture. Antoine conveys a world in which novelists become playwrights, dramatists become critics, a world of petty rivalries and squabbles where enemies of the Théâtre Libre are won over to eventually become supporters but where, conversely, those who were once friends turn to attack him, occasionally resorting to 'underhand campaigns' of protest. As well as 'bringing to life' a number of well-known figures whose names and contributions we might recognize, Antoine introduces the reader to a range of other less familiar individuals who had a part to play in the battle over Naturalism.

Early days and development

The picture we begin to draw is of an individual who, in his youth, was determined, hardworking, and capable of recognizing and capitalizing on opportunities as they revealed themselves. He was someone who, as Carlson notes, made conscious decisions for his future, but little could he have imagined when, at the age of 13, he was sent out to work as an errand boy, he was embarking on a journey which would lead him to be one of the most significant contributors to the development of Naturalism.

The oldest of four children, Antoine was sent out to work to supplement the family income. Ceasing his formal studies, he now began a rather different education and, with the few pennies he had to spend, he indulged in 'low-priced literature' containing, as it did in those days, contributions from well-known authors. This prompted in him a 'great thirst for reading and an enormous eagerness to see and learn' (Antoine, 1977: 5). A little later, he took up an apprenticeship with a firm of publishers, Firmin-Didot, situated on the left bank of Paris. Here, as Antoine acknowledges, surroundings and chance played a role in his destiny. Befriended and guided by a colleague, who Antoine credits with opening up 'the horizons of thought and art to me' (5), he frequented book shops, libraries, art galleries and museums during his lunch hours and very often in the evenings. Thus Antoine continued his period of 'self education', progressively developing his knowledge in literature and fine art, whilst simultaneously familiarizing himself with the modern impulses of the milieu and the various 'artistic' debates being explored in the newspapers and journals, which introduced him to figures like Émile Zola. It was, as he says, 'the sort of culture that most young men of my age had left behind them in school' (6). Hippolyte Taine, who had exercised such an influence on Zola's ideas, similarly proved to be 'the guiding thread' for Antoine. A result of happenstance led Antoine to enrol on Taine's History of Art course where, as we might imagine, he was introduced first hand to a number of Naturalist ideas. Indeed, on hearing of Taine's death in March 1893, Antoine acknowledged he was 'one of the men to whom I owe the most' (218).

Where then did Antoine, whose upbringing it seems was 'quite devoid of art' (Antoine, 1977: 4) develop an understanding of theatre so acute that it would see him become one of the key figures of 'modern' theatre? In his memoirs, he recalls a number of theatre outings that had made a profound impression on him in his childhood. Whether it was the acting of the great Paul Félix Taillade (1826–1898), or the opportunity to see behind the scenes at the Théâtre de la Gaîté, these events ignited a passion in the young boy that would continue. As an errand boy he continued to read the theatre notices which he had done as a child, picturing in his imagination the productions which he could never attend. Working at the publishers he spent his spare time reading 'all the famous plays of the last fifty years' (6) in an old reading room he regularly frequented. By now earning his own living, he was able to further indulge in his passion with regular theatre visits. Antoine slowly began to immerse himself in the world of the theatre; firstly by working as an assistant claqueur, an applauder, which had the added benefit of reduced ticket prices to performances, and latterly working as an extra at the Comédie-Française, where it seems he managed to make an appearance in the whole repertoire, as well as appearing at a number of the other main playhouses in Paris.

These combined experiences provided him with a first-hand education of Parisian theatre, affording him the opportunity to closely observe the actors who had so impressed him and at the same time providing a degree of insight into the technical workings of the theatre. It is unsurprising, then, that Antoine harboured ambitions to become a professional actor and, to this end, enrolled 'at a small school of oratory' being run by Marius Laisné in the hope that he might eventually gain entry to the Conservatoire de Paris to pursue a formal actor training. Antoine failed the entry examination to the prestigious school which, upon reflection, he felt was 'wishful thinking to hope to pass that threshold without individual recommendation' (Antoine, 1977: 8).

Although Antoine claims that common sense prevailed and he renounced his ambition to become an actor, the 'set-back' as he interestingly refers to it, coincides with his call up for military service and he was to spend the next five years in North Africa. Jean Chothia notes that even during this enforced absence, Antoine's correspondence reveals his 'obsessive interest in the French theatre' (1991: 6). Following his return to France, Antoine was employed as a clerk at the Gas Company where, once again, a colleague was to exercise an important influence on his future by introducing him to the Cercle Gaulois, a group of amateurs who met regularly each month after work to give 'little dramatic presentations' in the hand-built auditorium located at 37 Passage de l'Elysée-des-Beaux-Arts. Here Antoine 'rediscovered the lost dreams of my youth' (8) and quickly established himself as a key member of the group who, somewhat motivated by a sense of competition with the successful and more affluent rival group, the Cercle Pigalle, became increasingly proactive.

In the first instance he undertook to 'renovate the repertoire' (Antoine, 1977: 9) of plays produced by the group which had hitherto largely been drawn from the popular and entertaining 'Scribean' models. Antoine advocated the introduction of more modern plays in anticipation that this would secure a unique reputation for the group, surpassing that of the rival Pigalle. His ambition from the outset was to cultivate the emergence of new playwrights, who he hoped would be encouraged to produce work in the knowledge that there now existed an opportunity to have their work performed by the Cercle Gaulois, without the necessity of the censor's licence.

The idea was commendable and generally greeted favourably, but the problem facing Antoine and the group was where to find these playwrights. Chance, once again, had a role to play in his future because, as luck would have it, a close friend was able to provide the first of several significant introductions. Within days of having been first introduced to Arthur Byl, whose unpublished play Antoine had agreed to perform, he found himself meeting two influential literary figures, Jules Vidal and Paul Alexis, the latter of whom was a close friend of Émile Zola and whose connections within the Medan literary circle would have a decisive influence on the future of Antoine's venture.

These introductions enabled Antoine to establish the first of what would soon be the Théâtre Libre, programmes comprising four unpublished, one-act plays which included *Jacques Damour*, an adaptation by Leon Hennique based on Zola's novel of the same name. Paul Alexis had been instrumental in persuading Hennique, also a member of Medan, to submit his play for presentation. As Antoine discovered, the association with Zola was, on the one hand, an unexpected coup which he recognized would guarantee publicity and interest in the programme. On the other, Zola's notoriety proved extremely problematic for several members of the group, with the result that the president and founder member abdicated from all responsibility for the project, withdrawing the use of the name Cercle Gaulois, all financial support and rehearsal facilities at the theatre. His one concession was to rent out the theatre for the performances.

The birth of Théâtre Libre

This unexpected reversal of fortune not only signalled the birth of the Théâtre Libre, the newly chosen name, it firmly placed on Antoine's shoulders full responsibility for the experiment. Antoine thus found himself negotiating the demands of his day job at the Gas Company with the increasing demands of the forthcoming launch of the theatre during his lunch hours and in the evenings.

For the newly appointed director, the financial implications, which were to be a continual source of anxiety, were felt immediately. With resources on which he had been reliant now withdrawn, he found himself responsible for all potential production costs as well as the 100 francs due for rental of the venue. In addition he was now charged with finding alternative rehearsal space.

The developing picture of Antoine increasingly reveals an extremely resourceful individual, who quickly managed to reach an agreement with a local bar owner to use the billiard room free of charge, guaranteeing that in return everyone would buy a drink. He, similarly, organized the printing of the programme for a reasonable sum, and, together with one of the group, delivered all the invitations to the performance by hand. With no money to spare for the rental of props, he quite sensibly persuaded his mother to lend him several pieces of dining-room furniture. Renting a handcart, he collected the items and delivered them to the theatre for the stage rehearsals, which took place during the evenings leading up to the performances, the date of which had been determined by pay day when he would have sufficient funds to pay the rent on the theatre.

Antoine, for whom at the start of his project 'the prospect of moving in literary circles made my head swim' (Antoine, 1977: 9), now felt able to personally approach Jules Prével, the theatre critic of *Figaro*, hoping to persuade him to provide some advance publicity for the venture. He pleaded his case successfully and, much to Antoine's surprise, an announcement appeared in the paper the following morning:

> A special presentation of four new and quite unusual unpublished one-act plays will be given in the near future, behind closed doors, for critics and men of letters. The evening will be free of charge and by invitation, and is of unusual interest, due to the names on its program – Émile Zola, Léon Hennique, Paul Alexis and the late lamented novelist, Duranty.
>
> The four new plays will be:
>
> *Jacques Damour*, a drama in one act by M. Léon Hennique, based on a novel by M. Zola which appeared in the *Figaro*.
> *Mlle. Pomme*, a farce in one act by Duranty and M. Paul Alexis.
> *The Sub-prefect*, a tragedy in one act by M. Arthur Byl.
> *The Cockade*, a comedy in one act by M. Jules Vidal.
>
> The plays are being energetically rehearsed, and they will be performed as soon as they are perfected, probably before the end of the month.
>
> The Actors are members of the Cercle Pigalle, the Cercle Gaulois, and the Cercle de la Butte, and performers from various theatres.
>
> If this experiment succeeds – and the organizer M. Antoine, a young leading man, is taking great pains to succeed – then it will surely be followed

by others, and young writers will gain a wonderful outlet for their work, and
be able to present their plays in living form to the directors, instead of on a
sterile manuscript. (16)

The announcement is telling in that it reveals what would become the working
method of the Théâtre Libre. We see here the type of audience Antoine hoped to
draw and that attendance would be by invitation, later to develop into membership
by subscription. It not only advertises the nature of Antoine's experimental theatre
but it draws attention to the contributors and the interesting nature of the
programming, combining as it did different styles of drama. Several other Parisian
newspapers were prompted to follow suit in announcing the programme, thus
signalling a suitably impressive marketing campaign for a novice, the importance
of which he was to remain conscious of for the duration of the Théâtre Libre.

On 30 March 1887, some six years after Zola had produced his *Naturalism in
the Theatre* manifesto, the inaugural programme of the Théâtre Libre was
presented at the little theatre in the Passage de l'Elysée-des-Beaux-Arts, a venue
described by Jules Lemaître in an article he wrote following the performances and
cited by Antoine:

> The auditorium is very small, rather amateurishly daubed with paint, and
> resembling the concert halls found in the chief towns of some districts. One
> could shake hands with the actors across the footlights, and stretch out one's
> legs over the prompter's box. The stage is so small that only the simplest
> scenery can be set up on it, and so near the audience that scenic illusion is
> impossible. If such illusion were born in us, it was because we created it
> ourselves, as the good spectators did in the time of Shakespeare, seeing what
> the writer asked them to see, or in the time of Molière, when the illusion was
> not broken at all by the coming and going of the candle snuffer. (1977: 47)

Significantly, Lemaître concludes his review: 'The naturalness of these amateurs
sets them apart from the playing of many professional actors' (48). The first
programme exceeded all Antoine's expectations, largely due, it has to be said, to
the inclusion of Hennique's adaptation of Zola's novel, which he acknowledged
'created an enormous effect'. Antoine recalls that few critics attended but the
response from those who did, combined with the mounting interest in his venture,
was enough to persuade Antoine to produce a second programme two months
later. It is worth noting the remarks of those critics who did attend. Henry
Fouquier, writing in *Figaro*, was struck by the 'real literary interest and life in this
obscure little theatre lost in the wilds of Montmarte' (Antoine, 1977: 21). In the
République française, Denayrouze was moved by Hennique's play, which he urged
Porel, director of the Odéon theatre, to produce, taunting him with the comment
that: 'since the play has the taint of Zola on it, we might as well ask the director of

the second Théâtre-Français to put dynamite under his official chair' (20). He concludes his review: '[...] if the naturalist theatre produces many plays like this one, it can rest easy about its future' (21). In the event Porel, who had previously declined Hennique's play, now accepted it with the result that the Théâtre Libre had, in its first programme, succeeded in facilitating the transfer of a new piece of drama to one of the main Parisian theatres, and one 'tainted' with the name of Zola.

It is worth considering *Jacques Damour* in a little more detail because this early performance provides us with an indication of the innovations in staging and acting that Antoine would develop further in his work at the Théâtre Libre. Jean Chothia (1991) draws attention to a number of important Naturalist qualities that were already evident in this production. Compared to the extravagant settings audiences were used to, the simplicity and authenticity of Antoine's staging and costume contributed to an overall effect of environment rather than simply providing a backdrop to the action. It is entirely possible that the intimacy of the stage on which Lemaître comments, 'scenic illusion is impossible', actually contributed to this. For the audience, this produced a sense that 'real, lived lives' were being played out in front of them providing a more 'experiential' engagement with the performance. The 'naturalness' of the actors which Lemaître noted, drew the attention of a number of other commentators who found much to praise in relation to Antoine's skills of 'gesture', 'expression' and notably his use of 'silences' in representing the character of Jacques Damour. Chothia cites the actor Charles Mosnier who had seen a touring production of the play and it is worth repeating this for the impression it conveys of Antoine's skills:

> The vision of Antoine on the threshold nailed me to my seat, I will always remember the life-likeness of his slow arrival. I recall that his silences were held a long time and as to his expression [...] when he began to speak between his teeth, what truth and what beauty. (1991: 9)

We see from Denayrouze's review, mentioned earlier, that he immediately establishes the Théâtre Libre as a 'naturalist' theatre but what is clear from Antoine's recollections, and indeed borne out in his programming, was an awareness that to focus solely on the work of the Naturalists might conceivably signal the failure of his venture. He remained convinced that Théâtre Libre should: 'remain quite ready to welcome everyone' (Antoine, 1977: 109). The success of this first experiment clarified in Antoine's mind the necessity to continue the pattern of programming he had just established. All future programmes would include new work from a well-known figure whose contribution, alongside that of the newly emerging dramatist, would attract the initial 'curiosity and attention of the press', on which he would depend for the duration of the Théâtre Libre. An awareness that he would need to offer a range of interesting material led him to fall out with

Byl and Vidal, two of the original contributors, whose work he would not include a second time. Antoine recalls that this led to 'hostility', and for a short while, a parting of company during which time they attempted to set up their own rival theatre. Rather tellingly Antoine writes 'I gave them to understand that I intend to remain the master of my venture' (23).

The most pressing of Antoine's concerns was how to finance a second programme. The first had been realized at a personal cost of some 400 francs and he needed to find ways to generate an income in order for the Théâtre Libre to continue. In this respect, one of the group, Émile Paz, was able to assist by suggesting a form of subscription which, combined with Antoine's salary, would provide the budget for a second programme.

Only two months later on 30 May 1887, the Théâtre Libre presented the second programme comprising a play by the unknown Oscar Méténier and one contributed by the well-known writer and journalist Émile Bergerat:

> 1st A realistic play in one act and in prose, entitled *In the Family*,
> 2nd A tragi-comedy (in the old style), three acts in verse, entitled *The Berga-masque Night*.
> (Antoine, 1977: 27)

On this occasion, the press turned out in full force and the reviews were once again favourable, although predictably Oscar Méténier's *In The Family*, the naturalistic drama, generated some of the more disparaging comments. Sarcey, the 'leading critic' and defender of the more conventional theatre tradition, had missed the first programme but kept his promise to Antoine to attend the next. In his subsequent review, he noted in the actors' 'extraordinary perfection in details' (28), although, unsurprisingly, he was less enthused by Méténier's play. It is significant that Sarcey's attention should be drawn to the quality of acting and it is worth reminding ourselves that the actors to whom he is referring were mainly amateurs, who had full-time jobs ranging from cane sellers to book-keepers and were thus confined to rehearsing during the evenings at the end of their working day. From the outset, Antoine had been clear that he intended to avoid the 'effects' that trained actors employed in their performances. Throughout his memoirs, he regularly refers to performances he has witnessed on the main stages of Paris, complaining of the tendency for actors to perform to the audience, the actors' stage voices and exchanges of dialogue between characters who do not look at each other.

Drawing on three photographs of a scene from *En Famille* (which incidentally are the first extant photographs of a play in performance), and Antoine's prompt book for *The Bergamasque Night*, Jean Chothia notes a number of interesting innovations in relation to both acting and staging in these two contrasting performances. The sequence of photographs illustrate a group of five characters sitting around a table laid with glasses and bottles and whilst these images convey

Antoine's early attempts at a 'realist set' representing the cramped and cluttered second-hand shop, more revealing is the impression of: 'actors being absorbed in his or her part by responding with eyes and bearing to the speaker [...]' (1991: 11). It is a testament to Antoine's skills in training his ensemble that a number of the actors reappeared after the interval in Bergerat's play, which as noted earlier was a 'tragi-comedy of the old kind' and written in verse. Antoine's prompt book reveals scrupulous attention being paid to the staging of *The Bergamasque Night*. The play demanded an altogether different interpretation and Antoine, acutely aware of the 'tone' of the play, noted his own detailed stage directions on separate sheets of paper, occasionally crossing out Bergerat's original directions. Interestingly, Antoine is more experimental in his staging of this play, and in placing the boudoir scene at an angle to facilitate the practical demands of the play, he introduces the 'angled set' which anticipates Strindberg's setting in *Miss Julie* (Chothia, 1991).

The success of the two 'experimental' programmes convinced Antoine that the Théâtre Libre: 'must become a solid and permanent organisation' (1977: 29). The summer of 1887 saw Antoine putting together plans for the first season and resolutely committed to the pattern of 'coupling the work of an established author with that of a beginner'(33), he set about finding these authors. Buoyed by the interest now being shown in the Théâtre Libre, Antoine felt a great deal more confident to approach well-known literary figures with a view to persuading them to contribute work to future programmes. Meanwhile, presumably with a degree of calculation, he wrote to Sarcey asking him to forward him any plays he thought suitable for the Théâtre Libre. In a gesture that was to be repeated on a number of occasions in the future, Sarcey included the letter in his column at the *Temps*, thereby ensuring Antoine a wide public appeal. The letter had the desired effect with the result that Sarcey was swamped with enquiries.

The summer also saw a number of significant changes in the organization. In July, Antoine took the decision to resign from his job at the Gas Company to commit more fully to the running of the Théâtre Libre. Two colleagues took on more formal roles, Baston from the Cercle Gaulois became the stage manager with Rudolphe Darzens as the fencing master and archivist. By August, Antoine had acquired a large studio which became the registered offices and rehearsal space, replacing the billiard room in which they had previously worked.

In October, however, Antoine faced a serious setback when the Cercle Gaulois withdrew use of the little theatre on which he had obviously been relying for the forthcoming season. Astonishingly, within a matter of some four days, Antoine had managed to secure a new venue, a theatre located in the suburbs of the left bank in Montparnasse. The disadvantages of location, which some of the group felt would deter audiences, were outweighed by the facilities Antoine would now have at his disposal, including access to scenery stored in the warehouse, 'In vain I described the theatre – a real one, with stage, settings and lighting' (1977: 46).

The programme for the 1887/88 season was, of course, a great deal fuller, but once again carefully compiled to include a range of new writing. The season included work from the Parnassian poets, adaptations of novels from the Goncourt Brothers and Zola, the first play by Jean Jullien (who would in 1890 produce his own theories on Naturalism, coining the term 'a slice of life'), and significantly the first of the foreign plays to be produced at the Théâtre Libre, Tolstoy's *The Power of Darkness* written in 1866. The play, which had been banned in Russia, proved to be a 'large undertaking'. Antoine recalls that the view held among contemporary dramatists (Dumas fils, Sardou and Augier) was that it would prove impossible to stage. Carlson, in his notes to Antoine's entry of 6 February 1888, draws attention to the fact that the response here was not in antic-ipation of a failed production, but rather a response to the published translation by Halpérine, which Antoine similarly regarded as problematic. Indeed, as Chothia (1991) points out, so concerned was Antoine about the literal quality of dialogue which tended to be 'stiff' and 'academic', and lacking the 'French equiv-alents for Tolstoy's idiomatic phrases' that he commissioned a new translation and adaptation which proved to be 'a much rougher and more colloquial text' (1991: 41). This demonstrates Antoine's acute awareness of what Chothia refers to as the 'integral text' and the importance of the director's role in achieving this.

The production which took place on 12 February 1888 proved to be one of the high points of the season. In preparation, Antoine and his carefully chosen ensemble of amateur actors visited 'refugees living on the left bank' from whom he acquired authentic costumes and 'real Russian objects for properties' (Antoine, 1977: 60) Interestingly, we find here methods that Stanislavksy would later employ in his work as a director. Antoine was able to make good use of the theatre's stock of staging materials for the settings with the result that the production was, in Antoine's words, 'a triumph' and the play 'universally hailed as a masterpiece' (61). Reviewing the presentation Melchior de Vogue commented on the total absorp-tion of the audience for the four-hour duration of the performance: 'For the first time a setting and costumes truly borrowed from the daily customs of Russian life appeared on the French stage without comic opera embellishments and without that predilection for tinsel and falsity which seems inherent in our theatrical atmosphere' (64). Once again, it was not simply the authenticity of staging which marked the production as a 'triumph' but the quality of ensemble acting within the 'Russian peasant' environment Antoine had created. Critics not only judged Antoine's interpretation of the role of Akim to be convincing in its detail but also those of the other actors. The cast, as Chothia (1991) notes, worked hard in rehearsals to understand the 'psychological developments' of their char-acters and the environmental pressures on their lives. So successful was the production that Antoine was persuaded to give a second, and on this occasion, public performance a week later. The ticket sales went extremely well but a heavy snowfall on the morning of the performance caused Antoine a great deal of anxiety, convinced as he was that the audience would be put off from attending by the remoteness of the theatre and the weather. To his enormous surprise the theatre was 'filled to overflowing'. The other significant success of the season was Théodore de Banville's play *The Kiss*, which was subsequently accepted by the Comédie-Française.

It was on a business trip to Brussels in July of the same year that Antoine witnessed several performances of the Saxe-Meiningen Company whose staging innovations were, unsurprisingly, the subject of a number of articles in the press. Antoine, having seen for himself the measure of these innovations, wrote a lengthy letter to Sarcey admonishing him for not having attended the productions and, further, for his audaciousness in relying on the observations made in Jules Claretie's essay for his own commentary. In his record of 23 July, Antoine reproduces the letter which had been published in the *Temps* and which provides for the reader a valuable account of his impression of the work of the Meiningen. As we will see, Antoine had already been experimenting with a number of these innovations, but in other respects what he witnessed would have an important influence on his own practice as director and actor.

Antoine makes a number of important points about the realism of the crowd scenes with which the troupe have tended to be primarily associated. Writing with a degree of authority in this respect, he reminds Sarcey of his first-hand experience working as an extra at the Comédie Française:

> Do you know what the difference is?
>
> Their crowds are not, like ours, made up of elements put together at random – or people hired during the dress rehearsals, badly dressed and quite untrained, to wear bizarre or constricting costumes, especially when these demand precision. Our theatres almost always demand that the extras stand stock still, while those of the Meininger must act and portray their characters. Do not assume therefore that they attract attention and divert the emphasis from the principals. No, the scene is an organic whole, and wherever one looks, he is struck by a detail in situation or character. This lends an incomparable power to certain moments.
>
> The Meininger troupe contains about seventy artists of both sexes. Everyone who does not have a part is kept as an extra and so appears every evening. If twenty actors are needed, the fifty others – without exception, the stars included – appear on stage in the crowd scenes. (82)

In comparison, the French theatre used the services of enthusiastic individuals 'who scarcely know what they are doing or why they are there' (82). The idea that a leading actor in France might play a key role in one play and join the ranks of the extras in another seemed entirely unimaginable to Antoine at the time. Of the other innovations, Antoine goes on to describe a scene from *William Tell* in which the actors playing the parts of a beggar and his two children had their backs to the audience:

> I am sure this scene would have convinced you that a properly shown back is most effective in giving the audience the impression that the actors are not aware of their presence and that the action is really taking place.   (83)

Antoine notes a number of other features which contributed to the overall realism of the performances, the auditorium remained in darkness, important scenes were played upstage with the extras turning their backs to watch the actors performing, actors were forbidden to move beyond the frame and look into the auditorium. He was particularly impressed by the fact that none of the actors move towards the prompter.

Antoine was not uncritical of the performances commenting on the 'oddly designed settings' and the 'shocking taste' evident in the choice of costume. In terms of the technical elements, he berates the troupe for their lack of attention to the detail shown in other respects. Of the various examples, he notes: 'The lighting effects, although often striking, are handled with epic naïveté' (1977: 84). He was particularly irritated by the poor handling of effects: 'after an extraordinary torrential rain, achieved by electric projections, I was annoyed to see the water stop abruptly without any transition' (84). Interestingly, Antoine was not overly impressed by the actors, who he viewed as 'adequate and nothing more' (84). One of his main criticisms is levelled at the 'false and heavy-handed' (83) way in which the lines written for the crowd were handled in *William Tell*. Rather than everyone crying out at the same time, as had occurred, Antoine offers a very detailed description of how he would approach the scene, breaking up the groups and dividing the lines between the extras, arguably demonstrating his rather more perceptive skills of interpretation. What comes across in these criticisms is an acute awareness of the possibilities that exist for a more fluid and realistic performance. He writes to Sarcey, 'Of course, you are aware of the stimulating innovations in all this. Why don't we try to appropriate what is good among them?' (86).

Throughout Antoine's recollections of the 1888/89 season, we get the impression of him doing exactly what he advocated in his letter to Sarcey, both appropriating what he felt was innovative about the Meiningen approach but also developing on the staging possibilities he felt were neglected in their performances. Having had to relocate once again, the Théâtre Libre was now producing its monthly performances at the Menus-Plaisirs, a theatre in the Boulevard de Strasbourg. Whilst the location was much more central, Antoine lost access to the staging materials he had previously been able to draw on in Montparnasse and he now found himself incurring additional expenses as he invested more into the staging of the Théâtre Libre productions.

For the opening of the 1888/89 season the Théâtre Libre presented *The Butchers*, a play written by Fernand Icres and for which Antoine recalls he wanted 'a realistic setting and hung up actual quarters of meat, which created a sensation' (1977: 80). It is worth noting Claude Schumacher's point that the play: 'is written in impassioned verse and that Antoine, far from re-creating the neat and clinical aspect of a village butcher's shop, had strewn the stage with offal: offal everywhere, even on the ground. There is a term to describe such heightened theatrical imagery, and that term is "expressionism"' (1996: 5). On 12 December 1888, Antoine produced Hennique's 'historical' play, *The Death of the Duke of Enghein*, and here we note special attention given to the lighting: 'The council of war in the third act, illuminated only by the lanterns placed on the table, created an effect so new and unexpected that everyone is talking about it' (Antoine, 1977: 94). Antoine notes that the production marked a renaissance for the historical play, largely due to the realism: 'Not only was there a definite attempt to reconstruct the feeling of an age, but the setting contributed greatly to the success of this attempt' (94). It is also worth mentioning that Antoine managed to rent authentic costumes for the performance which, of course, contributed to the realism of the piece not simply because they accurately reflected the historical period, but more importantly because, as Chothia notes, 'he used the tired, faded quality of the actual clothes to demonstrate the straitened circumstances as well as the historical period of his aristocrats in exile' (1991: 66).

The play was extremely well received and news of the production spread to England, with the result that the Théâtre Libre was invited to London in early February 1889 to give a 'series of performances' at the Royalty Theatre in London. Whilst there, Antoine had the opportunity to attend a number of performances including that of *Macbeth* at the Lyceum Theatre in which Henry Irving was performing. Of the production, Antoine recalls he was not particularly 'dazzled' by the great actor's performance, but rather he was far more impressed by the stage technology in relation to both setting and lighting which he felt surpassed that of the French theatre. What particularly impressed Antoine was that: 'in Irving's production a shaft of moonlight or sun would always appear on the face of the leading character, one hardly knew how or why, but it was fine all the same' (Antoine quoted in Chothia, 1991: 70).

Writing in May and again in July 1889, Antoine notes that the season had been a difficult one. The theatre was in debt and, overall, he felt that, with the exception of some notable contributions, the content had been unequal to that of the preceding season. He writes: 'I am beginning to realize that the Théâtre Libre must follow new currents; I only wonder if the results will be sufficient to assure a sustained and fruitful campaign (Antoine, 1977: 113)

The following season saw the emergence of a new playwright Eugène Brieux (1858–1932) in whom Antoine placed a great deal of confidence, not least because his work as a journalist and editor-in-chief of the *Nouvelliste* in Rouen provided him with a grounded sense of reality and public life. Brieux, who had made a number of attempts to have his work performed in Paris, saw his first play *Artists' Households* presented by the Théâtre Libre in March 1890 and, although it met with rather a poor reception from the critics, Antoine went on to produce his second play *Blanchette* on 2 February 1892 which, in contrast, was an outstanding triumph. Shortly afterwards, the play was given public performances in Rouen and Le Havre. In his memoirs Antoine often refers to the presence of the dramatist at rehearsals, a practice established as early as *Jacques Damour* when Zola attended the rehearsal, and indeed Antoine recalls that Brieux made a number of trips from Rouen to attend rehearsals of his first play. The significance of this, as Chothia notes, is that dramatists were not only offered the opportunity to witness Antoine's interpretation of their work, it simultaneously offered the opportunity to develop their own practice. In this respect, Antoine fostered: 'a sense of mutual learning and development' (Chothia, 1991: 80). Although Antoine and Brieux subsequently fell out over *Blanchette*, Brieux proved to be one of Antoine's 'most important discoveries' and the play went on to be produced at two leading French theatres a few years later.

For Antoine it was a victory to see Théâtre Libre productions accepted by the boulevard theatres. By 1890 a substantial number of plays which had originated at the Théâtre Libre had been taken up by the main theatres and performed for the theatre-going public. Unhappily for Antoine, the quality of these productions was often underwhelming compared to the original productions. He noted as early as September 1887, following his attendance at the Odéon to see the dress rehearsal of *Jacques Damour*: 'Realism can only assert itself if from now on we follow a different interpretation from the current practice in the theatre – one of simplicity, naturalness, and restrained emotion' (Antoine, 1977: 42) He was disappointed to find that the play which had been the outstanding success in the Théâtre Libre's first programme 'did not recapture the great emotion which it aroused at our theatre'(42). This was similarly the case when Antoine attended the premiere of Banville's play *The Kiss* at the Comédie Française, where he felt the actors were less 'spirited and spontaneous' and had a tendency to overplay their roles. In 1890 a number of damning reviews of Henri Beque's play *The Woman of Paris* at the Théâtre Française, which had also originated at the Théâtre Libre, prompted a public response from Antoine. Linking the failure of this production to two others, *The Master* by Jean Jullien at the Nouveautés (again, a Théâtre Libre play) and Ancey's play *The Grandmother* at the Odéon, Antoine felt it was no coincidence that the plays, 'conceived in the spirit of renewal which activates the new school' (149), should fail on the main stage. In the knowledge that his statement would be published, Antoine articulated his ideas on interpretation more clearly and more forcefully in a letter written to Sarcey. The letter was primarily directed to the theatre profession and, importantly, to 'far-sighted actors concerned about their art and about the present-day theatre movement' (150).

It is worth considering in detail a number of comments he has to make in relation to the 'inadequate interpretation' of acting and staging. The lengthy letter set out Antoine's analysis of the causes behind these 'repeated failures' and provides us with a document which, in many respects, develops on the objectives Zola set out in his manifesto of 1881 and, interestingly, pre-empts a number of the ideas Stanislavsky would later articulate:

> Well! The simple reason for this triple coincidence – of actors who are ordinarily excellent being judged mediocre for one evening, and for this evening alone – is that not one of these three works was set or acted in its true sense. What the new (or renewed) theatre demands is new (or renewed) interpreters. One cannot play works based on observation (or pretended observation, if you prefer) as one would play the traditional repertoire, or comedies based on the imagination. One must get under the skin of these modern characters, and leave the old baggage behind. A work which is *true* must be played *truly*, just as a classic play should above all be *recited*, since the character more often than not is only an abstraction or a synthesis, without material life. The characters in *The Woman of Paris* or in *Grandmother* are people like us who do not live in vast rooms with the dimensions of cathedrals, but in interiors like our own – beside the fire, under the lamp, around a table, but never (as in the old repertoire) before the prompter's box. They have voices like ours; their language is that of our own daily life, with its elisions and its familiar turns, and not the rhetoric and noble style of our classics.   (Antoine, 1977: 150).

The actors, Antoine felt, had simply resorted to their 'stage voices', misrepresenting the quality of Becque's dialogue and thereby the characters they were playing. He goes on to say:

> The characteristic of the new theatre is always that the characters are unconscious of themselves, is it not? Like any of us, they make foolish and ridiculous mistakes without being aware of them. When most of our actors come on stage, they bring their own personalities instead of those of the figures they are to bring to life; they do not enter their character, their character enters them.   (151)

Antoine is particularly critical of the approach to setting which comes only as a secondary consideration:

> In modern works, created amid a movement of truth and realism in which the theory of the environment and the influence of exterior things play so large a part, isn't the setting an indispensable complement of the action?

> Shouldn't the setting be as important in the theatre as description is in the novel. Isn't it one kind of exposition of the play? Of course it can never be made completely real, because it is in the theatre [...]. (151)

The actors' movements on stage were equally misunderstood: 'they were not determined by the text or the sense of the scene, but according to the desire or the whim of the actors, each of whom played for himself, with no concern for the others' (152).

A little later in the letter he draws on his own experience of a recent rehearsal, making the point that the actors had found it difficult to carry out normal everyday activities without looking at the audience or affecting a theatrical walk, concluding that, like the highly skilled actors in Becque's play: 'they have lost the simple touch, and the ability to act naturally, *as if no one were watching*' (Antoine, 1977: 154). Their traditional training now inhibits them in their interpretation of the new drama and the possibility of truthful acting. What was an excellent training for a bygone era now becomes detrimental to the new drama being produced and Antoine urges the readers whom he is addressing to turn their attention to this problem: 'You will be struck by the discord between the works incorporating the new tendencies and the interpreters they encounter. It is an important problem, and a curious aspect of the current theatre movement' (154).

When in July 1889 Antoine wrote of seeking 'new currents' to sustain the life of the Théâtre Libre, he may well have had in mind presenting Ibsen's *Ghosts*. Although it is rather unclear exactly when Antoine was first acquainted with the work of Ibsen (Carlson points out in his notes that two articles on Ibsen written by Jacques Saint-Cère had appeared as early as the spring of 1887 and one assumes Antoine would probably have read them), he was certainly aware of *Ghosts* during the summer of 1888 when he saw the Meiningen company in Brussels. In his letter to Sarcey on the subject of their performances, he mentions:

> At Meiningen they even gave Henrik Ibsen's *Ghosts*, which I have in translation. It was the Duke's idea to give the play in private before the author and invited critics from the German press – much in the manner of the Théâtre Libre. The play could not be given publicly, for it is quite subversive, and I am sure that in October you too will be rather astonished by it. (Antoine, 1977: 83)

It would seem from this that Antoine's intention was to produce it later that year. However, it is not until his recollections for 1890 that we find further mention of Ibsen when he recalls Zola drawing attention to the play in January. By early February it seems it is Zola who is urging Antoine to produce it at the Théâtre Libre, offering to arrange for the translation. In spite of these inconsistencies it is clear that the translation, when it did arrive, was not without problems, and Antoine notes:

I have read *Ghosts*. It is like nothing in our theatre; a study of heredity, the third act of which has the somber grandeur of a Greek tragedy. But it seems too long to me – which may be due to the translation into French from a German text, itself an adaptation from Norwegian. Apparently this is what slows down and obscures the dialogue, but even so, we should not hesitate.

(123)

Antoine was not alone in his reservations about the length of the play, other members of the group felt it was impossible to stage, needed cutting or required a prologue to contextualize the content. Although now aware of the furore surrounding Grein's recent performance of *Ghosts* in London, he remained committed to producing the play at the Théâtre Libre. Still concerned about the translation, Antoine sought to find someone who could translate it directly from Norwegian to French. Rodolphe Darzens, the archivist and fencing master at the Théâtre Libre, undertook to arrange this and when the new manuscript was finally produced in April it was, as Antoine had instinctively felt it would be, greatly different to the translation in his possession. As he had done with Tolstoy's *The Power of Darkness,* Antoine submitted the play to the dramatist for his blessing and received the following reply from Ibsen:

Since the founding of the Théâtre Libre, I have followed the activity of this interesting enterprise with the closest attention, and I was very pleased to learn, two years ago, that you were planning to present my play *Ghosts* in the theatre which you direct.

The translation which M. Darzens made and sent to me seems most suitable and conforms closely to the original. Despite my obligations to M. de Prozor, therefore, I see no objections to giving my consent – which you have so graciously requested – to the presentation of M. Darzen's translation at the Théâtre Libre.

I await the fruits of your labours with great interest. In thanking you for the warm welcome you have given my work, I remain, etc.

(Antoine, 1977: 133)

Although Antoine in his recollections admits to some cuts, according to Jean Chothia the text that Antoine eventually used for the performance was more like an adaptation of the play. It is not entirely clear why, but he chose to cut a number of speeches, some quite considerably, particularly those of Pastor Manders and Mrs Alving (Chothia, 1991: 50). The first of Ibsen's plays to be presented in France took place on 30 May 1890 with Antoine taking the role of Oswald, which he recalled was 'one of the best roles an actor could play'. Of the performance he recalls:

We gave *Ghosts* last evening. I think its effect was profound in some quarters but the majority of the audience went from wonder to boredom, although a real agony gripped the room in the closing scenes. I can say no more of it except by hearsay, for I myself underwent an experience totally new to me – an almost complete loss of my own personality. After the second act I remember nothing, neither the audience nor the effect of the production, and, shaking and weakened, I was some time getting hold of myself again after the final curtain had fallen.   (1977: 138)

What we note here is the audience's reception to the play and Antoine's absorption in his role. As Antoine acknowledged, Ibsen introduced 'a new kind of drama' to the French stage both in terms of the content and the demands on the actors representing the characters. In spite of the mixed reviews, Antoine went on to present *The Wild Duck* in April 1891. Keen to continue to present the work of foreign dramatists which 'could stimulate the interest and curiosity of the literary youth' (204), he turned to another Scandinavian playwright, August Strindberg. On 15 January 1893 the Théâtre Libre presented Strindberg's *Miss Julie*; the performance, Antoine recalls: 'made an enormous sensation. Everything stimulated the audience, the subject, the setting and the packing into a single act an hour and a half in length enough action to sustain a full-length French play. Of course, there were sneers and protests, but it was, after all, something quite new' (216). Interestingly, Antoine arranged to translate and distribute Strindberg's Preface to the audience, although as we have seen in an earlier chapter many of the techniques and ideas advocated had already been put into practice by Antoine. In May of the same year, we find Antoine in rehearsals for Hauptmann's *The Weavers*. As we might imagine, the production, which involved five settings and a large number of actors, proved to be a huge undertaking and an extremely expensive one. Indeed, the costly production, which Carlson notes took place on 29 and 30 May, relied on a substantial advance subscription from a friend . It was an enormous success: 'the aroused house cheered it from beginning to end. It is a masterpiece of the developing social theatre' (219). For Antoine, the interpretation by the actors was 'outstanding', the second act in Baumert's home 'enormously effective' and the: 'over-running of the manufacturer's home in the fourth act generated such terror that the entire orchestra rose to their feet' (219).

It is clear that by now Antoine was beginning to tire: 'To get this far, I have utilized every talent and ability possessed by myself as well as my friends – authors and actors alike – but the one thing we cannot create is money' (219). Other factors contributed to the weariness he must have felt, for some time the troupe had been progressively breaking up, several of the leading actors had been engaged by the main Parisian theatres, and artistically he had begun to feel that the Théâtre Libre had started to reach the end of its experiment. The work of the foreign dramatists had fulfilled their usefulness and the 'native authors' were now able to produce work elsewhere. Had it not been for the fact he had drawn on the following season's subscriptions, one forms the impression that he would have closed down the Théâtre Libre immediately. In fact it was to continue under his directorship for a further year, during which time he travelled to Berlin to see Hauptmann's play *Hannele*, taking advantage of the opportunity to see a number of other performances whilst he was there. Antoine was particularly struck by the interpretation of Hauptman's play and that directors from other theatres attended the performance with a view to staging the play in their own theatres in other German cities.

On his return Antoine produced *A Bankruptcy*, the work of another Norwegian, Bjørnson Bjørnstern, and in early 1894 presented Hauptmann's *Hannele* which, once again, proved to be a costly production. By April 1894 the debts were increasing, and Antoine felt 'strangled' by the lack of money available to him. He had achieved his objective to provide an outlet for new playwrights, many of whom were now well established. His ensemble of actors had progressively departed to work and, indeed, 'triumph' on the main stages of Paris. Finally, in the summer of 1894, Antoine passed control of the Théâtre Libre into the hands of a theatre devotee and son of a former actor and director.

Théâtre Antoine

Of course Antoine's career did not stop here, he went on in 1897 to open the Théâtre Antoine in Paris. In what he regards as the second phase of his development he 'won over the general public'. It had long been his hope that one day he might have an 'open' theatre where he would have the opportunity of producing plays for the public on a regular basis. In contrast to the policy of long runs which the other theatres adopted, Antoine aimed to produce at least 50 plays each season. The first programme opened with Brieux's play *Blanchette* and a number of other plays which had earlier been presented at the Théâtre Libre (Chothia, 1991). Having made amends with Brieux following their earlier falling out, Antoine went on to present his new full-length plays. Less well known today outside France, Brieux was in fact the dramatist best known as a Naturalist playwright. His plays *Les Trois Filles de M. Dupont* (The Three Daughters of Monsieur Dupont) (1887), *Les Avariés* (Damaged Goods) (1901), *Maternity* (1903), and *La Femme Seule* (Woman on Her Own) (1913) explore the prevailing milieu and, as Furst and Skrine note, by choosing a specific subject to focus on in each of the plays Brieux provides 'a dramatic survey of contemporary society' (1971: 62). The two plays most often referred to are *Damaged Goods* and *Maternity*, largely because the subjects Brieux had chosen to explore produced such an outcry: venereal disease in the first and birth control in the second. These plays are of particular interest in terms of Naturalism in that they are 'ruthlessly objective', possibly as a result of Brieux's experience as a journalist, presenting as they do case studies which draw on factual evidence in the content. In many respects Brieux's approach fulfils Zola's aim for a 'scientific methodology'. Furst and Skrine perceptively note the similarity between these plays and the 'probing social documentaries' we are used to seeing on television.

CHAPTER SUMMARY

- The establishment by André Antoine of the Théâtre Libre, Paris, in 1887 was a key moment in the development of Naturalism.
- Antoine was part of the unique artistic and literary environment of Paris but was initially an amateur in regard to the theatre.
- Antoine's early experience with an amateur theatre group gave him the opportunity to refresh and revitalize the repertoire without financial constraints.
- He embarked on a search for new plays.
- The Théâtre Libre was a small, intimate space and critics immediately remarked on the 'naturalness' of the acting.
- Adaptations of Zola's novels and Tolstoy's *The Power of Darkness* were early successes in an expanding enterprise that involved Antoine in full-time work.
- Antoine saw the work of the Meiningen company and was generally impressed with some reservations about the dialogue and settings.
- He greatly admired Irving's use of stage technology and revolutionized the settings and acting styles of his company to create a much more 'natural' effect.

SEMINAR AND WORKSHOP TOPICS

1 Antoine's Théâtre Libre was, perhaps, the first small theatre established by amateurs for the performance of new or experimental plays. What other examples can you give?
2 What aspects of contemporary performance did Antoine find unsatisfactory and how did he attempt to remedy them?
3 Antoine is often credited with creating the concept of the 'fourth wall'. What is this and how did he employ it?
4 Which plays mentioned elsewhere in this book were produced at the Théâtre Libre? What is the significance of this?
5 How important is it to use 'real' props in a play?
6 Take a scene from *Thérèse Raquin* and rehearse it as if you were Antoine.
7 Design a stage setting for *Ghosts* or *The Weavers* that would satisfy Antoine's principles.

FURTHER READING

Antoine, A. (1964/77) *Memories of the Théâtre Libre*, trans. M. Carlson, Miami: University of Miami Press. This supplies a vivid impression of Antoine's passion, frustrations and ambitions.

Chothia, J. (1991) *André Antoine*, Cambridge: Cambridge University Press. An invaluable text which provides a very detailed and sympathetic view of Antoine's career.

Cole, T. and Chinoy, H. (1953/70) *Directors on Directing*, New York: Crown. The section on Antoine and particularly his article 'Beyond the Fourth Wall' remains the most useful introduction to Antoine's work.

CHAPTER 7

Otto Brahm and the Freie Bühne

Anna Miller in *The Independent Theatre in Europe* (1931) draws on the sentiments of the novelist, Michael Georg Conrad (1846–1927), to illustrate the view of a number of young German writers and intellectuals in the final decades of the nineteenth century: 'Since the seventies', mourned Conrad, 'we have not had a single name in the story, the novel, the epic, or the drama reach the consideration of Europe. It is as if the German triumph of literature stopped at the new German boundary [...].' (1931: 98).

The 'boundary' Conrad is referring to is the one marked by two events, the end of the Franco-Prussian War in which France was defeated and the subsequent unification of the German states, finally achieved by Otto von Bismarck in 1871. Wilhelm I of Prussia was crowned Emperor and Bismarck became Chancellor of the new German Empire or Second Reich as it became known. Understandably, unification had a significant impact on the political, economic and social structures of the 'new' Germany. Under the new government headed by Bismarck, the country entered into a period of 'relative political stability' and, in spite of the stock-market crash of 1873 and subsequent depression, economic prosperity. Industrialization, which had taken a foothold earlier in the century, expanded rapidly, turning the country into one of the leading manufacturing nations.

The 'boundary' that very quickly established Germany as a major European power provides a useful starting point for our discussion of German Naturalism. What, then, was the state of German theatre in the decade following unification? A theatre which had in the eighteenth century produced such celebrated playwrights and 'pioneers' of theatre reform as Lessing (1729–1781), Schiller (1759–1805) and Goethe (1749–1832) and the 'Sturm und Drang' (Storm and Stress) drama of the 1770s. A theatre that produced the Meiningen Company and the first 'modern' stage director only some years earlier.

Certainly the view of Conrad and his fellow writers was of a theatre driven by the demands of the box office, and catering to an audience who largely sought pleasure and entertainment. Miller (1931) suggests that with the exception of the Austrian playwright Ludwig Anzengruber (1839–1889), whose most notable play *Das Vierte Gebot* (1877) draws on the life of the lower classes in the urban environment of Vienna, there were no 'native' dramatists of any particular note in the decade following unification. It seems that in common with other European countries, the theatre repertoire of the latter decades of the nineteenth century was largely dominated by adaptations and translations of the French 'well-made play' and the work of a group of German playwrights who relied on that model as the basis for their own 'native' drama. The most notable of these German playwrights was Paul Lindau (1839–1919) who would later go on to become director of the Meiningen Court Theatre. John Osborne in *Gerhart Hauptman and The Naturalist Drama* (1998) notes that, whilst there is a moderate degree of 'social realism' evident in the work of these playwrights and an attempt to explore the effect of 'social conditions' on the individual, this exploration is limited to bourgeois concerns and problems. There was a decided reluctance on the part of these 'bourgeois dramatists' to expand their subject matter to less attractive concerns, namely working-class social problems. By way of example, Osborne notes Paul Lindau's response as a critic to the working-class drama *Vater Brahm*, by Heinrich Shaufert. Lindau's view is that working-class social problems, however grave, were 'not the concern of the dramatist' (1998: 8). For Lindau these problems were best left to experts to solve and, furthermore, plays of this nature had the potential to incite 'discontent'.

The development of Naturalist drama

We should note here that the tendency toward 'social realism' was not something new in German drama. As Miller (1931) notes, there is evidence of an emerging 'dramatic realism' in the work of the eighteenth-century playwrights mentioned earlier and it is worth exploring this briefly. Lessing holds a particular place in the history of German theatre for establishing a 'national German drama'. In his efforts to break away from the 'neo-classic constraints' of the French models of drama and acting introduced earlier in the century he was innovatory. Perhaps one of the most interesting of his experiments was undertaken in 1749 when he attempted to produce a drama which took as its subject the Swiss journalist Samuel Henzi, who had been arrested and later executed along with two of his companions on 17 July 1749. Written in verse and comprising only one and a half acts, the 'fragment' *Samuel Henzi* is, as Gertrud Mander (Hayman,1975) argues, 'a landmark' in eighteenth-century German theatre. In order to understand this landmark we need to consider that Germany in the eighteenth century comprised hundreds of principalities, each ruled by absolute monarchs and their coterie of state officials. The rising middle classes were excluded from matters of state and struggling to find their identity and place within the social structure of the time. In his choice to represent a contemporary subject and 'bourgeois hero' on the stage, Lessing is 'daring' to challenge the prevailing conventions of drama. Credited with producing the first German 'bourgeois tragedy', *Miss Sara Sampson* (1755), it is Lessing's later domestic tragedy *Emilia Galotti* (1772) that would have a decisive influence on the development of German drama. Whilst the play, as Ladislaus Löb (Hayman, 1975) tells us, relies on the prototypes of virtuous and villainous characters and extols middle-class values, it simultaneously provides a critique on the ruling classes. The characters of the court are revealed as corrupt, weak and irresponsible. Interpreted as an 'anti-absolutist' play, it was taken up as the dramatic model for the 'Storm and Stress' movement which emerged in the 1770s and took its title from a play of the same name. The drama produced by the movement was revolutionary both in its emphasis on social reality and the introduction of more 'life-like' language. Although Schiller and Goethe are generally regarded as 'classicists', both were 'young rebels' in the movement in the earlier stages of their respective writing careers and both made an important contribution to the development of dramatic realism. Of particular note is Schiller's play *Love and Intrigue* (1784) which, set in contemporary Germany, presents characters whose lives are determined by their social conditions (Löb in Hayman, 1975). What we find in the eighteenth century, then, is an increasing attempt to both represent the social reality of the emerging middle classes and to reproduce the language of this class.

Most commentators tend to agree that, with some notable exceptions, the theatre repertoire of the nineteenth century until the emergence of Naturalism was predictable. Of the notable exceptions are a number of playwrights whose work demonstrates a greater degree of 'dramatic realism' and, more significantly, the early traces of Naturalist ideas. This is partly explained by the influence of a group of 'politically active' writers in the 1830s, *Das Junge Deutschland*, 'The Young Germans'. Inspired by the French revolutions of 1789 and 1830 and the earlier Storm and Stress movement, these writers attempted a greater degree of realism and political radicalism in their work. Arguably, the most important of these early nineteenth-century writers was the dramatist Georg Büchner (1813–1837). Büchner produced only three plays in his short lifetime *Danton's Death* (1935), *Leonce and Lena* (1936) and the unfinished *Woyzeck* (1937). Interestingly, *Woyzeck* was not published until 1879 and neither *Danton's Death* nor *Woyzeck* were performed until the following century. Whilst the form of Büchner's plays lend themselves more easily to an expressionistic presentation, they anticipate a number of the Naturalist concerns and, indeed, Gerhart Hauptmann cites Büchner's work as an important influence on his own writing. Interestingly, as Nicholas Boyle notes, Büchner draws on documentary evidence to inform the content of both *Danton's Death* and *Woyzeck*. In the first, 'verbatim extracts from revolutionary speeches' and in the second 'medical reports' on a soldier executed for murder in spite of his plea 'of diminished responsibility due to insanity' (2008: 86–7). It comes as no surprise to find that Büchner studied science and, whilst Darwin's theories were yet to be published, we find in these plays an underlying determinism that would be a characteristic of Naturalist drama. Büchner represents characters more complex than had hitherto been depicted, characters at the mercy of the social conditions in which they find themselves, their lives and behaviour determined by the environmental forces and pressure of circumstances. In *Woyzeck* particularly, Büchner demonstrates a remarkable ability to experiment with language, capturing the inarticulacy of the victim soldier Woyzeck. Where Lessing had in the previous century attempted to bring the bourgeois hero to the stage, Büchner in the nineteenth century brought the 'proletarian hero' to the stage.

Of the other notable dramatists whose work would influence the future Naturalists we should include Otto Ludwig (1813–1865) and Friedrich Hebbel (1813–1863). Ludwig whose detailed realism is evident in both his novels and drama is also noted for having developed his own theory of 'Poetic Realism' which, as John Osborne (1998) tells us, marks 'midway' point between the earlier idealism exhibited in drama and the Naturalism that would be developed later in the century. Hebbel's play *Maria Magdalene* (1844) is for Ladislau Löb 'a masterpiece' in dramatic realism and a turning point in German theatre as the domestic drama of the eighteenth century gives way to a decidedly social drama. The contemporary setting, the accuracy of speech and characters who are 'convincingly shaped' by environmental factors do, indeed, anticipate Naturalist ideas and techniques. Whilst we can trace an increasing tendency towards a 'social realism' at various stages in the nineteenth century and, indeed, some very important influences on the development of German Naturalism, it would not be until 1889 that German Naturalist drama would arrive on the stage.

Seen within the context of Unification and the 'nationalistic euphoria' following the defeat of the French we can, perhaps, better understand Conrad's lament for a new and similarly triumphant German 'literature'. What we do find throughout the decade following unification is an increasing dissatisfaction with the 'stagnate' state of literature and drama. As we enter the 1880s, we find what Anna Miller refers to as 'the sparks of a new literary art' emerging. This spark is ignited by a group of writers and intellectuals who, taking their name from the earlier 'Young Germany' group established in the 1830s, significantly call themselves the 'Youngest Germans'. As the name implies these young intellectuals clearly regarded themselves as revolutionary and had similar aims to produce a literature which would reflect the tensions and conflicts inherent in the prevailing milieu. The immediate influences on these young intellectuals and the development of Naturalism came from abroad. The 'Youngest Germans' would have been aware of the new ideas and theories which had been developing elsewhere in Europe and by now had been translated into German. They would also have become acquainted with the translated work of the French and Russian novelists, and the published plays of Ibsen. We should also note that the writings and theories of Schopenhauer, Nietzsche and Marx would also have a bearing on the new ideas emerging at this time. However, the most important influence on these young intellectuals as the Naturalist movement started to develop was Emile Zola both in his translated novels and in his theoretical writing (Miller, 1931).

As most commentators agree, the development of Naturalism in Germany is an extremely complex one and in the first instance we should note that there were two centres of activity – Munich and Berlin. In Munich, Michael Georg Conrad became the 'figurehead' for the group, which included Karl Bleibtreu and Herman Conradi, whilst in Berlin the group included among others, Heinrich and Julius Hart, Otto Brahm, Gerhart Hauptmann and Arno Holtz. As John Osborne notes, the eighties was a 'confused' decade in which 'no single figure or group succeeded in securing a dominant position' (1998: 3). We can broadly divide the concerns of the two groups. In Munich, Conrad, a particularly keen advocate of Zola's theory and writing, concentrated on the development of Naturalist literature, whereas the Berlin group tended to be more associated with the development of Naturalist drama. We can further divide the emergence of Naturalism into two phases, in the first we find an 'outpouring' of theory, dramatic criticism and novels, and in the second phase a decisive focus on drama. The activities of both groups throughout the 1880s and early 1890s were largely centred around theorizing, and during this period a prodigious amount of theoretical writing was produced in the form of manifestos and critical essays. A plethora of new journals emerged to provide an outlet for these new ideas and theories and although many were shortlived, the most important include the Hart brothers' *Kritische Waffengänge* and Conrad's *Die Gesellschaft*, which for a number of years became the main Naturalist journal. Various societies and groups were formed, the most notable of which was the Durch circle established by Leo Berg and Julius Türk. We should note, however, that the contributors to this outpouring of theory were by no means united in their ideas on Naturalism or, indeed, their criticism of the prevailing conventions. Whilst Zola's influence was without doubt the most important, the response to his theories was as varied as the individuals who made up the group of young intellectuals and writers (Furst and Skrine, 1971).

Of these individuals there are a number of important figures who made a significant contribution to the development of Naturalist drama. The Hart brothers, Julius and Heinrich, are two of the earliest Naturalists to express their views. Critical of the theatre repertoire, one of their first tasks, as Osborne notes, was to 'overthrow' contemporary playwrights whose work relied on the methods of the French dramatists, specifically the type of drama produced by Paul Lindau, and a great deal of their dramatic criticism is directed towards this. They sought to encourage writers to develop new material which more clearly focused on an authentic representation of contemporary reality, exploring the struggles and conflicts evident in all areas of society and not simply the 'bourgeois' concerns that largely provided the content for contemporary playwrights. To this end, they endeavoured to address the 'prejudices' and 'moral objections' expressed by those who criticized the Naturalists for the baseness of their material. Of the two brothers, it is Heinrich Hart who is most noted for the Naturalist theories he produced in his journal *Kritische Waffengänge* (Osborne, 1998). For Naturalists like the Hart brothers, the influence of Zola's novels and his ideas for a more accurate representation of society chimed with their own experience of the urban environment and some of the socialist ideas they had been introduced to at the various societies they frequented.

What the German Naturalists had more difficulty in coming to terms with, and where opinion was sharply divided, was Zola's emphasis on the relationship between science and literature and the ideas he expressed in *The Experimental Novel* in relation to a scientific methodology. John Osborne notes that for many Naturalists, the notion of applying a scientific methodology and developing a greater knowledge of the natural sciences was embraced. For others, Zola's theory is an impossibility and they share Heinrich Hart's view: 'In art and literature personality is dominant. A work of art is a spontaneous spiritual creation and that has nothing to do with the verification of natural phenomena, in which we can have no creative role' (Hart quoted in Osborne, 1998: 20).

Osborne goes on to draw attention to Georg Brandes's essay of 1886, in which Brandes clarifies the view of a number of the many other young intellectuals who were more influenced by Zola's creative writing than by his theories on scientific objectivity and literature. In this Brandes uses Zola's definition of art as 'un coin de la nature vu à travers un temperament' (a corner of nature seen through temperament) and interprets the word 'temperament' to be the 'personal contribution of the artist' equating it with the artist's 'taste' and 'imagination' (Brand quoted in Osborne, 1998: 22). For Georg Brandes : '[…] Naturalism too cannot avoid that re-shaping of reality which is an essential feature of art' (22). In fact, as we noted in an earlier section, Zola's aim was as to be as objective as possible in representing reality with as little personal input as possible.

Of the young writers who more fully embraced Zola's ideas of a scientific methodology, Arno Holtz (1863–1929) is one of the more radical German Naturalists to emerge. Noted for his attempts to achieve a more extreme Naturalism in his work – a style known as 'consistent naturalism' – Holtz similarly takes Zola's definition of art to produce his own definition:

> Art has the tendency to be nature again. It becomes nature in proportion to the conditions for imitation and the way they are handled.
>
> (Holz quoted in Furst and Skrine, 1971: 39)

which is further reduced to an equation 'art = nature − x', in which x represents 'any deficiency in the artist's imitative skill' (39). From this, we might reasonably deduce that art should represent reality as mimetically as possible and that 'temperament' should be 'eliminated'. Whilst Holz's equation is generally accepted as an illustration of his view that Zola's theories didn't 'go far enough', we should note, as Osborne points out, that Holz had misinterpreted what Zola meant by 'temperament'. Rather like Brandes, he too took it to mean the imagination and taste of the creative artist. Interestingly, it seems that some years later Holz claimed: 'he had never advocated the confinement of mimetic realism, and had never sought to restrict the freedom of artistic individuality in the slightest degree' (Osborne, 1998: 47).

None the less, Holz clearly advocated in his theories an emphasis on the objectivity of the artist and a precision in the detail of representation, both of which are demonstrated in the work he produced in collaboration with Johannes Schlaf (1862–1941), *Papa Hamlet* (1889) and *Die Familie Selicke* (1890). Regarded as 'seminal' Naturalist works, *Papa Hamlet* is a series of short sketches which, in terms of form, consist almost entirely of dialogue. The later work, *Die Familie Selicke*, is their first drama. In both pieces of writing Holz and Schlaf explore Naturalist concerns but as examples of 'consistent naturalism', the works are particularly noted for the degree to which they attempt to represent authentic speech. Their aim was to precisely and accurately reproduce the minutiae of detail one might observe in everyday speech in a style known as Sekundenstil (second-by-second) in order to more naturalistically represent their characters. Their explorations were not simply confined to the authenticity of the spoken word but equally to the accompanying non-verbal physical gestures, something Schlaf went on to articulate more fully in his essay *On Intimate Theatre* (1898).

Notwithstanding Holz and Schlaf's experiments, much of the theory produced by the Naturalists offered very little in the way of practical realization and it was not until 1887 that German Naturalism can be said to enter the second phase of its development. It was the first public performance of *Ghosts* at the Residenztheater in Berlin in 1887 which marked a turning point in the development of German drama and we now find Ibsen replacing Zola as the 'great foreign model'. Although Ibsen's plays had, in fact, been translated into German as early as 1872, and the first production of his work, *The Pillars of Society,* took place in 1878 followed two years later by the German versions of *A Doll's House*, and *Nora* he was, as John Osborne notes, a 'neglected dramatist'.

In the same way as we find Archer and Shaw championing the work of Ibsen in England, so too we find the theatre critic Otto Brahm (1856–1912) campaigning for Ibsen in Germany. According to Osborne, Brahm was rather ambivalent about Ibsen's drama until in 1884 he discovered a published version of *Ghosts*. Drawn to the challenging 'new material' and the social realism of the play, Brahm embarked on 'a long and loyal campaign on behalf of Ibsen', which included an important essay on the dramatist written in 1886 and, it would seem, some advance campaigning for the Berlin performance of *Ghosts*. The play was an enormous success, not least for establishing Berlin as the centre of the Naturalist movement. The effect of the performance was felt in other respects, Ibsen's play had demonstrated the possibilities for a 'native' Naturalist drama which had hitherto largely been unexplored. For the young Naturalists this represented an important moment and the focus of their efforts now turned towards the theatre (Osborne, 1998: 35–8).

The founding of the Freie Bühne

Influenced by André Antoine's Théâtre Libre, ideas for a similar venture started to emerge amongst the young writers of Berlin. Two journalists Theodor Wolff and Maximilian Harden are credited with initiating the idea of a German independent theatre, although it seems early discussions also included the critic Paul Schlenther who would later become one of the founding members:

> We are united in the purpose of forming, independent of the management of the established theatre and without entering into rivalry with it, a theatre free from conventions, theatre censorship and commercial aims. During this theatre-year, this group shall give in one of the first theatre houses of Berlin some ten productions of modern plays of decided interest which in their very nature the established stages find difficult to undertake. The aim of a living art shall be opposed to that of the patterns and masters alike in the choice of the dramatic works and in their presentations.
>
> (Schlenther cited in Miller, 1931: 111)

As Anna Miller tells us, the organization of the theatre was run along the lines of two forms of membership. There were to be ten 'regular' members, including among others Schlenther, the Hart brothers, who were responsible for both the artistic and financial organization, and Otto Brahm. Brahm was elected as president and responsible for the programming, choice of actors and publicity. The 'extraordinary' members comprised individuals who, for a 'modest' annual subscription, attended the performances. Prior to the opening, three members resigned including the two founders Wolff and Harden. Of the three replacements, Gerhart Hauptmann was elected to the group. Unlike Antoine's theatre in France, the Freie Bühne had no theatre or company of actors. The support for the venture was astonishing; Oscar Blumenthal offered the use of the Lessing Theatre for productions, and a variety of other notable individuals offered their assistance as managers, actors and directors. Subscriptions were taken up with enthusiasm and numbered 360 before the first performance, rising to around a thousand once it had become firmly established (Miller, 1931: 112–13). The Freie Bühne also produced its own periodical *Free Stage for the Developmental Struggle of the Time*, which included plays written by members of the group and essays on a range of topical issues.

The Freie Bühne opened with a matinee performance on Sunday, 29 September 1889 and, not surprisingly, *Ghosts* was chosen to inaugurate the new independent theatre. Brahm produced his own manifesto, announcing in the opening statement:

> 'To Begin' We are launching a Free Stage for Modern Life. Art shall be the object of our strivings – the new art, which fixes its attention on reality and contemporary existence [...].　　　(Brahm cited in Bentley, 1968: 373)

There were, of course, criticisms from those who felt that the Freie Bühne should be producing 'native drama' and encouraging new German playwrights. The second programme addressed this by including a new play, *Before Sunrise* by Gerhart Hauptmann, which had earlier been declined for publication in the journal *Die Gesellschaft*. In order to create some advance publicity, the play was quickly published prior to the performance which took place on Sunday 20 October 1889. With most of the audience already decided in their opinion, it was, as Osborne describes it, 'one of the noisiest and most violent premieres in the history of German theatre' (1998, 87).

The third programme included Anzengruber's *Das Vierte Gebot* and introduced the work of Tolstoy, Holz and Schlaf to the stage with their play *Die Familie Selicke*, which, as Miller notes, was more successful with the literary critics than the public, who grew impatient with 'slightness of action and over-abundance of details' (Miller, 1931: 120). The Freie Bühne during the two seasons it was active produced, among many others, two subsequent Hauptmann plays, Strindberg's *The Father* and Zola's *Thérèse Raquin*. The Freie Bühne closed at the end of the second season largely because it had paved the way for performances to take place in the main theatres. It had as Miller notes succeeded in many of its objectives by introducing the foreign drama of the Naturalist playwrights, encouraging new writing to some degree, and raising the standards of commercial theatre: 'It lies in the nature of the experiment that its greatest victory is its end' (Brahm cited in Miller, 1931: 125). It did, however, form again to produce Strindberg's *Miss Julie* in 1892 and Gerhart Hauptmann's *The Weavers* in 1893 (119–24).

Of course, one of the most important contributions the Freie Bühne made to German Naturalism was to bring Gerhart Hauptman's plays to the stage, notably *Before Sunrise* and *The Weavers*. Both plays differ significantly from the Naturalist drama we have explored elsewhere in the book. In his chapter 'Theatre as a political Forum', Raymond Williams notes:

> There was an early crisis within the chosen form of modernist Naturalism. Its version of the environment within which human lives were formed and deformed – the domestic bourgeois household in which the social and financial insecurities and above all the sexual tensions were most immediately experienced – was at once physically convincing and intellectually insufficient. Beyond this key site of the living room there were, in opposite directions, crucial areas of experience which the language and behaviour of the living room could not articulate or fully interpret. Social and economic crises in the wider society had their effects back in the living room, but dramatically only as reports from elsewhere, off-stage, or at best as things seen from the window or as shouts from the street   (1989: 85)

In fact, Williams goes on to discuss the subsequent development of modern drama in the work of Artaud and Brecht, but it is worth considering Hauptman's play in the light of Williams's comments. *Before Sunrise*, which had created such a furore on the opening night, is the first of his plays to be set in Silesia, now part of Poland. Briefly, Hauptman addresses the effect of industrialization on a farming community who have profited from the recent discovery of coal. He quite brilliantly uses the character of Loth, a socialist and economist who has been sent to the town to study the conditions of the local community, to expose the wider implications of the newly found prosperity. The social crises in Hauptman's play unfold on stage, one of the main concerns in the play is an exploration of alcoholism, which at the time was widely believed to be hereditary. Whilst we might argue that the play has a number of flaws in it, Hauptman makes a bold attempt to explore the effect of the environment on the community and, indeed, Loth, who for all his socialist ideas, cannot bring himself to stay, abandoning Helene with whom he has fallen in love and who commits suicide (Osborne, 1998: 87–92).

Hauptmann's *The Weavers* is further removed from the bourgeois domestic household to address the plight of the working-class weavers. The play represents on stage the events that led to an uprising which actually took place in Silesia in 1844. Written in 1891 in Silesian dialect, Hauptman later produced a version which was closer to standard German. The play, an on-going source of controversy from the date of publication in 1892, had been banned by the authorities, with the result that the Freie Bühne reformed to produce the first performance on 26 February 1893 at the Neues Theatre in Berlin.

Opinion of Hauptman's play, which takes as its subject the 'spontaneous revolt' of the Silesian weavers in 1844, was sharply divided. The Conservatives regarded *The Weavers* as a piece of socialist propaganda which had the potential to incite the audience, whilst the Social Democrats greeted it with enthusiasm as a piece of drama which drew attention to the proletariat. We should note that Hauptmann vehemently denied that the play was a socialist one. A number of the Naturalists found themselves in the difficult position of, on the one hand, admiring Hauptman's genius as a Naturalist playwright, but on the other a reluctance to be associated with the political left. Julius Hart's rather conservative view of the play as 'the manifestation of universal humanitarianism' in which 'Everything political and socialist has been refined into the purest artistic creation and into a humanitarianism that rises above naked self-interest' is indicative of the position taken by the more conservative Naturalists (Hart quoted in Mehring, 1893).

Franz Mehring, one of the earliest Marxist literary critics, wrote his article in response to Hart's view which he found untenable, the purpose of his article was to draw attention to 'just how deeply embedded *The Weavers* is in '"the steam and vapour of political partisanship"'(Mehring, 1893: 185). The reason for this, as Mehring makes clear, is that Hauptmann based his play on Wilhelm Wolff's published account of the weavers' uprising. Wolff, 'a genuine Social Democrat' according to Mehring, not only presented a picture of the weavers' plight in the middle of the nineteenth century, it relied on verbatim accounts from eye-witnesses. Mehring provides a detailed overview of Wolff's account, quoting several lengthy extracts from the text before going on to compare it to Haupt-mann's play. It is, as Mehring argues 'abundantly clear just how much Wolff's account has furnished the skeleton for Hauptmann's drama' (187). Notwith-standing the main purpose in the article, Mehring acknowledges that 'what Hauptmann was undertaking constituted a departure from all previous dramatic technique', going on to say that 'None of the other literary achievements of German Naturalism can remotely compare with *The Weavers*' (188).

Born in Silesia in 1862 to a family of innkeepers, Hauptman's grandfather had been a weaver before setting up the family business. Hauptman not only had a close affinity with the people of Silesia and their dialect, he was also familiar with the weaving industry. Although Wolff's account provides the 'skeleton' for the play, it seems Hauptman also drew on Alfred Zimmermann's later historical account and undertook several visits to the area to conduct research.

For Furst and Skrine (1971), Hauptman succeeded in this play 'where all other Naturalists failed' and it is worth exploring why this might be. In drawing on the evidence provided in the historical documentation, there is little opportunity for any personal contribution from the dramatist and, to this extent, Hauptman achieves the objectivity required by the Naturalists. The 'facts', as Osborne notes, have a 'disciplinary effect' and what we find in place of the 'logic' of plot is 'a logic' of actual events represented over five acts. In each of these Hauptman relo-cates to a different environment. The setting of Act I, described in detail, takes place in the manufacturer's workroom where the weavers bring their webs and wait for payment. Hauptman produces on stage a 'picture' in which the weavers' plight is immediately evident to the audience. Waiting in line are '*A large number of young and old weavers and weaver women*' (Hauptmann, 1980: 28). Hauptman describes their physical appearance in detail: '*They look disheveled, haunted, over-worked and their clothes are in tatters*' (29). The extent of their suffering and their impoverished circumstances are gradually revealed as the Act unfolds and we discover weavers begging for advances in order to survive, deductions made from their wages and the collapse of a starving child who has journeyed some seven miles to deliver webs to the manufacturer. There are no characters in the tradi-tional sense, but rather representatives of the proletariat and capitalists. Dreis-siger, the manufacturer and his employees stand for manufacturers as a wider group. Their treatment of the weavers is harsh, Pfeifer the manager and once a weaver himself, shows no compassion: 'If you don't like it, just don't take no more warp. There are enough people who'd walk their shoes off their feet to get it' (33). At one point Dreissiger 'holds forth' on the problems facing manufacturers in general and attempts to draw attention to the effect of foreign competition on the weaving industry. However, little sympathy can be felt for a manufacturer whose offer of work to unemployed weavers will result in a reduction of pay for existing ones.

In Act II, Hauptmann relocates to the home of one of the weaver families: '*the room is narrow and less than six feet high*' (1980: 41). The stage picture of a dimly lit room with women working at their looms, which produce the sound of 'heavy thumping' and 'monotonous humming', immediately conveys the appalling conditions in which the weavers live and work, the most shocking illustration of their circumstances is that they must resort to eating their dog. Act III is set in an inn, and here Hauptman has chosen a public place in which various characters come and go to reveal the extent of the weavers' exploitation in which the clergy, farmers, tradesmen are complicit. Up until this point the uprising has gradually been brewing, the Bielau weaver Bäcker has already voiced disconnect in the first act. Jäger, a returning soldier, has appeared in the second act and introduced the words of the weavers' song, words that prompt a gradual realization in the weavers of their own circumstances: 'Whoever's written that know the truth' (53). Momentum towards the revolt occurs when Jäger and Bäcker enter the inn. In Act IV, Hauptmann relocates again to the home of the manufacturer, where the weavers storm the house. In the final act Hauptman moves location to the town of Langenbielau and the weaving room of old Hilse, where the family are 'saying their morning prayers'. The misery is once again evident, but the suffering is borne in the knowledge that reward will be found in heaven: 'Give us patience, heavenly Father so after this suffering we can partake of your eternal bliss. Amen' (86). Against the 'backdrop' of the approaching revolutionaries in which he sees his daughter-in-law join the mob, he resolutely refuses to participate: 'This is where my Heavenly Father put me. Ain't that so Mother?' (Hauptmann, 1980: 101). As he returns to his loom a stray bullet ends his life and the play.

In many respects Hauptman's skilful treatment of the uprising resembles a documentary to the extent he exposes the 'ceaseless pressure' of the social environment from a number of different angles. Hauptman represents on stage what he has found in the evidence with the objectivity of an impartial reporter.

CHAPTER SUMMARY

- The eighties 'ignited the sparks of a new literary art' (Miller, 1931: 107) with the emergence of the 'Youngest Germany' group of writers.
- The decisive influences on the development of Naturalism in Germany came from the translated work of the French and Russian novelists, the plays of Ibsen and the writings of Zola, who was to be the most influential figure.
- In the same way that Archer and Shaw championed the work of Ibsen in England, the theatre critic Otto Brahm campaigned for Ibsen in Germany.

- The figure with whom we tend to associate German Naturalism is Arno Holtz, not least because of his formula for Naturalism 'art = nature − x'.
- Influenced by André Antoine's Théâtre Libre, ideas for a similar venture start to emerge in Berlin: two journalists Theodor Wolff and Maximilian Harden are credited with initiating the idea.
- Otto Brahm, the elected president, was responsible for programming and produced his own manifesto for the new independent theatre.
- The Freie Bühne produced its own periodical *Free Stage for the Developmental Struggle of the Time*, which included plays written by members of the group.
- *Ghosts* was chosen to inaugurate the venture and the project to produce significant new plays continued for two seasons
- The Freie Bühne did not entirely disband and met again to produce Strindberg's *Miss Julie* in 1892 and also Gerhart Hauptmann's *The Weavers*, which had been banned. This proved to be one of the high watermarks of Naturalist theatre

SEMINAR AND WORKSHOP TOPICS

1 Why did the Freie Bühne elect to open with *Ghosts*?
2 Take a scene from *The Weavers* and, after a rehearsed reading/performance, discuss how the writer conveys the drudgery of work.
3 Repeat this scene in movement only, working to create a sense of mechanical and repetitive tasks.
4 How does Brahm's 'Manifesto' compare with those of Zola and Strindberg? What are the common issues?
5 Why did a 'new' form of drama emerge in Germany in the 1880s?
6 Research the real events dealt with in *The Weavers*. How do these reflect issues described in our chapters on Naturalism in Context?
7 Plot a diagram or make a table of all those practitioners influenced by the Meininger and indicate the nature of that influence.

FURTHER READING

Furst, L. R. and Skrine, P. N. (1971) *Naturalism The Critical Idiom*, London: Methuen. Cited frequently in this book and regarded as an accessible and helpful guide.
Lustig, T. H., trans. (1961) *Five Plays by Gerhart Hauptmann*, New York: Bantam.
Osborne, J. (1998) *Gerhart Hauptmann and the Naturalist Drama*, rev. edn, London: Routledge. An excellent study of the development of German Naturalism and Hauptman's key plays.

Schumacher, C. ed., (1996) *Naturalism and Symbolism in European Theatre 1850–1918*, Cambridge: Cambridge University Press. An invaluable source of documentary evidence contextualizing the development of Naturalism in Europe.

Skrine, P. (1989) *Hauptmann, Wedekind and Schnitzler*, London: Macmillan Education. Provides a thoughtful analysis of these writers and their plays.

CHAPTER 8
Moscow Art Theatre

An overview of the Russian theatre

As we have seen elsewhere in Europe, Russian theatre in the latter decades of the nineteenth century was 'inundated' with adaptations and translations of foreign plays. David Magarshack, noted for his extensive writing on Anton Chekhov, Stanislavsky and a number of Russian novelists, draws on Chekhov's sketch *The Dramatist* to illustrate the situation. Written in 1886, Anton Chekhov represents his view of the prevailing Russian dramatists in the character of 'the playwright' who, upon visiting 'the doctor', is asked to describe his writing process: 'First of all, I get hold of some French or German piece either by accident or through some friends [...]. If the play is any good I take it to my sister or hire a student for five roubles. They translate it for me and I, you see, adapt it for the Russian stage: I substitute Russian names for the names of the characters and so on' (Chekhov cited in Magarshack, 1953: 31). In fact, what we find in Russia is a situation quite unlike that of the other European countries we have considered and in terms of theatre the situation was far worse. We should remind ourselves that Russia was until 1905 an autocracy under the absolute rule of the Russian tzar. As Edward Braun notes in *The Director and The Stage*, until 1882 a state monopoly: 'forbade the existence of any public theatres in Moscow and Petersburg save those few under the direct control of the Imperial Court' (1982: 59). This meant that the Maly Theatre in Moscow and the Alexandrinsky in Petersburg were, in effect, the only theatres regularly producing drama and, significantly, only drama which met the imperial censor's approval. This was a censor who: 'exercised his prerogative not only in the field of morals and politics, but in questions of artistic taste as well' (59). The obvious consequence of this situation was that until 1882, when the monopoly was abolished, there was: 'absolutely no competition to stimulate innovation' (59). Of the commercial theatres that did open in Moscow after 1882, we find numerous references to three main theatres; the Pushkin Theatre, the Solodovnikov Theatre, and a privately owned stage in the hands of F. A. Korsch. These managers were, of course, primarily concerned with financial profit and hence relied on drama that would attract audiences and fill their houses: 'all experiments were left to amateur societies' (59).

This overview of the Russian theatre is necessarily a rather simplified account and it is important to bear in mind that, just as we find elsewhere, there had been attempts to develop drama, the style of acting and stage production, all of which would contribute to the evolution of a modern Russian theatre and many of the principles later developed by the Moscow Art Theatre. Of particular note in this respect are two individuals, the actor Mikhail Shchepkin (1788–1863) and the renowned playwright Alexander Ostrovsky (1823–1886).

Until the emancipation of the serfs in 1861, Russia was a feudal state. Born into serfdom 'on an estate in the Ukraine in 1788', Mikhail Shchepkin went on to become a professional actor, working in the 'serf theatres' where his reputation as the leading actor eventually led to an invitation to join the Maly Theatre in Moscow. As we have already seen (see Chapter 4), Shchepkin was particularly influenced by the 'lifelike' performances of Prince Meshchersky which he had seen as a young man. In a letter written in March 1848 we find his ideas are remarkably similar to those which would later be articulated by other key figures:

> Get under the skin of your character, so to speak, study his particular ideas well, if he has any, and do not overlook the social influences on his past life. When all this has been analysed, then whatever situations may be drawn from life, you will not fail to depict them truthfully.
>
> (Shchepkin cited in Schumacher, 1996: 195)

It was Shchepkin who, as Magarshack notes, was responsible for raising the standards of the Maly to become: 'one of the foremost theatres in the country not only by his own acting but also by training a large number of actors and actresses who became famous on its stage' (1950: 142).

The playwright Alexander Ostrovsky, noted for his attempt at a more 'realistic' representation of Russian society in his drama, worked closely with the actors at the Maly Theatre. After Shchepkin's death, he took over responsibility for actor training and instilling a degree of 'stage discipline' into the Maly productions. Increasingly, Ostrovsky found himself at loggerheads with the theatre authorities who, driven by the pressure for high box-office returns, were largely unconcerned about the quality of drama being produced. The traditions that had been built up at the theatre by Shchepkin and Ostrovsky started to erode. Concerned by the decline of the Maly, Ostrovsky made a number of representations to the authorities outlining the problems as he saw them and proposing changes to the organization and repertoire along the lines of a 'national theatre'. Ostrovsky envisaged a theatre which would be open to a wider audience, and one that would invest its resources into the training of actors and be overseen by a producer who was an expert in his field. These ideas would anticipate many of the Moscow Art Theatre principles but at the time were ignored and the Maly steadily continued in its decline (Magarshack, 1950: 144–5).

In *A Boring Story* written in 1889, Chekhov once again expressed his view of theatre, this time through the hero of the story, an old professor of medicine:

I don't know what theatre will be like in fifty or a hundred years, but under present conditions it can serve only as entertainment, and as entertainment it is too expensive to be worthwhile […]. Not to mention the sheer waste of money and the moral injury suffered by the public from seeing a wrongly presented case of murder, adultery or libel on the stage.

(Chekhov quoted in Magarshack, 1953: 24)

Russian theatre at the end of the nineteenth century was in a 'moribund' state and badly in need of reform; the two figures with whom we associate this reform are Konstantin Stanislavsky (1863–1938) and Vladimir Nemirovich-Danchenko (1858–1943). Stanislavsky, the son of a wealthy manufacturer, was fortunate enough to be born into a family with strong connections to, and an interest in, the arts. His maternal grandmother was a renowned French actress which probably explains the family's keen interest in theatre and opera, and their continued support for his dramatic enterprises. As a teenager he organized the Alexeyev Circle, a small amateur group largely comprised of family members and friends. As we have discussed elsewhere, the group approached their amateur productions with a startling degree of professionalism. Although Stanislavsky joined the family business, he continued to pursue his interest in theatre, regularly attending performances at the Maly Theatre for the purpose of researching and analysing the productions with the Circle members.

At one point Stanislavsky attempted to combine his work commitments with a more formal actor training by enrolling at a newly opened drama school, this proved to be a rather underwhelming experience and he left after only three weeks. Over time the Circle gradually dissolved and Stanislavsky found himself having to join other amateur groups in order to continue acting in what he describes in *My Life In Art* (2008) as 'chance performances'. Despite having to perform with unreliable and unprepared members in the cast, and very often in poor surroundings, Stanislavsky had no option but to continue: 'There was nowhere else I could act and I had to act or I would die' (2008: 85). At one of these 'chance performances' Stanislavsky was 'stopped in his tracks' by the sight of his parents in the audience. Their experience of the evening's performance caused his father to remark the following day: 'If you want to do some acting in your own free time, then create your own circle and your own repertoire, but don't play any old filth with God knows who' (85). As it happened, circumstances arose which enabled Stanislavsky to do exactly what his father had advocated. He managed to secure the lead role in a Gogol play which was being produced by Aleksandr Fedotov, 'famous in his day as a director' (89). The performance was an enormous success with the result that the individuals involved did not want to split up: 'we talked about setting up a large society which would bring together all the amateur and dramatic circles and everyone working in other theatres and arts in one single drama circle where there was to be no card-playing' (89). Stanislavsky duly brought together Alexandr Fedotov, Fyodor

Kommissarzhevsky and Fyodor Sollogub to found The Society of Art and Literature in 1888, a year after Antoine had established the Théâtre Libre in Paris.

The society was, in many respects, the first experimental theatre in Russia. Stanislavsky invested a substantial sum of money he had unexpectedly received into acquiring and refurbishing suitable premises which, upon completion, contained an auditorium, foyer and meeting place. Here Stanislavsky together with several of the more reliable amateur actors he had become acquainted with, and subsequently introduced to the Society, were able to experiment and develop their skills under the guidance of Fedotov, Sollogub and latterly Fedotov's ex-wife, the acclaimed Maly actress Glikeria Fedotova. It was during this period that Stanislavsky saw the work of the Meiningen troupe on their second visit to Moscow in 1890, and like Antoine who had seen them Brussels, Stanislavsky was similarly impressed by the performances: 'I did not miss a single show. I not only saw them, I studied them' (2008: 113). The Meiningen innovations proved to be extremely influential on the development of Stanislavsky's own ideas and it is significant that Stanislavsky now started directing productions. Among the plays produced by the Society was a private performance of Tolstoy's *The Fruits of Knowledge* – Stanislavsky's directorial debut. Tolstoy was so impressed by the performance, he later offered Stanislavsky the opportunity to produce *The Power of Darkness*, which had been banned by the censor. It was whilst directing for the Society that Stanislavsky undertook the much referenced trip to Venice to research costumes and buy props for the production of *Othello,* a practice he would continue later at the Art Theatre. Already we find in these early years of the Society the stirrings of Russia's first stage-director (Braun, 1982: 60).

The Society increasingly gained a reputation for their performances which, largely due to Stanislavsky's direction, achieved 'unprecedented standards' in staging and ensemble acting. Although the Society was somewhat constrained by a commitment to produce weekly performances for the Moscow Hunting Club, to whom, for financial reasons, they had been forced to let out their premises, they still managed to produce one play each season for which they would invest in a lengthy rehearsal process. In late 1895 and early 1896 Stanislavsky took advantage of the opportunity to direct on the main stage of the Solodovnikov theatre for the Russian impresario Mikhail Lentovsky, these productions included *Othello,* mentioned earlier, and Hauptmann's *Hannele.* The last of the plays he directed for the Society was Hauptmann's *The Sunken Bell* and this production was particularly significant in that, as Magarshack notes, Stanislavsky drew for the first time on the skills of scenic designer Victor Simov. They worked together exploring the essence of the play in an attempt to improve on Stanislavsky's original ideas for staging, illustrated in the 'fairy tale' like scale models he had made and which they both felt were inadequate. According to Magarshack, when Simov arrived with the model of his new design Stanislavsky asked: 'Where did you get such a knowledge of the stage? To feel it like that is a great achievement' (1950: 132). The working relationship established between designer and director during this production would prove to be fundamental to the creative approach of the Moscow Art Theatre. As Stanislavsky acknowledged:

> To our good fortune we found in Simov a designer who could meet the actor and director halfway. He had that rare ability for the time that he was not only gifted and well informed in his own field but also in matters of directing. Simov was interested not only in the decor in the play itself, [but] its interpretation and the director's and actor's tasks. He was able to subordinate himself, as a designer, to the overall idea behind the stage.
>
> (Stanislavsky, 1980, 168)

The founding of the Moscow Art Theatre

Vladimir Ivanovich Nemirovich-Danchenko was an extremely well known figure in Russian literary circles. He had earned himself a reputation as a novelist and critic as well as being a very successful playwright whose work had been produced at the Maly Theatre. In 1895 he was the recipient of the prestigious Griboyedov prize for his play *The Price of Life* which, at the time, he felt to be rather misjudged, requesting that instead the judges award it to his friend Anton Chekhov for *The Seagull* – something they were not minded to do. At this point he was working as stage director and acting teacher at the drama school attached to the Moscow Philharmonic Society, where 'he threw himself with great zest into the work of training a new generation of actors who should be free from the stale and outworn traditions of the stage' (Magarshack, 1950: 150). Magarshack notes that Nemirovich-Danchenko was a writer of the 'psychological school' and as such he focused on developing the 'psychological undertones in the acting of the pupils, and his first great success in that particular line was the production at his school of Ibsen's *A Doll's House* in 1896' (150).

In the opening paragraphs of his autobiography *My Life in Russian Theatre*, Nemirovich-Danchenko writes:

> Finally, one of my biographers affirms that the will of my entire life was directed toward one object: the creation of the Art Theatre; that everything I had sought as a dramatist, author, journalist, stage director, theatrical pedagogue, and even amateur actor in my youth – everything aspired toward the historical meeting with Stanislavsky which developed into an eighteen-hour conversation giving birth to the Art Theatre.
>
> (1936: 3)

Nemirovich-Danchenko wrote to Stanislavsky in June 1897 asking to meet with a view to discussing 'a new theatre which I would enter with my group of amateurs and he with his group of graduating students. To this nucleus we would add his former pupils Moskvin and Roksanova and other actors from Petersburg, Moscow and the provinces' (Stanislavsky, 2008: 159). They duly met on 22 June 1897 for the famous 18-hour meeting during which Nemirovich-Danchenko recalls: 'The most remarkable thing about this conversation was that we did not once disagree' (1936: 83).

They considered and laid out: 'the bases of our new enterprise: purely artistic questions, our aesthetic ideals, ethics, organization, repertoire and our mutual relations' (Stanislavsky, 2008: 159). In *My Life in Art*, Stanislavsky describes at length a number of decisions reached in the meeting. One of their main intentions was to create a popular theatre along the lines of those envisaged earlier by Ostrovsky. They hoped to encourage a wider audience to their productions and the original name for the theatre was the Moscow Popular Art Theatre. However, as they discovered, the limitations imposed by the censor on the repertoire of popular theatres would mean compromising their 'artistic intentions', leading them instead to make the Art Theatre an 'open' one where anyone might go. Actors would not simply be chosen on the basis of their talent, but rather: 'Because he has ideals and fights for them. He is not happy with things as they are. He's a man of ideas' (160). They agreed that Nemirovich-Danchenko would take responsibility for the organizational aspects but would have the right of veto over matters relating to literature whilst Stanislavsky would have the same right over artistic matters. Actors had a right to work in conditions 'fit for educated human beings' if they were expected to behave decently and work creatively. Finance to support the venture would be sought in the form of shares and the first of their monies would be spent refurbishing premises to a suitable standard for work to take place:

> Then we talked about professional ethics and we wrote our decisions into the minutes in sentences and aphorisms such as, 'There are no small parts, only small actors'
> or
> 'Today, Hamlet, tomorrow, an extra, but as an extra he must be an artist'
> 'The author, the actor, the designer, the wardrobe master, the stagehand all have one goal, given by the writer as the basis of his play'
> 'Any disruption in the creative life of the theatre is a crime'
> 'Lateness, laziness, wilfulness, hysterics, bad character, not knowing the lines, having to do the same thing twice, is damaging to our work and must be banished. (163)

The repertoire for the first season was compiled by Nemirovich-Danchenko and included amongst the plays selected Tolstoy's *Tsar Fyodor* and Chekhov's *The Seagull*. Chekhov had written the play in 1895 and the first production had taken place at the Alexandrinsky Theatre in Petersburg on 17 October 1895. Chekhov, who had arrived in Petersburg ten days earlier, was dismayed to find that rehearsals had only just started, there were last minute changes to the cast, actors who didn't know their lines and who overacted when they did. He wrote to his sister Marya, 'the acting in *The Seagull* is poor [...] I'm afraid it's not going to be a cheerful , but rather a gloomy performance' (quoted in Magarshack, 1953: 292). The opening night of the play was not a success, the audience responded with laughter and booing and Chekhov left the auditorium after the second act. Writing to Nemirovich-Danchenko a month later, he says: 'Yes, my *Seagull* was a huge failure. The theatre breathed malice, the air was compressed with hatred, and in accordance with the law of physics, I was thrown out of Petersburg like a bomb' (quoted by Fen in Chekhov, 1951: 22). In fact, had Chekhov remained in Petersburg he would have seen, as Magarshack points out, that the subsequent performances were far better received, although this did not prevent the management from withdrawing the play after only five performances.

Nemirovich-Danchenko clearly held *The Seagull* in high regard, as he had demonstrated some years earlier. Convinced its failure had been due to poor interpretation, he saw potential in it that chimed with the artistic vision of the new Moscow Art Theatre. Nemirovich-Danchenko had to work hard to persuade Chekhov to give his permission to include it in the first season, his initial request was met 'with a categorical refusal' (1936: 140). Eventually, after several exchanges of correspondence, Chekhov finally agreed: 'The public is not yet capable and perhaps never will be capable of yielding to the mood of the play; it is necessary that it should have a strong vehicle for conveying it. We will do our best!' (Nemirovich-Danchenko, 1936: 143).

Stanislavsky similarly required persuading, he admitted he found the play strange and boring, and had to retreat to a friend's estate to do the preparatory work. As he describes in *My Life in Art*, his approach to the production plan was prescriptive, he provided sketches of the set, costume and makeup, and made notes for the actors detailing every action, mannerism and tone of voice, in the genuine belief that: 'it was possible to tell someone else what to live and feel. I gave directions to everyone at every moment of the action and they were binding' (2008: 176). One of the qualities Stanislavsky did discover in his exploration of *The Seagull* and later in the other Chekhov plays was that: 'Their fascination is not conveyed by words themselves, but by what is hidden behind them or in the pauses, or the way the actors look at each other or in the way they radiate inner feeling' (192). Stanislavsky elaborates further: 'His plays are full of action, not outwardly but inwardly. The most inactive people the writer has created conceal highly complex inner action' (193).

Rehearsals for the forthcoming season commenced during the summer of 1898, in a converted barn in Pushkino whilst the company awaited access to the Hermitage theatre they had rented. The theatre, when they did gain entry, proved to be a huge disappointment and the group had to set about restoring a semblance of order to what Stanislavsky describes as a 'kind of slum' in time for the opening performance. The first performance of the Moscow Art Theatre took place on 14 October 1898 with Tolstoy's *Tsar Fyodor* (1875). The first of what Stanislavsky refers to as the 'historico-realist' line of productions by the Art Theatre was a great success, the like of which the audience had not previously seen on a Moscow stage. The authenticity of staging, costume and props 'enthralled' the audience and the time and energy invested into detailed research, the purchase of genuine materials for props and costume, and expeditions to Russian towns, particularly Rostov, to inhabit the atmosphere of ancient fortifications made for a 'spectacular production'. The opening success was to be short-lived, the subsequent plays included in the first programme resulted in failures and the theatre was on the 'verge of collapse', the future of the Moscow Art Theatre rested on the success of the final production, *The Seagull*. Nemirovich-Danchenko, in his biography, recalls there was little to give them confidence and the house was 'by no means full' on the evening of 17 December (Stanislavsky, 2008: 184). Of the actual performance, he writes: 'There was on the stage that of which litterateurs who love the theatre had long dreamed: the life they now beheld in these simple human contacts on the stage was "real", not "theatrical"' (186). The scene which had provoked laughter in Petersburg, now: 'resounded in the deep, tense silence and held attention' (187). Confidence was restored in Nemirovich-Danchenko as the audience showed themselves to be capable of 'yielding to the mood' and understanding the play. As the curtain closed on the first act Nemirovich-Danchenko recalls:

> [...] something occurred which can occur in a theatre only once in a decade: the curtain closed and there was silence, a complete silence both in the theatre and on the stage; it was as though all held their breath, as though no one quite understood; had it been a vision? [...] Then, suddenly, in the auditorium, something happened. It was as if a dam had burst, or a bomb had exploded – all at once there was a deafening crash of applause from all: from friends and from enemies. (1936: 188)

Chekhov who was in Yalta at the time, did not attend the performance but heard about the reception the play had received in a telegram signed by the company: 'We have just finished performance of Sea Gull. A colossal success. From the first act the play so possessed every one that there followed a series of triumphs. Endless curtain calls. [...] We are mad with happiness' (1936: 189). The Moscow Art Theatre had established itself, and as Edward Braun notes: 'If *Tsar Fyodor* secured the Art Theatre a public, it was *The Seagull* which enabled the company to find its identity' (1982: 62). In a show of public recognition for Chekhov's contribution, the Art Theatre chose the seagull as its official emblem.

For Chekhov, too, the production had been an important one, not only did it establish his reputation as a dramatist and his relationship with the Art Theatre, it was where he met his future wife Olga Knipper. Chekhov's biographical details have been dealt with extensively in various accounts of his life and works but it is worth reminding ourselves of some background information. Chekhov, born on 17 January 1860, was one of six children born to Paviel and Yevghenia Chekhov, a family of shopkeepers in Taganrog, a provincial town and trading port situated on the Azov Sea. Accounts of Chekhov's life indicate that his upbringing was a harsh one, Paviel Chekhov was an ineffectual businessman who, with a large family to support, struggled to make ends meet. From Chekhov's own accounts of his childhood, his father was a bully who 'destroyed his mother's youth' and spoiled both his childhood and that of his siblings. Paviel Chekhov finally went bankrupt with the result that the family left hastily for Moscow, leaving behind the young Chekhov to continue his education. During this period it seems he thrived, his school work improved, he edited the school magazine and earned a small income coaching younger school boys (Fen in Chekhov, 1951: 12). According to David Magarshack in his book *Chekhov The Dramatist* (1980), Chekhov had, in his youth, appeared in a number of amateur and professional productions. Not only was he regarded as a 'talented actor', he was in Magarshack's view 'a born playwright' producing a number of full-length plays in his teens and early twenties. The first of these, *The Fatherless*, was written in 1877 at the age of 17, but it would not be until some ten years later that he would develop his work more fully as a dramatist. In 1879, Chekhov rejoined the family in Moscow and enrolled to study medicine at Moscow University. The writing of short-stories with which his early career is most commonly associated was borne out of financial necessity in an effort to support his family. The first of these was published in 1880 and he continued to write what he referred to as 'pot boilers' for the next seven years, producing regularly and prodigiously for a number of journals.

Magarshack notes that as early as 1881 Chekhov was also revealing himself to be an astute theatre critic, writing several articles for the *Onlooker*, a Moscow journal. In two of these, Chekhov critiqued Sarah Bernhardt's performance during a recent tour in Russia. In his review, he found: 'not a glimmer of talent in all her acting, but just an enormous amount of hard work' (Chekhov quoted in Magarshack, 1953: 25). For all her 'great industry', which he was clearly impressed by, Chekhov remained of the view that Bernhardt transformed: 'everyone of her heroines into the same kind of unusual woman she is herself' (25). Her acting was spoilt by: 'that confounded artificiality, those deliberate conjuring tricks and overemphasis' (26). What Chekhov did note, however, was the way in which the whole company listened to each other on stage in contrast to the Russian actor who, when required to listen to another character: 'has his eyes fixed on some far-away point and keeps coughing impatiently' (26). Chekhov wrote his first major play *Platonov* in the same year, submitting it to the Maly Theatre for consideration. It was rejected and returned to him in the post.

With his studies complete, Chekhov began practising as a doctor in 1884, managing to combine his profession with his writing. 'Medicine', he said, was his lawful wife and literature only his 'mistress'. Writing to Professor Rossolimo towards the end of his life Chekhov recalls:

> I do not doubt but that the study of medicine has had a great influence on my literary work; it has considerably widened the field of my observations and enriched my knowledge [...]. I suppose, it is because of my knowledge of medicine that I have succeeded in avoiding making many mistakes. An acquaintance with the natural sciences and the scientific method always kept me on the look out for such mistakes, and wherever possible I tried to take the scientific data into account; and where it was not possible I preferred not write at all [...]. (quoted in Magarshack, 1953: 48)

By 1887 Chekhov had started to devote more time to writing drama, and critics tend to divide the work produced between 1887 and 1890 into two groups, the vaudevilles and the earliest of his full-length plays, *Ivanov* and *The Wood Demon* (which would later be adapted to *Uncle Vanya*). As we have seen, many European dramatists writing in the nineteenth century intended their plays to be read first as literary works. Chekhov, as Magarshack points out, clearly wrote his plays in anticipation of their being staged and, furthermore, envisaged an active role in the rehearsal period during which he would have the opportunity to make revisions. In a letter Chekhov wrote in 1889 responding to a request to publish his play *The Wood Demon*, he writes: 'I never consider a play ready for publication until it has been revised during rehearsals' (quoted in Magarshack, 1953: 21). In the case of these two full-length plays, *Ivanov* was a success with the Moscow audience and, on the whole, greeted favourably by critics in spite of Chekhov's reservations about the standard of the performance, and it subsequently went on to be performed at the Alexandrinsky in Petersburg. *The Wood Demon* produced in Moscow in 1889 was, in contrast, a complete failure and, as Fen notes: 'The critics accused Chekhov of merely reproducing on the stage a slice of life which did not even have the interest of being original or exciting' (Fen in Chekhov, 1951: 20). It would be some five years before Chekhov would write another full-length play; in late 1895 he completed *The Seagull*, and the following year completed the rewritten version of *The Wood Demon*, now renamed *Uncle Vanya*.

Following the success of the Moscow Art Theatre production of *The Seagull*, Nemirovich-Danchenko approached Chekhov with a view to producing *Uncle Vanya*. Although the play had already been promised elsewhere, circumstances arose which meant he was able to give the play to the Art Theatre for their forthcoming season. Chekhov was in the Crimea when the play opened on 26 October 1899 and once again heard about the somewhat 'mixed' reception by telegram. Writing to a friend shortly after the performance, he says: 'They expected to have a sensational success and, having only got a moderate one, they are worried. I have been writing for twenty-one years and I know that a moderate success is the best kind of success for a writer and actor' (quoted in Magarshack 1953: 346).

Stanislavsky recalls: 'After the success of *The Seagull* and *Uncle Vanya* we could not do without another play from Chekhov. Our future was in his hands. If there was a play, there would be a season' (2008: 204). Chekhov's next play was the first to be written for the Art Theatre, with roles developed for specific actors. Writing from the Crimea to the actor A. L. Vishnevsky on 5 August 1900, Chekhov says:

> I'm writing a play, I've already written a lot but I can't judge it till I'm in Moscow. Perhaps what I'm producing isn't a play, but boring Crimean rubbish. It's called 'Three Sisters' (as you already know) and I've done a part for you in it, that of second master at a high school, the husband of one of the sisters. You will wear a schoolmaster's regulation frock-coat and have a medal on a ribbon round your neck.
>
> (Chekhov quoted in Lyman, 1976: 161)

In a letter to Maxim Gorky in October he acknowledged how hard it had been to write the play. Chekhov was becoming increasingly more frail as the Tuberculosis, from which he had suffered since his early twenties, became more invasive. In October 1900, Chekhov arrived in Moscow to personally deliver the play. Stanislavsky describes the reading at which Chekhov and all members of the company, including stage hands and ushers, were present: 'He kept getting up from his chair pacing about, especially when the dialogue took, in his opinion, a false or simply disagreeable direction' (2008: 204). At the end of the reading Chekhov left without any explanation, the cause of which Stanislavsky found out later was because he felt the play had been misunderstood: 'He was convinced that he had written a happy comedy but when it was read everyone took it as a drama and wept' (205). We should note here that there is some doubt over Stanislavsky's interpretation of Chekhov's intention. A number of critics make the point that when Chekhov intended a comedy, he always referred to the work as such – something he never does with *Three Sisters*. Regardless of this, there was clearly a misunderstanding over interpretation at the reading. Chekhov's concerns regarding Stanislavsky's interpretation of his plays were not new. He had by now seen a private performance of *The Seagull* in Moscow in May 1899, where the acting and interpretation of the characters proved to be a disappointment to him. When the Art Theatre toured the Crimea in April of the following year, he had the opportunity to see *Uncle Vanya*, which clearly surpassed the poor expectations which he had expressed in a letter to Nemirovich-Danchenko some six months earlier: 'The thought of Alexeyev's acting fills me with so much gloom that I can't shake it off, and I just can't believe that he acts well in *Uncle Vanya*, though everybody writes to me that he is not only good but very good' (quoted in Magarshack, 1953: 339)

Clearly anticipating problems with *Three Sisters*, he wrote to Olga Knipper whilst he was writing the play: 'I've absolutely got to be at rehearsals, I've got to! Four responsible female parts, four educated young women, I can't leave them to Stanislavsky, with all my respect for his talent and understanding. I must at least look in on rehearsals' (Chekhov quoted in Lyman, 1976: 162). Stanislavsky's approach was, once again, to begin with a detailed *mise en scène* outlining: 'who must cross to where and why, what he was feeling, doing, how he should look around him, etc.' (2008: 205). Rehearsals started whilst Chekhov was still in Moscow and he attended them again on a short return visit to deliver a number of revisions he had made whilst living in Nice. Interestingly, Nemirovich-Danchenko recalls that Chekhov was more precise in his advice and explanations in his letters than he was when he was present at rehearsals. Certainly, his letters to Olga Knipper and others members of the Art Theatre convey the precision Nemirovich-Danchenko refers to, in a letter to Knipper who plays Masha, he writes: 'Don't look sad in any of the acts. You can look angry, that's all right, but not sad. People who have been unhappy for a long time, and grown used to it, don't get beyond whistling and are often wrapped up in their thoughts. So mind you look thoughtful fairly often on the stage during the conversations. Do you understand?' (quoted in Lyman, 1976: 2).

Nearing the end of the rehearsal period and faced with the imminent dress rehearsal and public performance, Stanislavsky and the actors felt: 'the play had no resonance, no life, it was long and boring. It lacked something' (2008: 205). Rehearsals, as Stanislavsky eloquently describes them, became tortuous as the company explored the 'tone' of the play in an attempt to discover what was missing from the performance. Working late into the night at one particular rehearsal, the company, overcome by despondency, sat silently in the dimly lit rehearsal room, the only sound to be heard was that of someone scratching 'nervously' on the wooden bench on which he was sitting. The sound triggered in Stanislavsky a moment of inspiration, a stirring of something in his emotional memory touched him, and he now began to understand what had been missing:

> The stage was a good place to be. Chekhov's people came to life. They do not wallow in their misery. No, they look for happiness, laughter, well being. They want to live and not vegetate. I felt that this was the right approach to Chekhov's characters, it encouraged me and I intuitively understood what I had to do. (2008: 206)

The first performance of *Three Sisters* took place at the Moscow Art Theatre on 31 January 1901. Stanislavsky recalls that: 'In terms of the acting and directing this production was one of the best things we had done' (207). In terms of the audience response, however, it seemed to be a failure. The first act was successful, resulting in a number of curtain calls, the subsequent acts and end of the play drew 'applause so sparse' that the actors could only take one curtain call (207).

Chekhov was, once again, absent but returned to take an active role in the rehearsals later that year when the play was revived.

Chekhov's final play *The Cherry Orchard*, a comedy in four acts, was written during 1903 when Chekhov was extremely ill and increasingly becoming even more frail. He clearly found work on this play particularly difficult and drawn out, eventually submitting it to the Art Theatre in October. It was immediately evident to Chekhov that there would be problems regarding interpretation, not least because Stanislavsky viewed it as a 'tragedy'. As Fen notes, Chekhov clearly had in mind a comedy from the outset: 'The next play I write for the Art Theatre will definitely be funny, very funny – at least in intention' (Chekhov, 1951: 28). On the advice of a specialist, Chekhov relocated to Moscow for the winter which meant he was able to attend the rehearsals, where he hoped to persuade Stanislavsky otherwise. By all accounts this final collaboration was extremely difficult and, in spite of Chekhov's protestations and explanations, he finally gave way to Stanislavsky's interpretation. The play was produced by the Art Theatre on 17 January 1904, to coincide with Chekhov's birthday and 25 years as a published writer. Special preparations were made to celebrate these events after the performance. Ill health and a reluctance to attend the celebrations prevented him from attending until half-way through the performance. Taking to the stage after the curtain had closed, Chekhov was seized by an 'uncontrollable fit of coughing' and Stanislavsky recalls: 'The celebration was a triumph but it left a heavy impression. It smacked of a funeral and our hearts were heavy' (2008: 237). Chekhov died during the night on 1 July 1904.

It is interesting to note Edward Braun's reference to what Nemirovich-Danchenko wrote some 25 years later:

> There is no denying that our theatre was at fault in failing to grasp the full meaning of Chekhov, his sensitive style and his amazingly delicate outlines [...]. *Chekhov refined his realism to the point where it became symbolic,* and it was a long time before we succeeded in conveying the subtle texture of his work; maybe the theatre simply handled him too roughly.
>
> (Nemirovich-Danchenko quoted in Braun, 1982: 73)

For Raymond Williams it came as no surprise to find that Chekhov was often dissatisfied with what was being done to his plays by Stanislavsky and Nemirovich-Danchenko. Chekhov's drama was clearly ahead of its time, he was in Williams's view: 'a writer of genius beginning to create a new dramatic form [...]. It is now seen as the triumph, but must also be seen as the crisis, of the naturalist drama and theatre' (1987a: 111). 'High' Naturalism as Williams refers to it was remarkably short-lived and, as we have seen, Naturalist playwrights like Ibsen, Strindberg and Hauptman turned to other forms. Russian theatre director Georgii Tovstonogov (1915–1989) pointed out in an article in the 1960s discussing his direction of *Three Sisters*: 'The form which the MAT found for Chekhov was the only accurate one possible at the time' (*The Drama Review*, 1968, 147). For Arnold Aronson in his chapter 'The scenography of Chekhov': 'Chekhov was a Symbolist playwright trapped in a Naturalist theatre' (Gottlieb and Allain, 2002: 134) and this is certainly a view which has been expressed by a number of other critics. It is worth reminding ourselves that other experiments in drama were taking place alongside those of Antoine and his Théâtre Libre and these were concerned with the development of symbolist drama. The two figures with whom we associate this form of theatre are Paul Fort and his Théâtre d'Art founded in 1890 and Aurélien Lugné-Poe who founded the Theatre de l'Oeuvre in 1893.

What then do we find in *Three Sisters* to persuade us of its Naturalism? *Three Sisters* offers the audience a glimpse into the lives of the Prozorov family and a number of other characters who are or become closely associated with the family. As Styan (1971) notes in his very detailed analysis of the play, Chekhov does not focus on any one individual but rather presents the characters as a 'group', we are not drawn to any one particular story but rather observe the behaviour and responses of the group to the changing circumstances around them. There is no plot in the traditional sense but rather a series of moments, or snapshots, rather like those taken at the start and end of the play, when the audience is invited to view the group. In many respects this fulfils Zola's earlier objective in that the audience is presented with a 'case study' of a family living in a provincial town in Russia. The audience is there to observe and analyse these ordinary 'human' subjects, upon whom the past has inevitably had a bearing, and the future remains to be seen. Raymond Williams in discussing what he refers to as the 'structure of feeling' in the play notes:

> As Chekhov explores his world, he finds not deadlock – the active struggle in which no outcome is possible – but stalemate – the collective recognition, as it were before the struggle, that this is so. Virtually everyone wants change; virtually no-one believes it is possible. It is the sensibility of a generation which sits up all night talking about the need for revolution, and is then too tired next morning to do anything at all, even about its own immediate problems.
> (Williams, 1987a: 107)

Three Sisters is a play in four acts, and Chekhov's approach to the structure of the play is an interesting one, the action takes place in the Prozorov home over a number of years, he is never explicit about the passage of time which is left to the audience to determine in relation to what is said or occurs on stage. Between Acts I and II we discover that Natasha and Andrey have married and have a child, Irena has a job at the post office, Andrey works for Protopopov at the local council, and Vershini and Masha have established a more 'intimate' relationship. In the second act, the audience is left to observe the effect of these events as they have become absorbed into the ordinary flow of life. The passage of time in the successive acts reveals Natasha's and, indeed, Protopopov's progressive takeover of the Prozorov home. In the final act there is a second child, Protopopov's, who will shortly take over Andrey's room, and the regiment are leaving the town.

The Naturalist representation of the environment which Simov achieved in his construction of a complete section of the family house may not have been what Chekhov had wanted, but it certainly provided the 'lived in space' that enabled the actors to achieve the quality of acting Chekhov required from his actors.

The setting for the play reflects Chekhov's structure and visually reinforces the progressive 'dispossession' of the sisters and Andrey. The first two acts take place in: '*A drawing-room in the Prozorovs' house; it is separated from a large ballroom at the back by a row of columns*' (Chekhov, 1951: 250). The separation of the space is important, particularly in the first act, where at a practical level it enables Chekhov to deal with the number of characters on stage. More interesting is the way in which Chekhov uses the defined spaces for simultaneous action on stage. Early in the play we find Chebutykin, Toozenbach and Soliony behind the columns, by the table. The significance of this is evident when we examine the dialogue:

OLGA:	[...] I felt so moved and so happy! I felt such a longing to get back home to Moscow.
CHEBUTYKIN:	(*to* TOOZENBACH) The devil you have!
TOOZENBACH:	It's nonsense I agree.

And shortly afterwards:

OLGA:	Yes Moscow! As soon as we possibly can.	
(CHEBUTYKIN *and* TOOZENBACH *laugh*)		(256)

The separation also enables Chekhov to foreground characters. As the group withdraw to the dining table: '(*Only* IRENA *and* TOOZENBACH *remain in the drawing room*)'(267). Later, as the act draws to a close, Chekhov again foregrounds the characters: '(*Loud laughter.* NATASHA *runs out into the drawing room*, ANDREY *follows her*)' (267).

The darkness of the second act provides a contrast to the warmth and light of the previous act: '(*The stage is unlit. Enter* NATASHA *in a dressing gown carrying a candle.*)' (272) and it is on the dimly lit stage that the anxious and loving mother now reveals herself to be mistress of the home: 'NATASHA: Yes it's their house as well.' (273). Act III takes place in: '(*A bedroom now shared by* OLGA *and* IRENA.)' (294) as Irena has made way for Bobik. The final act is set outside in the garden and we find the battalion withdrawing, and the family dispossessed:

NATASHA: So tomorrow I'll be alone here. (*sighs*). I'll have this fir-tree avenue cut down first, then that maple tree over there [...].   (1954: 328)

As Stanislavsky discovered, Chekhov's characters are finely detailed studies of the human subject, each an individual with an extraordinary degree of psychological depth. Chekhov reveals the 'subtleties' and 'nuances' of the characters through the dialogue, gestures and – importantly – through what remains unsaid. This, of course, is the subtext which is so crucial to the representation of the characters on stage.

Writing to the novelist Alexander Tikhonov in 1902, Chekhov says: 'All I wanted to say honestly to people: Have a look at yourselves and see how bad and dreary your lives are! The important thing is that people should realize that, for when they do, they will most certainly create another and better life for themselves. I will not see it, but I know that it will be quite different, quite unlike our present life' (Chekhov quoted in Magarshack, 1980: 14).

CHAPTER SUMMARY

- Until 1882 a state monopoly 'forbade the existence of any public theatres in Moscow and Petersburg save those few under the direct control of the Imperial Court'.
- Shchepkin was largely responsible for raising the standards of the Maly, the State Theatre, 'not only by his own acting but also by training a large number of actors and actresses who became famous on its stage' (Magarshack, 1950: 142)
- Russian theatre was in a 'moribund' state and badly in need of reform. The two key figures with whom we associate this 'reform' are Konstantin Stanislavsky and Nemirovich-Danchenko.
- Stanislavsky saw the work of the Meiningen troupe on their second visit to Moscow in 1890.
- Stanislavsky brought together Alexander Fedotov, Fyodor Kommissarzhevsky and Fyodor Sollogub to found The Society of Art and Literature in 1888, a year after Antoine had established the Théâtre Libre in Paris.
- In 1897 the Moscow Art Theatre was founded and the opening season included a production of Chekhov's *The Seagull*.
- Nemirovich-Danchenko was a writer of the 'psychological school' and, as such, he focused on developing the 'psychological undertones in the acting of pupils, and his first great success in that particular line had been the production at his school of Ibsen's *A Doll's House* in 1896.
- For Chekhov , the production of *The Seagull* had been very important, not only did it establish his reputation as a dramatist and relationship with the Art Theatre, it was where he met his future wife Olga Knipper.

- The Art Theatre subsequently produced all of Chekhov's major plays. In the process, Stanislavsky begun to develop the approaches to acting that still form the basis of much modern actor-training.
- As Stanislavsky discovered, Chekhov's characters are finely detailed studies of the human subject, each an individual with an extraordinary degree of psychological depth, 'His plays are full of action, not outwardly but inwardly' (2008: 193).

SEMINAR AND WORKSHOP TOPICS

1 Reread our chapter on 'The Search for Truth' and explore the ideas developed by Stanislavsky.
2 What were the major influences that led to a more naturalistic acting style in the Russian Theatre?
3 Take the opening scene from *Three Sisters* and work on the sense that meaning is lying beneath the surface.
4 Why do the plays of Chekhov require 'truthfulness' in performance?
5 Select statements from this and other chapters which illustrate the principles of Naturalism.

FURTHER READING

Braun, E. (1982) *The Director and the Stage: From Naturalism to Grotowski*, London: Methuen. This is a classic guide to the work of major directors in the period we are discussing.

Chekhov, A. (1951/1954), *Anton Chekhov Plays*, trans. E. Fen, Harmondsworth: Penguin. One of a number of good translations of the plays which avoid the fustiness of earlier versions.

Gottleib V. and Allain P., eds (2002) *The Cambridge Companion to Chekhov*, Cambridge: Cambridge University Press. A wonderfully rich source of information.

Lyman, J., ed. (1976) *Perspectives on Plays*, London: Routledge & Kegan Paul. Stimulating discussion of texts.

Magarshack, D. (1953/1980) *Chekhov, A Life*, Westport, CT: Greenwood Press. This provides an illuminating discussion.

Magarshack, D. (1980) *Chekhov the Dramatist*, London: Eyre Methuen

Miller, A. (1931) *The Independent Theatre in Europe*, New York: Blom.

Nemirovich-Dantchenko, V. (1936) *My Life in the Russian Theatre*, New York: Theatre Art Books. This provides fascinating insights into the work of the Art Theatre.

Stanislavsky, K. (2008) *My Life in Art*, trans. and ed. J. Benedetti, London: Routledge.

PART IV

The Legacy

CHAPTER 9

The Immediate Legacy

The quintessence of Ibsenism

In a small book simply entitled *Drama* published in 1926, the English theatre manager Ashley Dukes said that 'more than any other writer' the Norwegian playwright Ibsen had 'influenced the stage of our times' (107). Nearly sixty years later, the actor and playwright Ronald Harwood reiterated this claim in his informative television series and accompanying book *All the World's a Stage* (1984). 'Generations of playwrights have laboured in his shadow', he says, 'it was Ibsen's work that restored vitality to the theatre' (215), and later he asserts: 'the influence of Ibsen pervades modern drama. In his own lifetime, his work was argued, analysed and discussed all over Europe' (223).

In this chapter we shall be exploring the truth of these statements and tracing the ways in which Ibsen and his ideas on Naturalism have continued to shape approaches to theatre. Describing a production of *Nora*, Ingmar Bergman's adaptation of Ibsen's *A Doll's House*, the *Guardian* critic Lyn Gardner pointed out in 2012 that 'Ibsen's play might be 130 years old but it retains the power to both shock and grip audiences and its examination of the contracts and compromises of marriage often seems startlingly modern.' This extraordinary sense that Ibsen and his ideas on Naturalism are our contemporary has continued to permeate drama, film and television on either side of the Atlantic. It has now spread to the rest of the English-speaking world, including the Indian subcontinent where a version of *A Doll's House* has been used by the actress Usha Ganguli as the basis of her play *The Journey Within*.

London

Early performances of Ibsen's *Ghosts* were invariably met with outrage and opprobrium from the critics and the first production in England was no exception. It took place as an 'invitation performance' in 1891 as the first production of the Independent Theatre of London, founded by the critic, playwright and theatre manager Jack Grein. Based initially at the Royalty Theatre, and inspired by the work of Antoine at the Théâtre Libre in France, Grein's organization was devoted to mounting plays of artistic and literary merit rather than of commercial value

ILLUSTRATION 7
The legacy. This illustration of a recent production of Ibsen's *Hedda Gabler* in South Korea
demonstrates the playwright's continuing influence on modern theatre practice (direction
and photo by Park Yung Hee)

and in the years that followed, mounted a substantial number of the new 'plays of ideas' that had grown out of the influences from mainland Europe.

Ghosts was not the first play by Ibsen to have been performed in England. That was *The Pillars of Society*, performed in 1880 and, like *Ghosts*, in an English translation by William Archer. It is a frequently told story, but worth repeating, that Archer, who spent many hours at work in the Reading Room of the British Museum, found himself frequently sitting next to the eccentrically dressed figure of George Bernard Shaw, who might be reading anything from the works of Karl Marx to the score of a Wagner Opera. They struck up a friendship that was to have a profound effect on the direction of English theatre. Archer introduced Shaw to the plays of Ibsen and Shaw fell under their spell: in 1886 at a private reading of *A Doll's House* in a house near the British Museum, Shaw played Krogstad and Karl Marx's youngest daughter played Nora, and in 1889 Shaw became infatuated by the actress Janet Achurch, who had achieved a triumph in the role of Nora in its first major production. Writing in his diary, Shaw wrote that his 'next effort in fiction will be a play'. He certainly fulfilled his promise and continued to write plays well into his nineties!

It is, perhaps, difficult for us now to imagine that this 'eccentric and able London socialist, essayist, music critic, Ibsenite, and wearer of grey flannel clothes (*The Times,* quoted *in The Oxford Companion to Theatre)* was, with the exception of Shakespeare, the most frequently performed playwright throughout the world for a substantial part of the twentieth century. His prodigious output, the result of what Nietzsche would have called a 'Dionysian' creative exuberance, has now become somewhat neglected and, indeed, it is more likely that we can see a revival of one of his contemporaries' plays in the modern theatre than one of his. However, Shaw, whose play, *Man and Superman,* is a comment on Nietzsche's concept of the 'Ubermann', was a major force in the theatre of his day. His contribution to the concept that drama is a suitable vehicle for serious issues, ideas and debate is immeasurable and his energetic championing of 'new drama', much of which he directed himself, was a key factor in the encouragement of Naturalism in the English theatre.

Before Shaw was able to complete his first play he turned to writing an essay: *The Quintessence of Ibsenism* (1891), which argued that Ibsen had demonstrated the possibility that drama could change the moral and social order and thus bring about a change in humankind. Many subsequent critics, such as Ronald Harwood (1984), point out that this was, in fact, a misreading of Ibsen, who believed that plays could transform the nature of humankind and, hence, the moral and social order. Nevertheless, even though many of the aspects of Ibsen's writing were overlooked by Shaw, he did highlight the playwright's ability to expose and destroy false ideals and provided valuable insights into many of the lesser known plays. This impetus was much needed for, as J. C. Trewin reported in his revision of Allardyce Nicoll's *British Drama*, one critic sneered: 'To conceive of Ibsen Drama

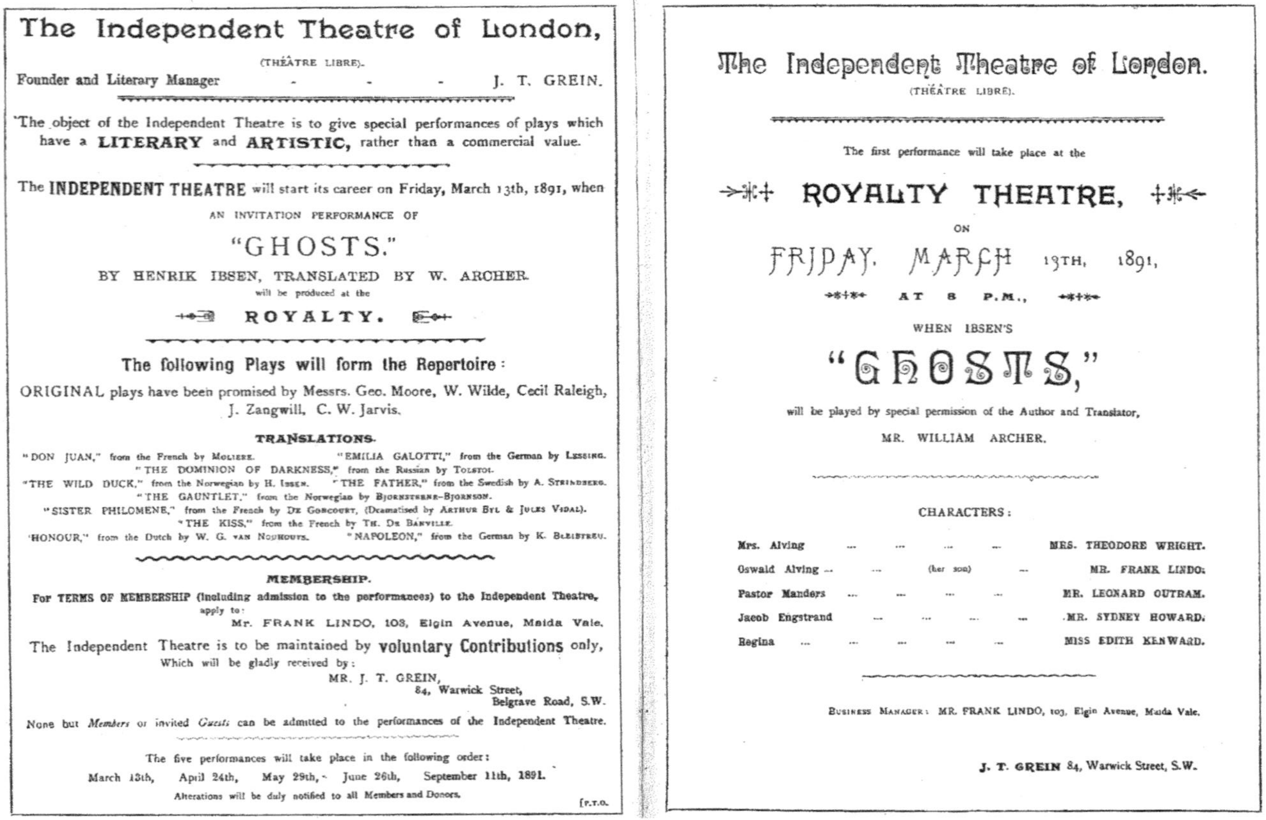

The Independent Theatre of London,

(THÉÂTRE LIBRE).

Founder and Literary Manager - - - J. T. GREIN.

The object of the Independent Theatre is to give special performances of plays which have a **LITERARY** and **ARTISTIC,** rather than a commercial value.

The **INDEPENDENT THEATRE** will start its career on Friday, March 13th, 1891, when

AN INVITATION PERFORMANCE OF

"GHOSTS."

BY HENRIK IBSEN, TRANSLATED BY W. ARCHER.

will be produced at the

ROYALTY.

The following Plays will form the Repertoire:

ORIGINAL plays have been promised by Messrs. Geo. Moore, W. Wilde, Cecil Raleigh, J. Zangwill, C. W. Jarvis.

TRANSLATIONS.

"DON JUAN," from the French by Molière. "EMILIA GALOTTI," from the German by Lessing.
"THE DOMINION OF DARKNESS," from the Russian by Tolstoi.
"THE WILD DUCK," from the Norwegian by H. Ibsen. "THE FATHER," from the Swedish by A. Strindberg.
"THE GAUNTLET," from the Norwegian by Bjornstierne-Bjornson.
"SISTER PHILOMENE," from the French by De Goncourt, (Dramatised by Arthur Byl & Jules Vidal).
"THE KISS," from the French by Th. De Banville.
"HONOUR," from the Dutch by W. G. van Nouhouys. "NAPOLEON," from the German by K. Bleibtreu.

MEMBERSHIP.

For **TERMS OF MEMBERSHIP (including admission to the performances) to the Independent Theatre,** apply to:
Mr. FRANK LINDO, 108, Elgin Avenue, Maida Vale.

The Independent Theatre is to be maintained by **voluntary Contributions** only,
Which will be gladly received by:
MR. J. T. GREIN,
84, Warwick Street,
Belgrave Road, S.W.

None but *Members* or invited *Guests* can be admitted to the performances of the Independent Theatre.

The five performances will take place in the following order:
March 13th, April 24th, May 29th, June 26th, September 11th, 1891.
Alterations will be duly notified to all Members and Donors.

[P.T.O.

The Independent Theatre of London.

(THÉÂTRE LIBRE).

The first performance will take place at the

ROYALTY THEATRE,

ON

FRIDAY, MARCH 13TH, 1891,

AT 8 P.M.,

WHEN IBSEN'S

"GHOSTS,"

will be played by special permission of the Author and Translator,

MR. WILLIAM ARCHER.

CHARACTERS:

Mrs. Alving	...	MRS. THEODORE WRIGHT.
Oswald Alving	(her son)	MR. FRANK LINDO.
Pastor Manders	...	MR. LEONARD OUTRAM.
Jacob Engstrand	...	MR. SYDNEY HOWARD.
Regina	...	MISS EDITH KENWARD.

Business Manager: MR. FRANK LINDO, 103, Elgin Avenue, Maida Vale.

J. T. GREIN 84, Warwick Street, S.W.

ILLUSTRATION 8

Play bill for Ibsen's Ghosts at The Independent Theatre (1891), reproduced from *J. T. Grein – The Story of a Pioneer, 1862–1935*, by his wife Alice Augusta Greeven Grein (London: J. Murray, 1936) gaining an extensive or permanent foothold on the stage is hardly possible' (1978: 194), and another critic was reported by the Irish poet and playwright W. B. Yeats (1904) to have said of the first performance of *A Doll's House*: 'It is but a series of conversations terminated by an accident' (quoted in Cole, 1961: 38).

It took some time for Shaw to complete his first play, *Widower's Houses*. He had begun writing it in 1885, but he finished it in 1892 when he was able to attend its first performance at the Royalty Theatre as part of Grein's Independent Theatre season. He was not pleased with the result but appears to have enjoyed the experience of seeing his plays performed and being the target of criticism, and immediately embarked upon an ambitious period of playwriting, attacking and exposing many of what he considered to be the social evils of his day: prostitution, the arms trade, unscrupulous slum landlords, organized religion, public health provision to name but a few.

The major period of popularity for Shaw's plays was the period from 1904 to 1907 when the initiative of Grein with the Independent Theatre was continued at the Court Theatre (now the Royal Court Theatre) in Sloane Square. The 'thousand performances', as these years have sometimes been named, were the result of a collaboration between the young actor and director, Harley Granville-Barker (who had met Shaw at the Stage Society) and J. E. Vedrenne, the manager of the Court. The Stage Society had been founded to enable new or controversial plays to be given private performances and, encouraged by William Archer, Barker developed Grein's vision to establish a season at the Court that he hoped would include plays by Hauptmann, Sudermann, Ibsen, Schnitzler, Shaw and Brieux.

The play chosen to open the first season was, in fact, Shaw's *Candida* and of the further 31 plays presented at the Court, another ten were to be by Shaw. *Candida* was to remain one of his most popular plays on both sides of the Atlantic, mainly because the characters and their dilemmas are of genuine human interest. The role of Candida provides a challenging and satisfying part for an actress and her husband, the Rev. James Mavor Morell is based on a then well-known figure in the Arts: Stuart Headlam, a Socialist clergyman who opposed the censorious attitude of the Church towards the Theatre.

Many of Shaw's plays have the trappings of Naturalism: detailed descriptions of the characters and settings which (like Arthur Miller's later) often run to several pages; precise stage directions for the performers; some realistic dialogue; and a four- or five-act structure. Shaw clearly aimed to be like Brieux, whose work he admired, 'a ruthless revealer of hidden truth and a mighty destroyer of idols' (Cole and Chinoy, 1970: 57) but he lacked Ibsen's economy and directness or Chekhov's ability to allow meanings to lurk beneath the surface, even though he attempted to imitate both of them. His plays were frequently vehicles for promoting his own socialist ideas and failed to allow audiences to observe human beings struggling with relationships, ideas and moral dilemmas. Remarking on Shaw's work, the famous director Max Beerbohm said that if Shaw had been confronted with the parable of the prodigal son, he would have said that the son was quite right not to work under the dangerous industrial conditions described and that they should be abolished: thus missing the point of the entire story! (quoted in Nicoll, 1978: 199).

By contrast, another of the dramatists to be promoted and 'discovered' by the Court was John Galsworthy, who wrote what John Worthen in an essay on the drama of D. H. Lawrence somewhat condescendingly described as 'what passed at that period for naturalistic drama' (2001: 139). Galsworthy's Court play, *The Silver Box*, which explores ideas of social injustice and the class system, revealed a very considerable ability to create intriguing situations, sympathetic characters and believable dialogue. The sheer craftsmanship of his play and the extent to which Galsworthy embraced the themes explored by other Naturalist playwrights can be demonstrated by examining the way in which he feeds information to the audience in one scene alone. The following issues are hinted at in four pages of Act I, Scene 3:

> The emergence of the Labour Party into British politics.
> The apparent complacency of Liberal and Conservative Parties.
> The threat of socialist ideas to the 'Upper Classes'.
> The concept of patriotism.
> The question of education and its effect on the 'class' system.
> Women's suffrage.
> The idea of trusting the people.
> Attitudes towards women.
> The concept of being 'in service'.
> Over-protective mothers.
> Debt and disgrace.
> The importance of 'name' and 'saving face'.
> The generation gap and fathers claiming that they did not live like their sons.
> Responsibility and irresponsibility in finance.
> Relationships outside the accepted 'social circle'.
> The power and influence of money; even in respect of the law.

In spite of this plethora of ideas, the play never seems contrived or didactic: the audience is simply confronted with human beings in their physical and social environment. In discussing playwriting, Galsworthy made some significant statements concerning his technique and of naturalistic writing in general: 'Good dialogue is character, marshalled so as continually to stimulate interest of excitement' and suggests that, nevertheless, the dialogue must not be divorced from the 'spiritual action' which he defines as the 'progress of events, or towards events which are significant of character'. He warns against twisting character to 'suit his moral or plot' and concludes that the first principle of playwriting is to embrace 'that truth to Nature which alone invests Art with handmade quality' ((*Some Platitudes Concerning Drama*, 1909).

Whilst we may not agree with J. C. Trewin that two of Galsworthy's subsequent plays: *Strife* (1909) and *Justice* (1910) were 'masterpieces' (Nicholl, 1978: 206) and note that none of his work was successful in the United States, these plays, none the less, stirred the public conscience and brought about changes in legislation, ensuring that naturalistic techniques were increasingly seen as powerful modes of theatrical expression in England before the First World War.

Other important plays from the Court period included some significant feminist pieces; all of which relied on naturalistic techniques and centred on the concept of the 'New Woman' in some way. *Votes for Women* (1907) by Elizabeth Robins was a very popular play and placed the Court at the centre of political debate; Cicely Hamilton's *Diana of Dobson's* (1908), which portrayed marriage as a financial takeover, and Elizabeth Baker's *Chains*, which juxtaposed the tyranny of the workplace with the equally intolerable restrictions of domesticity, were equally provocative. J. M. Barrie's one-act *The Twelve Pound Look*, which celebrated the emancipating nature of the typewriter for many women, probably deserves the title of 'masterpiece'.

The problem play and the Manchester School

Many of the plays presented at the Court, including those by St John Hankin and Granville-Barker (which have enjoyed recent revivals) along with those of Shaw, Ibsen and Galsworthy, have been described by critics as 'problem plays' or even 'thesis plays'. A problem play identifies a social problem as its main dramatic thrust but does not necessarily offer a solution. 'It is not my task to answer', wrote Chekhov and, indeed, like Brecht, playwrights of naturalistic plays, which present 'real' situations, have often left it to audiences to provide solutions. The idea of a thesis play is taken from the French *pièce a thèse* and suggests a more prescriptive position taken by the writer in response to the dilemmas of the characters: some would argue that Shaw's or Brecht's plays fall into this category because they seem to advocate a socialist or Marxist solution. Whatever label we attach to the plays written in the early years of the twentieth century, there can be no doubt that more realistic representations of the lives of ordinary, often working, people became central to the energy of the English theatre. This was, by no means restricted to London and one of its most impressive manifestations was what Worthen calls the 'straightforward Naturalism of the Manchester School' (2001: 132).

The creation of a second venue for new drama in a northern city in England was the brainchild of the remarkable Annie Horniman, who was described by Shaw as 'the lady who *really* started the modern movement' and who had already financed the Abbey Theatre in Dublin as a centre for new Irish drama. Not only did Annie Horniman use her own personal fortune to refurbish an old circus and music hall, the Gaiety Theatre on St Peter's Street in Manchester, as a centre for new drama in 1908, she also established the pattern for what was to become the British repertory system in the twentieth and twenty-first centuries.

Annie Horniman was, in many respects, the epitome of the 'new woman': she studied at the Slade School of Art in the 1880s (the first art school to admit women on equal terms with men), had her own apartment, smoked, and rode a bicycle across the continent and over the Alps, and addressed meetings of women's suffrage organizations She was passionate about theatre: had seen her first Ibsen play in German in 1889 and was present when Ibsen himself attended the first performance of *Hedda Gabler* in Munich in 1890.

Manchester, with its rich cultural life and industrial wealth was an ideal centre for Annie Horniman's ambitions to emulate the Court and her first season opened with two Court successes, Shaw's *Candida* and St John Hankin's *The Return of the Prodigal*. However, she was determined to promote new playwriting with a Northern bias and she advertised for new scripts dealing with current, local issues from local writers and promised to read them all herself. Of the writers who responded, Stanley Houghton (1881–1913), Harold Brighouse (1882–1958) and Allan Monkhouse (1858–1936) all produced plays of robust Naturalism and challenging explorations of aspects of contemporary life. These, together with stagings of the plays *Women's Rights* and *Votes for Women*, established the Gaiety Theatre as a major centre for social comment.

Stanley Houghton's play *Independent Means* argues strongly in favour of women's suffrage through the articulate and passionate protagonist, Sidney, and her clear and unbiased view is contrasted vividly with the deeply conservative attitudes of her husband. But it was Houghton's play *Hindle Wakes* that audiences found particularly shocking because it explored ideas of the exploitation of working-class women and the polarities of industrial society that have a peculiar resonance today. It comes as no surprise that a series of very recent revivals of some of the Manchester plays at the Orange Tree Theatre in Richmond, together with supporting seminars, proved immensely popular and successful, for the plays of Houghton, Brighouse and Monkhouse present a realistic yet sympathetic picture of a deeply divided society: the prosperous middle class of mill owners, members of Parliament and business men, on the one hand, and the grossly underpaid and frequently exploited working class who, nevertheless, retain their standards, dignity and fierce sense of independence, on the other. In these plays we also see the issues that Ibsen wrestled with set in the context of a widening divide between the generations that cuts across class barriers. Middle-aged parents are shown as bewildered but conventional and narrow-minded, whilst being constantly obsessed with appearances and respectability, whereas their children appear rebellious, embracing ideas of freedom, especially in sexual matters, equality and increased opportunities. This is especially true of Harold Brighouse's *Hobson's Choice*, which is probably the best known and most frequently performed of the plays. Both *Hindle Wakes* and Alan Monkhouse's recently revived *Mary*

Broome take their starting point from a young girl in work or in service becoming pregnant by a middle-class young man to the confusion and dismay of both sets of parents, but the attitudes and outcomes expose the stubbornness, hypocrisy and sheer lack of communication that continue to victimize women.

The Abbey Theatre

The Abbey Theatre, which has been mentioned earlier, was established in 1904, the same year that Barker and Vedrenne embarked on their venture at the Court Theatre in London. The roots of the Abbey Theatre, as Rowell and Jackson note, lay in the Irish Literary Theatre formed in 1899 by W. B. Yeats, Lady Augusta Gregory and Edward Martyn. The subsequent merger in 1903 of the Literary Theatre and a company of Irish amateur actors run by W. G. Fay, and known as the Irish National Dramatic Society, resulted in the formation of the Irish National Theatre Society. The objectives of the newly formed society were:

> to create an Irish National Theatre, to act and produce plays in Irish and English, written by Irish writers, or on Irish subjects; and such dramatic works by foreign authors as would tend to educate and interest the public of this country in the higher aspects of dramatic art.
>
> (Rowell and Jackson, 1984: 32)

Annie Horniman had known Yeats for a number of years and been a keen admirer and supporter of his work. She continued in this respect, both involving herself in the work of the society and providing important financial assistance. Horniman funded a permanent theatre building for the society and the Abbey Theatre opened its doors on 17 December 1904. Prior to independence at that time, it was the first British repertory theatre to be established. Two years later the society became a professional company, with a board of directors comprising the play-wrights W. B. Yeats, Lady Augusta Gregory and J. M. Synge. Annie Horniman's relationship with the Abbey had not always been an easy one, various members of the society were resentful that an English woman provided the financial support necessary for its development. It was in 1906 with the formal registering of the society that Horniman ceased her involvement (32).

As Allardyce Nicoll notes in *Modern Drama* one of the key characteristics of the Abbey Theatre was: 'the way in which it built its repertory almost entirely from native plays' (1978: 250). The plays emerging from the Abbey playwrights dealt with 'local themes and characters', and more significantly drew on the 'various forms of native speech' which would have a profound influence on the work of English playwrights dealing in local dialect. D. H. Lawrence, discussed later in this volume, was an admirer of J. M. Synge's work and drew a distinction between his plays and other contemporary Irish work produced. For Raymond Williams, Synge's *Riders to the Sea* (1904) is: 'an especially pure naturalist tragedy', whereas *The Playboy of the Western World* (1907) is a: 'significantly localized naturalist comedy'. Synge who, in the Preface to *The Playboy*, dismisses Ibsen and Zola for: 'dealing with the reality of life in joyless and pallid words' (quoted in Williams, 1987: 130) sets his plays among the Irish peasants, a group who: 'from the tinkers to the clergy, have still a life, and a view of life, that are rich and genial and humorous' (130). Synge, whose plays are particularly noted for the quality of 'dramatic language', spent lengthy periods of time living among the 'country people' represented in his drama. During his various visits he assiduously made a record of the language and various phrases he heard:

> This matter, I think, is of importance, for in countries where the imagination of the people, and the language they use, is rich and living, it is possible for a writer to be rich and copious in his words, and at the same time to give the reality, which is the root of all poetry, in a comprehensive and natural form.
> (Williams, 1987: 130)

We should note, however, as Williams points out, that whilst the language Synge drew on was clearly rich and colourful in its authenticity, it is in the final analysis a 'literary product', reworked and shaped for the dramatic form.

Whilst Synge chose to represent the environment of the 'country people', Sean O'Casey in his three early plays focused on the Dublin working class. The plays share a number of characteristics in terms of setting, subject matter and characters drawn from the urban working class. In all three O'Casey presents a 'study' of contemporary life in the Dublin tenements set within the context of an Irish 'nationalism' and a particularly 'turbulent' time in Irish history. In each of the plays *The Shadow of a Gunman* (1922), *Juno and the Paycock* (1923), and *The Plough and the Stars* (1924–25), he selects a specific point during the 'troubles' to explore the pressure of these circumstances on the lives of the working-class inhabitants of the tenements. The first of his plays, *The Shadow of A Gunman*, produced at the Abbey in 1923, is set in May 1920 and draws on the struggle for Irish independence. The second, produced in 1924, is set two years earlier when Ireland, having achieved independence in 1921, is in the throes of a civil war which had broken out over the 'terms of settlement'. The final Dublin play, *The Plough and Stars*, is set earlier in 1915 and 1916, and focuses on the 1916 Easter Rising organized by the Irish Republicans. The production, which took place at the Abbey in 1926, resulted in riots at one of the performances and the subsequent performances necessitated a police guard.

As Ronald Ayling (1985) suggests, in terms of a representation of contemporary reality, O'Casey not only exposes the reality and struggles of 'tenement living' and the violence that invades the tenements both directly and indirectly, he dramatizes events which were very much 'alive' in the experience and 'national consciousness' of the Irish audience. At the time of the first performance of *The Shadow of a Gunman* Dublin was still 'plagued' by the effects of the Civil War and explosions and gunfire remained a feature of 'daily life' (Ayling, 1985). O'Casey clearly draws on his own background and familiarity with Dublin working-class life, as well as the Irish political life he was very much a part of; as Robert Lowery notes, his: 'role as a radical and militant agitator and organizer should not be underestimated' (Lowery in Ayling, 1985: 145)

What we find in these early plays are the detailed directions for setting which we have come to associate with Naturalism and which, as Christopher Murray notes in his introduction to Sean O'Casey's *Three Dublin Plays*: 'show how adept he was in naturalism, with its notion of character controlled by environment and the importance of "will" as a possible means of overcoming its power. Like Zola and Ibsen before him, O'Casey showed that environment was, tragically, all-powerful' (O'Casey, 1998: vii).

However, like Synge, it seems O'Casey also felt that Naturalists concentrated on the worst aspects of reality: 'as if life never had time for a dance, a laugh or a song' (O'Casey, 1998: viii) and the plays are particularly noted for the way in which O'Casey manages to blend the comic with the tragic, drawing on a number of dramatic styles to achieve this. Thus we find in the plays aspects of 'farce', and 'music-hall routine' integrated into the Naturalism. It seems that audiences responded enthusiastically to the humour and 'realistic' representation of the Dublin working-class characters and their 'Dublin dialogue'. In a review published in 1925 for *An Irish Quarterly Review*, the reviewer commenting on the first two of O'Casey's plays notes of the characters: 'It is these types chiefly that delight his audiences in Dublin because we in this city are familiar with them. We love to hear Dublin idioms, such as we listen to daily in our streets, spoken on the stage [...]' (WD, 1925: 494). Like Synge before him, O'Casey's skill lay in his ability to dramatize the Dublin 'proletarian Irish speech patterns' to produce an authentic dialogue which, the same reviewer remarks: 'is wonderfully natural and sponta-neous' (495). O'Casey's plays, which were performed in London and, indeed, America within a few years of their respective Abbey productions, quite possibly, as Ronald Ayling suggests in *O'Casey: The Dublin Trilogy*, paved the way for, and influenced the development of the 'indigenous working-class drama' in the late 1950s in Britain: 'as much as (if not more than) the earlier theatrical successes of the so-called Manchester School' (1985: 9).

Glasgow Rep and Joe Corrie

Following the Court venture and the establishment of Horniman's Gaiety theatre, we find a number of other repertory theatres starting to emerge. Alfred Wareing set up the Glasgow Repertory Theatre in 1909, in Birmingham Barry Jackson's Pilgrim Players evolved into the newly named Birmingham Repertory Company in 1911 and in the same year, the Liverpool Repertory was established. The Glasgow Rep, as Jan McDonald notes in *The Cambridge History of British Theatre: Volume 3*, drew its inspiration from the Court Theatre, both 'ideologically' and 'administratively'. Not only did many of the actors who had worked at the Court go on to work at the Rep, two of them became the principal directors. Not surprisingly the Court repertoire was 'adopted almost wholesale', although, notably, it produced the premiere of Chekhov's *The Seagull* in the year it opened. In other respects it was influenced by the Abbey Theatre who had visited two years earlier in 1907. The Glasgow Rep, similarly, sought to encourage the work of Scottish playwrights and succeeded in producing on average three new plays each season until the outbreak of the First World War when it closed (McDonald, 2004: 198). New playwrights continued to emerge in Scotland but, significantly, nearly all of these, as MacDonald notes, came from amateur societies. One of those playwrights to have emerged from within the amateur groups is Joe Corrie (1894–1968).

Corrie left school at the age of 14 to start work in the Bowhill pits, the conditions of which Linda Mackenney tells us in her introduction to Joe Corrie's *Plays, Poems and Theatre Writings* 'were amongst the worst in the country' (1985: 8). The end of the First World War saw a decline in the production of coal, with the result that Corrie found himself frequently 'on the dole' and it was at this point that he started writing articles, short-stories and poetry, a number of which were published in 'socialist newspapers and journals'. In 1926, Corrie produced his first play, *Hogmanay*, which represents the new year celebrations of a 'typical' mining family. The Bowhill Players, a group of amateurs from Corrie's home town comprised of local miners and their respective family members, toured the play to local mining communities. Late in1926, following the General Strike and subsequent 'lock-out', Corrie started on his first full-length play, *In Time O'Strife*, which he submitted to The Scottish National Players, an amateur company committed to producing and touring Scottish drama. Corrie's play was, in fact, rejected by the SNP, although it was successfully toured throughout Scotland during 1929 by the Bowhill Players under their new name, the Fife Miner Players (Mackenney in Corrie, 1985: 8–9).

In Time O'Strife represents the effects of the General Strike on a mining community by focusing on the Smith and Pettigrew families. The play is set in: 'the kitchen of the Smith's home' (1985: 25) into which the characters come and go, revealing as they do the full extent of their situation. The play examines the effect of these circumstances on the characters' subsequent choices and actions. The play, written in local Scottish dialect, exposes the harsh reality of the striking miners and their families as the strike goes on. With no money and facing starvation, a situation made worse by the withdrawal of Parish funds, the earlier 'unity' of the miners is seriously undermined. The divisions surface in the first act:

WULL: […] What about?

JOCK: What aboot what?

WULL: Makin' a start in the mornin' wi' the rest o' us?

JOCK: Eh! D'ye mean to tell me your canvassin' for blacklegs?

WULL: It's no' blackleggin'. You ken as weel as me that if it's left to the leaders it'll never be finished. The place is in ruination: if the pit doesna open soon it'll never open … A week's work would put you on your feet again.   (1985: 42)

At the end of the second act the family witness from their kitchen window the riots that have been triggered by Wull Baxter's return to work. In the third act set two weeks later, we find that the other young miner, Tam Anderson, who had joined in the riots, faces a three-year prison sentence. The play culminates in the ending of the strike which has seen one of the miners' wives die of starvation, Wull Baxter leaving for Canada without Jenny Smith to whom he had been engaged, and Tam Anderson in prison. Whilst in many respects the play might be regarded as a 'political drama', it is interesting to note Corrie's approach to what we might argue to be the 'political' elements. As McDonald notes, there is a degree of confusion in the miners' understanding of socialism and: 'Bob's repeated cry, "It's a revolution that's needed here", becomes a running gag, picked up by young Lizzie for dramatic effect. No one knows what the "dictatorship of the proletariat" really means' (2004: 202). The play is a fine example of Naturalism which tends to be overlooked in most accounts of Naturalist works. Similarly, Ena Lamont Stuart's *Men Should Weep*, written in 1947 for the Glasgow Unity Theatre and revived at the National Theatre in London in autumn 2010, is a play which also tends to be overlooked but is one which made an important contribution to the representation of working-class life. Lamont Stuart, who sets the play in 1930, represents the effects of the Depression on the lives of the working class living in the Glasgow tenements. As Nadine Holdsworth notes in her chapter 'Case study: Ena Lamont Stewart's Men Should Weep, 1947', Lamont Stewart was frustrated by the post-war Scottish theatre repertoire, wanting instead to see on stage: '"life". Real life. Real people. Ordinary People' (Holdsworth, 2004). Lamont Stewart drew on 'observations and overheard conversations' to achieve the 'broad Glaswegian dialect, idioms and local humour' (2004: 231). Whilst the play drew attention to the reality of working-class life and tenement living and for some was, as Holdsworth points out, a 'powerful sociological document', we should also note that Lamont Stewart was simultaneously criticized for compromising the authenticity of the representation, by overly focusing on tragic events and resorting to a melodramatic murder scene in the final act. Lamont Stewart rewrote the play in 1974, omitting the murder scene, and it was revived in 1982 by 7:84 Scotland along with Corrie's play.

D. H. Lawrence

It is somewhat of a paradox that in tracing the legacy of 'high' Naturalism in Britain during the early twentieth century, we might consider the most important Naturalist playwright to be one whose plays were, for the most part, unpublished and unperformed during his lifetime. D. H. Lawrence is, perhaps, best known as a novelist and poet, the author of novels such as *Sons and Lovers*, *The Rainbow*, *Women in Love* and *Lady Chatterley's Lover*, titles which these days might well be more familiar to the general public as dramatizations for television and film. Less well known is the fact that Lawrence wrote eight full-length plays which, as John Worthen notes, were so 'substantially forgotten' as to leave: 'even competent scholars doubtful about what he had written' (Worthen, 2001: 137). To some degree this is explained by the lack of interest in Lawrence's work as a dramatist whilst he was alive and, consequently, the focus of scholarly writing tended, until the mid-1960s, to concentrate on Lawrence's life and work as a novelist, with only a brief nod to his work as a dramatist. Certainly, as Simon Trussler (2001) points out in his introduction to the Oxford collection of Lawrence's plays, there seemed to be a misconception that Lawrence's drama was somewhat of a sideline and the view, even among the more notable drama scholars, was that Lawrence's plays were of little real significance in the canon of British drama. The perception of Lawrence as a novelist 'who fancied himself as a dramatist with largely unhappy consequences' (Eric Bentley quoted in Lawrence, 2001: xvi) was to prove an error of judgement when in 1965, the Royal Court produced *A Collier's Friday Night*. This event prompted the rediscovery of Lawrence as a playwright and, importantly, a complete 'reconsideration' of his dramatic work.

Sylvia Sklar, who in 1975 produced *The Plays of D. H. Lawrence*, a critical study of Lawrence's drama, draws attention to the difficulties she faced in providing an accurate chronology of Lawrence's early work, and indeed the plays with which we are concerned. As she notes, the evidence is often: 'confused and conflicting and Lawrence's habit of repeated revision makes the task of accurately dating these plays a particularly difficult one' (Sklar, 1975: 9). One of the main problems seems to be a scarcity of evidence in relation to Lawrence's work as a dramatist. Indeed, we only have to consider a collection of his surviving letters written between 1901 and 1913 to find that, whilst they provide a wealth of information about his life and novels, there is really very limited reference to his drama. To date, it seems that this is also the case in the memoirs and published letters of other parties with whom he had contact. As we shall see later in this section, Lawrence tended to simply refer to the 'play' in his correspondence and at times it is unclear which play he is discussing.

However, what we do know, from the careful piecing together of evidence that scholars have undertaken, is that of the eight plays Lawrence wrote, only three were published during his lifetime: *The Widowing of Mrs. Holroyd* (1914), probably written in 1910 ; *Touch and Go* (1920), written in 1918; and *David* (1926), written in 1925. Although Lawrence didn't actually attend the performances, two of his plays were produced, *The Widowing of Mrs. Holroyd* in 1920 and 1926, and *David* in 1927. Following his death in March 1930, the literary agent Edward Garnett published Lawrence's first play, *A Collier's Friday Night* (1909), in 1934. *The Daughter-in-Law* (1913) was discovered after his death, lying among various other manuscripts in his sister-in-law's possession. Seemingly unfinished and 'insufficiently theatrical', it ended up in the hands of the novelist Walter Green-wood who adapted it for production in 1936 under a different title *My Son's My Son* (Sagar, 1985: 59). It was not until 1965, when *The Complete Plays of D. H. Lawrence* was published, that *The Daughter-in-Law* made 'its first appearance'. The remaining plays, *The Fight for Barbara*, *The Merry Go Round* and *The Married Man* were published in various literary magazines from the mid-1930s (Sklar, 1975: 10).

Far from being the 'novelist who fancied himself as dramatist', it is worth noting that he was, in all likelihood, writing his first play at the same time as his first novel *The White Peacock*. Had the reception of his plays been more encouraging at the time of writing, he might well have achieved a reputation as dramatist. As most commentators now acknowledge, Lawrence fully intended each of his plays to be staged as, indeed, his letters reveal to us in *The Letters of D. H. Lawrence* (ed. Boulton, 1979). As early as 1910, Lawrence sent the manuscript for *The Widowing of Mrs. Holroyd* to a friend, Grace Crawford, with instructions to her to pass it on to Violet Hunt, his publisher's wife, in the hope that she would find it: 'fit for staging, after necessary clipping and tinting' (Lawrence quoted in Boulton, 1979: 188). The following year, in a letter to another friend Louie Burrows, we discover that his publisher, Ford Maddox Hueffer (later known as Ford Maddox Ford), had sent the play to Harley Granville-Barker, someone who we might well imagine would have seen merit in the work but who, nevertheless, returned it to Lawrence with the note: 'read it with much interest but afraid I don't want it' (298). On 6 October that year, Lawrence sent the play to his agent Edward Garnett, noting: 'This is the least literary – and the least unified of the three. I tried to write for the stage – I tried to make it end up stagily. – If I send it you at once you can read it at your leisure. The first scenes are good' (309). *The Widowing of Mrs. Holroyd* quite possibly underwent a number of revisions prior to its first performance in 1920, but if we consider the final published text it is certainly the more conventionally dramatic of the three plays. The focus of the play concerns Mrs Holroyd who, married to a miner and a drunkard, falls in love with Black-more, an electrician. Finally persuaded to take her children and move to London with Blackmore, Mrs Holroyd agrees to go with him on Saturday. In the final act, which takes place the following evening, news of Charles Holroyd's death in an accident reaches the family and shortly afterwards his body is brought home. Garnett and Hueffer clearly saw merit in the work, both for potential publication and staging. Indeed, there were a number of occasions when Lawrence seems tantalizingly close to having the early plays published and performed. In a subsequent letter to Louie Burrows, Lawrence confirms that Garnett intended to publish three of his plays but that two had been mislaid by Ford Maddox Hueffer. The missing plays, *A Collier's Friday Night* and *The Merry Go Round* were eventually located and returned to Lawrence in April 1912. In a letter to Garnett on 5 April 1912, Lawrence discusses the return of the plays:

> Mrs. Hueffer is 'so sorry the plays were delayed. They might have taken quite well, while the collieries are in the air. But perhaps it is not too late. You must get them published, with the aid of Mr. Garnett. So you see the fat's in the fire there. The plays are very interesting, but again formless.' Form will never be my strong point, she says, but I needn't be quite so bad. 'But never mind, Ford and I always call you a genius.' I have thanked her for the sarcasm.
>
> (381)

The 'collieries' Mrs. Hueffer mentions are, of course, a reference to Galsworthy's *Strife* which had by now been performed in London, Manchester and Liverpool repertory and which Lawrence had seen with his good friend Jessie Chambers some years earlier.

More frustrating for Lawrence was the initial interest Ben Iden Payne had shown in his work and which amounted to nothing. Iden Payne had collaborated with Annie Horniman, firstly at the Abbey Theatre in Dublin and then latterly worked as her General Manager and director at the Gaiety Theatre in Manchester, before running his own touring company. Lawrence wrote to Edward Garnett to tell him:

> It is huge to think of Iden Payne acting me on the stage: you are like a genius of Arabian Nights, to get me through. Of course I will alter and improve whatever I can, and Mr. Payne has fullest liberty to do entirely as he pleases with the play – you know that. And of course I don't expect to get money by it. But it's ripping to think of my being acted.   (Boulton, 1979: 384)

Lawrence did subsequently have a meeting with Payne in London in May 1912 to discuss the play. Given the reputation of the Manchester School for encouraging new writing and the emphasis on local drama, it now seems unimaginable that the play wasn't picked up by Payne, but then, once again, nothing further transpired. We should note here that there is a difference of opinion as to what play Iden Payne discussed with Lawrence. For Sklar it was *The Widowing of Mrs. Holroyd*, whereas Boulton, in his notes to Lawrence's letter, suggests it was probably *A Collier's Friday Night*, which seems to be Keith Sagar's view too. This serves to illustrate the confusion that accompanies the scarcity of evidence.

Irrespective of this, it is clear that *The Widowing of Mrs. Holroyd* was, as Lawrence had hoped, more appropriate for the stage. Writing to Edward Garnett from Lake Garda in February 1913, Lawrence is undeterred in his efforts to stage his plays:

> I believe that, just as an audience was found in Russia for Tchekhov, so an audience might be found in England for some of my stuff, if there were a man to whip'em in. It's the producer that is lacking, not the audience. I'm sure we are sick of the rather bony, bloodless drama we get nowadays – it is time for a reaction against Shaw and Galsworthy and Baker and Irishy (except Synge) people – the rule and measure mathematical folk [...]. Damn my impudence, but don't dislike me. But I don't want to write like Galsworthy nor Ibsen, nor Strindberg nor any of them, not even if I could. We have to hate our immediate predecessors, to get free from their authority.
>
> (Boulton, 1979: 509)

As Keith Sagar notes, two years later Lawrence was engaged in discussions with Esme Percy with a view to securing productions in Edinburgh, Glasgow and Manchester although, again, nothing came of it at the time. Finally, some five years later, the first performance of the *Widowing of Mrs. Holroyd* took place at the Altrincham Garrick Society performed by a group of amateur actors. The next performance, produced by Esme Percy, took place at the Kingsway theatre in London in 1926 by the 'amalgamated 300 club and the Stage Society'. George Bernard Shaw, who had attended the performance, is said to have commented: 'Compared with that, my prose is machine-made lace. You can hear the typewriter in it' (quoted in Sagar, 1985: 51). The play received mixed reviews, some finding it 'gloomy' and 'sombre', whilst others thought it a 'masterpiece' (Sagar, 1985: 49–50). The play would not be performed again until nearly 40 years later.

When Garnett finally published *A Collier's Friday Night* in 1934, he noted in his introduction that he found the play: 'a bit too artless and diffuse, too lacking in concentration and surprise' for a theatre piece' (quoted in Sklar, 1975: 37). The first of Lawrence's plays is generally regarded to have been written in 1909, although there is much to suggest that it had been written or begun as early as 1906, which coincides with the period in which he was writing and revising his first novel *The White Peacock*, finally published in January 1911. James Boulton, in his notes to one of Lawrence's letters, mentions that on the manuscript Lawrence had written in pencil: 'This was written when I was twenty-one – almost before I'd done anything. It's most horribly green. DHL' (1979: 381).

The exact date of writing is immaterial, what is impressive is that Lawrence had produced a first play of such quality, albeit unrecognized at the time, with very little experience of theatre. Jessie Chambers, Lawrence's closest friend whilst he lived in Eastwood, was responsible for bringing his writing to the attention of the publisher Ford Maddox Hueffer in 1909. She recalls in her memoirs, *D. H. Lawrence – A Personal Record* (1935), that whilst there were often play readings at Hags Farm, the Chambers family home where Lawrence spent a great deal of time, there were only very occasional theatre trips. She mentions only three that occurred whilst he lived in Eastwood, *Hamlet* and *Macbeth* and *La Dame aux Camelias*, which seems to be corroborated in other accounts of Lawrence's work.

There is enormous pleasure to be had in reading Jessie Chambers's memoirs, in which she recalls Lawrence's excitement after seeing the plays: 'Going to the theatre was the same as reading, Lawrence identified himself with the play and for the time being lived in its atmosphere' (1935: 109). In her chapter 'Literary Formation', Chambers provides the reader with a vivid account of their literary pursuits in these early years. Her recollections indicate the nature and scope of Lawrence's reading, a great admirer of Ibsen and Synge he read Balzac and Maupassant. He admired the technique of Flaubert, and Burrows's ability to integrate autobiography and fiction in a way: 'that the most astute critics could not be sure where one ended and the other began' (110). What fascinated Chambers about Lawrence's own early writing: 'was the way he would weave incidents from our daily life into it [...] described with amazing exactness and intensity of observation' (104).

Lawrence, the son of miner and 'a bright vivacious little woman, full of vitality and amusingly emphatic in her way of speaking' (Chambers, 1935: 24) had, at the age of 11, won a scholarship to the Nottingham High School. He left aged 15 to work as an apprentice clerk in a warehouse, which was to be a shortlived working experience interrupted as it was when he fell ill with a bout of pneumonia. Once recovered, Lawrence decided to return to his studies as a pupil teacher at the British School in Eastwood, later joining Jessie Chambers at the Ilkeston Pupil Teacher Centre in 1903. During this period Lawrence appears to have become Jessie's 'self-appointed mentor' helping her with her studies regularly on a Friday night at the Lawrence home: 'It was arranged that I should call at his home for my French lesson on Friday evenings as I returned from the Centre. Friday was the night when the little market was held in the open space in front of the Sun Inn, and we were often left alone while Mrs. Lawrence went to the market. The father I rarely saw. He was always out in the evenings' (56). She recalls: 'Our Friday evenings were not always undisturbed. Occasionally, one or other of the girls who drifted so casually in and out of the house would come in and sit quizzically and the atmosphere would become charged with curious cross-currents of feeling' (59).

In 1904, Lawrence sat the first of several exams, achieving a first in the King's Scholarship, and taught as an 'uncertified teacher' before enrolling at Nottingham University College in 1906, where he dropped the degree course in favour of the 'ordinary college course' which he passed with distinction. It was during his time at college that he concentrated on writing and rewriting his first novel, and quite possibly his first play. In the autumn of 1908, he accepted the post of assistant master at the Davidson Road School in Croydon. It was during a visit to Croydon in 1909 that Chambers first recalls Lawrence showing her his play, *A Collier's Friday Night*: 'There were poems, quite a number that I had not seen, and a play that was about his home on a Friday night. Sitting there in the tiny suburban room, it troubled me deeply to see his home put before me in his vivid phrases' (1935: 166).

The play is set in the Lambert's kitchen and living area, a mining-family home which Lawrence describes in very precise detail in his stage directions, the interior of which bears a remarkable resemblance to Jessie Chambers's recollections of visiting one of the Lawrence homes.. The action of the play takes place over a period of some four hours on the Friday night of the play's title. The play is, as Chambers noted when she read it, drawn from Lawrence's own life and, indeed, we only have to compare Chambers's recollections of the Lawrence family in her memoirs and the Friday nights mentioned above with Lawrence's characters, setting and action to confirm this.

Ernest returning home from college for the weekend would appear to be the figure of Lawrence and Maggie who visits the house for tutoring is clearly based on Jessie. Lambert would, similarly, appear to be drawn on Lawrence's father who, according to Jessie, was rarely seen: 'When he had washed and changed into his "shifting" clothes he went out to join his cronies in the public house' (1935: 35). Beatrice was probably one of the girls who Chambers recalled drifting in, Nellie was likely based on his own sister and, of course, the character of Mrs Lambert on his own mother:

> Mrs. Lawrence, though small was an arresting figure with shrewd grey eyes [...]. Her smallness was more than compensated for by her vigour and determination. All her energy was expended upon her children, who adored her; she was such a contrast to the poor, disinherited father. She was an excellent housewife [...] she could be vivid in speech, gay and amusing and in spite of a keen edge to her tongue, she was warm-hearted. She said quite frankly that she was interested mainly in her sons.
>
> (36)

Lawrence's life and the relationship with his mother is, of course, at the core of much of his writing and explored fully elsewhere in accounts of his life and works. Whilst we have drawn on biographical details in so far as they happen to provide the material of the play, it is important to separate ourselves from the biographical detail in order to recognize the qualities which make it a Naturalist piece of drama. To return to Chambers's memoirs as she draws to a close both in her book and, as it transpired, her relationship with Lawrence, she notes on reading an early version of *Sons and Lovers*:

> His descriptions of family life were so vivid, so exact, and so concerned with everyday things [...]. It was his power to transmute the common experiences

into significance that I always felt to be Lawrence's greatest gift. He did not distinguish between small and great happenings; the common [g]round was full of mystery, awaiting interpretation. Born and bred of working people, he had the rare gift of seeing them from within, and revealing them on their own plane [...]. I felt that Lawrence was coming into his true kingdom as a creative artist and an interpreter of the people to whom he belonged. (198)

Whilst she is writing of her impression of his work as a novelist, we might also say the same of his work as a dramatist where, equally, he demonstrates a 'rare gift of seeing them from within, and revealing them on their own plane'. Let us consider Lawrence's qualities as a dramatist.

As we have seen, the environmental setting is a key feature of Naturalist work, and in Lawrence's lengthy description we not only find what appears to be an 'authentic' representation of a miner's home at the turn of the century with all the attendant features of the working-class kitchen; stove, fire, items of clothing drying or waiting to be ironed, the table laid, bread, we also find a setting that reveals a great deal about the milieu in which the family were living. Within the mining community itself there were distinctions in class, and here in the Lambert home we find chintz, four shelves of books, a book case 'stained polished wood in imitation of mahogany', upon which are 'a Nuttall's dictionary and Cassell's French German and Latin dictionaries' and to the side, framed water-colour prints. As the play opens to offer the audience a brief glimpse into the world of the Lambert family on a Friday night, we find Mrs Lambert in a rocking-chair reading: 'The New Age. Now and again she looks over her paper at a piece of bread which standing on a hanging bar before the fire, propped up by a fork, toasting. There is a little pile of toast on a plate on the boiler hob beside a large saucepan [...]. The woman sees the piece of bread smoking, and takes it from the fire. She butters it ... ' (Lawrence, 2001: 4).

Within this domestic environment the characters progressively arrive, Nellie from the school where she teaches, Gertie eager for Nellie to join her to: 'go jinking off up town and wink at the boys' (6) in her search for someone better than a bacon sawyer or collier. The father 'a miner, black from the pit' arrives, and having deposited his tin bottle and food bag on the table and hung up his coat: 'pours out his tea into his saucer, blows it and sucks it up. Nellie looks up from her book and glowers at him with ferocity' (7). Following a confrontation between the father and his daughter, Ernest arrives home from college and, joining his father and mother, sits:

ERNEST: Give me a bit of paper, Father. You know the leaf I want: that with the reviews of on.

FATHER: Nay, I know nowt about reviews o'books. Here t'art. Ta'e it.

(*Father hands the newspaper to his son, who takes out two leaves and hands the rest back.*)

ERNEST: Here you are; I only want this.

FATHER: Nay, I non want it. I mun get me washed. We s'll ha'e th' men here directly.

ERNEST: I say, Mater, another seven-and-six up your sleeve?

MOTHER: I'm sure! And in the middle of the term too! What's if for *this* time?

ERNEST: *Piers the Ploughman*, that piffle, and two books of Horace, Quintus Horatius Flaccus, dear old chap.   (2001: Act I, 11–12)

This short extract is revealing in a number of ways, it illustrates the level of detail Lawrence provides in his directions for the characters' stage business. In this particular case it is only two lines but elsewhere it is far lengthier. It, none the less, provides an example of the degree of accuracy Lawrence was aiming for in the characters' interaction. The extract also reveals Lawrence's attention to dialogue and the production of authentic speech in relation to the individuals who form the group on stage. This is evident in obvious ways in the dialogue between the father and son, but also in a more interesting and subtler way as he refers to his mother as 'Mater' prior to explaining he needs to buy Latin books.

We find in Lawrence's work a determination to authentically reproduce the language of the Nottingham mining classes in their varying degrees of dialect, and speech patterns, an aspect that is developed further in *The Daughter-in-Law*. What we would also note if we compared *A Collier's Friday Night* to other plays written at the time and, indeed, the work of the early European Naturalists, is the absence of 'exposition'. Lawrence does not concern himself with filling in background details or providing explanations as to who characters are or their subsequent behaviour. The audience must determine this for themselves as a result of what they see and hear on stage. As Sylvia Sklar notes: 'Either intuitively or deliberately, Lawrence has here hit upon a way of presenting meaning which effectively reproduces the way in which meaning is generated in the experience of everyday life. We do not expect ordinary conversation to be fully informative' (1975: 56).

The first act draws to a close with the arrival of Barker and Carlin, fellow miners, who begin the process of dividing the money. Mrs Lambert: *'goes upstairs, it being tacitly understood that she shall not know how much money falls to her husband's share as chief "butt" in the weekly reckoning'* (16). The act ends in silence as:

They begin to reckon, first putting aside the wages of their day men; then the Father and Barker take four-and-threepence, as equivalent to Carlin's rent, which has been stopped; then the Father give a coin each, dividing the money in that way. It is occasionally a puzzling approach and needs the Ready Reckoner from the shelf behind.

(end of Act I, 16)

Within the kitchen setting the audience is introduced to characters who, in their action and dialogue, reveal the external reality and the social and economic environment in which their lives are situated and shaped. Lawrence represents not simply a working-class mining family, but rather a complex group of individuals who make up this family. The closing image is telling, Lawrence's instructions are detailed, providing clear information and motivation for the actors to 'naturalistically' distribute the money. The audience is then left to make of it what they will, there is no unnecessary dialogue to explain who gets what and why. There is no climax to the end of the act, and the second act picks up from the previous scene. In many respects, when we consider the play in the light of other work being produced at the time it comes as no surprise that Garnett and others found it formless and, as O'Casey suggested in his review in 1934, too much of an experiment with form to risk staging, that is until 1965.

A series of rather fortuitous events resulted in what we might now think of as the re/discovery of D. H. Lawrence the dramatist. Granada Television, which had launched the soap opera *Coronation Street* the previous year, produced 'an excellent adaptation' of Lawrence's *The Daughter-in-Law* on 23 March 1961 as part of the television 'play for today' series. Peter Gill, then a director at the Royal Court Theatre in London, had heard about this and requested a copy of the play but in error was sent *A Collier's Friday Night*. Clearly impressed by what he read, he went on to direct the 'first production of D. H. Lawrence's first play' as part of the English Stage Society's Sunday night performances 'without décor' on 8 August 1965. The complete plays of D. H, Lawrence were published in 1965 and Gill subsequently went on to direct *The Daughter-in-Law* in 1967, followed by the 'Lawrence Trilogy' which now included *The Widowing of Mrs. Holroyd* in repertoire at the Royal Court in 1968. Barry Hanson in his rehearsal logbook originally produced for the periodical *Plays and Players* in April 1968, and available on Peter Gill's website, provides an insightful account of the rehearsal process and visits to Nottingham to explore the Eastwood and Bestwood areas.

In his review of 2 March 1968, Irving Wardle, writing for *The Times*, said: 'In two years we have stopped treating Lawrence's plays as an insignificant by-product of his work as a novelist and begun to see it for what it is – British drama's closest relative to Strindberg'. Michael Billington in his review of *The Daughter-in-Law* six days later regarded it as: 'a superb example of stage naturalism at its microscopic best'. Wardle concluded his review with: 'he was born at the right time for the regional drama revival but the wrong place; a few miles farther north and he would have been swept into the Manchester repertory movement. In that case we might not have had the novels but we might have had a British *Miss Julie* and what a play that would have been.'

Wardle is echoing the sentiments of Sean O'Casey, the Irish dramatist associated with the Abbey Theatre in Dublin, and known for his 'working-class' drama, who reviewing the published text of *A Collier's Friday Night* in 1934 believed it to be:

'a play that was worth production when it was first written, and it is worth production now. Had Lawrence got the encouragement the play called for and deserved, England might have had a great dramatist'. But as O'Casey points out: 'the play is too good in essence to ensure a shower of gold into the manager's lap' (O'Casey quoted in Sklar, 1975: 37–8).

The United States: 'Art for Truth's Sake'

Eugene O'Neill's remarkable, semi-autobiographical play *Long Day's Journey into Night* (1941) opens with three pages of detailed stage directions before a word is spoken. The play is set in 1912, in the home of an actor, James Tyrone: an experienced performer of Shakespeare who has become identified with a particular role in a popular melodrama.

Like Ibsen in *Ghosts*, the playwright suggests that an important feature of the room is a collection of books but, in this case, he goes further and specifies the precise titles of the books that fill the bookcase, even though the likelihood of the audience's being able to see those titles is remote. The novels of Balzac and Zola and the plays of Ibsen, Shaw and Strindberg are among the many volumes that give the appearance of having been regularly read and reread. Thus, Tyrone's environment is created and the actor playing him inhabits it: a world of naturalistic drama and prose together with major works of nineteenth-century philosophy, sociology and poetry. Ironically, we discover that Tyrone has never, in fact, played roles from the new naturalistic plays because he has become identified with the more popular, but arguably less serious world of melodrama. This is clearly a source of inner tension and frustration for him.

Long Day's Journey into Night has many of the characteristics of the great European naturalistic plays: very careful attention to the quality of light; detailed stage settings; precise and clearly motivated instructions to the performers; deep psychological exploration and an all-pervading sense of inherited behavioural patterns. Added to this are themes of tedium, self-destruction and determinism that would not be out of place in a play by Zola, Ibsen, Chekhov or Strindberg.

O'Neill, who was probably the single most substantial and important dramatist in America during the first half of the twentieth century, had experimented with various theatrical forms and conventions, including some expressionist and one-act plays. However, he was a great admirer of Strindberg, Ibsen and the leading British dramatist of the day, Shaw, with whom he shared strong Irish roots. As a young man O'Neill had read Shaw's *The Quintessence of Ibsenism* and this had led him to explore the plays of Ibsen and all those authors whose works were on the shelves in James Tyrone's library.

Ibsen's plays had enjoyed a somewhat smoother passage in America than in England. This was partly because sizeable sections of the first-generation immigrant population of America had been able appreciate the plays in their own language rather that in the rather stilted English translations. For example, the world premiere of *Ghosts* in Chicago was performed in Norwegian and in 1892 the first American performance of *An Enemy of the People* was performed in German. This latter play was written as an angry riposte to the hostile reception accorded to *Ghosts* and its protagonist Dr Stockmann, who discovers that a town's water supply has been contaminated, had been one of Stanislavsky's most memorable roles as an actor. Lashing out at corruption and double standards, Stockmann indirectly voices Ibsen's fury at the supposedly enlightened and progressive public and critics who had been shocked by *Ghosts* and, casting doubt on the entire democratic principle, maintains that it is the 'minority' who is always right. The play's reception was key to the spread of Ibsen's influence throughout the international theatre world: some critics likened the role of Stockmann to Émile Zola, whereas the Moscow Art production coincided with the massacre in Kazansky Square and the words of Dr Stockman, 'never put on a new coat when one goes to fight for freedom and truth', had particular resonance. Perhaps more importantly for our purposes, the initial production of *An Enemy of the People* in Norway in 1882 provoked some of the clearest statements on the achieving of Naturalism in the theatre ever made by Ibsen. Writing to the manager of the Christiana Theatre concerning Act IV of the play he said:

> The stage director must here enjoin the greatest possible naturalism and strictly forbid any caricaturing or exaggeration [...] above all truthfulness to nature – the illusion that everything is real and that one is sitting and watching something that is actually taking place in real life.   (1980b:118)

So concerned was he that the first production of this play would in no way resemble the operettas, romantic melodramas and vaudeville performances that were popular at the time that he wrote again a few weeks later:

> [...] for in these the prime requirement is unqualified illusion; every member of the audience is fully conscious throughout the evening that he is merely sitting in a theatre watching a theatrical performance. But this should not be the case when *An Enemy of the People* is being acted. The spectator must feel as though he were invisibly presenting Dr Stockmann's living room.   (119)

It was principles like these that inspired theatre practitioners on both sides of the Atlantic to attempt to achieve what Ibsen had set out. It was also this play that was later to be adapted for a modern, English-speaking audience in America by the dramatist Arthur Miller.

Early indications of the search for truth in American theatre had occurred in 1891 in Boston where the writer Hamlin Garland put forward a proposal for a new kind of theatre that he wanted to call 'The First Independent Theater Association', with one of its objectives being 'to encourage truth and progress in American Dramatic Art'. In his prospectus he indicated that he would aim to introduce famous modern plays by the 'Best Dramatists in Europe' and that the Freie Bühne of Berlin, the Théâtre Libre in Paris and the Independent Theatre of London would be providing 'helpful hints'. Although Garland's plans did not materialize, it is significant that an awareness of very recent developments in Europe lay behind his ideas and it would appear that he also greatly admired the dramatist James A. Herne, who was Ibsen's earliest and initially most successful imitator in America. Herne had himself been encouraged by Garland and the critic and writer William Dean Howells (1837–1920) who has sometimes been called the 'Father of American Realism'. One-act plays by Howells had achieved some success in the late nineteenth century and, like Ibsen, whose work he was among the first to champion, he discovered that it was the language of everyday life that achieved the degree of realism he sought. Herne, however, went a good deal further and his articles and plays demonstrated a passion for truthfulness and detail.

Writing in *Arena* (1897), Herne entitled his article 'Art for Truth's Sake in Drama'. He argued that drama should both 'interest' and 'instruct' and that its 'supreme quality' must be 'truthfulness'. He insisted that: ' It must first express some *large* truth', 'it must always be representative'. In order for art to convey truth he maintained that it needed to be both 'serious' and able to 'perpetuate the life of its time': these qualities, he suggested, could only be achieved by an emphasis on 'humanity'. To these assertions he added: 'Truth is not always beautiful', and he went on to demonstrate this in his own plays.

Herne's earliest works for the stage had been melodramas, some written in collaboration with David Belasco who, like Henry Irving, was notorious for the scrupulous detail and spectacle of his productions. However, Herne maintained that: 'The domestic drama always appealed to me [...] the simpler the play the better for me', and he soon began to experiment with a more naturalistic style of writing. By the time he came to write his most celebrated play *Margaret Fleming* in 1890, he was showing a profound interest in Darwinism, heredity and determinism. Indeed, in applying many of the principles of Ibsen to his playwriting, he created a theatrical experience that was as devastating and shocking to contemporary audiences as *Ghosts* had proved.

The protagonist of the play, Margaret, is a highly sensitive woman who suffers from a disease which would result in blindness were she to receive a severe shock. By contrast, her husband Philip is a faithless philanderer whose attitude to his wife, child and business is of a doubtful moral nature and characterized by a 'live and let live' philosophy. The anticipated shock for Margaret comes when she discovers that the unmarried sister of her child's own nurse has died giving birth to Philip's baby, so, once again, we see the impact of infidelity involving a 'master of the house' and those 'in service'. The final act shows some similarities with

Ibsen's *A Doll's House* because it does not hint at reconciliation. Margaret is blind and Philip makes an ignominious return to the home of his wife and two children. However, the play ends with an enigmatic smile from Margaret that suggests her sense of both moral superiority and of hope.

Such was the disquiet expressed by critics and audiences after the first productions that Herne was persuaded to re-work the final act to climax in an ambiguous possibility of reconciliation. But, as Walter Meserve points out, in spite of its weaknesses, this play was to shape the direction of American drama in a profound way:

> Although the moralizing of Margaret's doctor, is extremely heavy-handed, the truthfulness of the dialects, scenes and the characters in particular is everywhere emphasized. Symbolism is effective in a song that Margaret sings as well as in the comments on the care of roses. The concept that Margaret reveals through her cry that 'truth has killed her' is a reference to Ibsen's work which appears again in Herne's commentary on double standards, medical practices and the scene during which Margaret unbuttons her blouse to nurse the newborn child.
>
> (Bogard, Moody and Meserve, 1977: 192)

Herne himself admitted to the play's faults but was equally aware of its significance: 'didactic in places', he wrote, 'but there has been nothing *just* like it given to the stage (1996: 7).

Much of the outrage caused by the breastfeeding scene was reminiscent of the reception accorded to *Ghosts*, which one critic had described as a 'dirty deed done in public'. But is also showed a playwright who, like Ibsen, was making a plea for freedom from the stifling respectability of Protestant values. For, whereas Ibsen wrote in the context of the severely puritanical Lutheran Church, Herne was constantly wrestling with his equally restricting Dutch Reformed background. *Margaret Fleming*, which had its first performances in a hired hall in Boston, was not a commercial success and its significance has only been appreciated relatively recently.

It was to be some years into the twentieth century before a distinctively American naturalistic drama was to appear on Broadway but the foundations were laid in the early years of the century by the work of a growing number of 'Little Theatres' and subsequently, 'Art Theatres'. The Little Theatres were invariably amateur or community theatres where groups of enthusiasts experimented with the new, naturalistic plays from Europe and successfully introduced the works of Strindberg, Hauptmann, Gorky, Ibsen, Shaw and Chekhov to American audiences. Writing in 1908, the critic Walter Clifford Eaton pointed out that the predominant influence on an emerging American drama was undoubtedly the plays of Ibsen: 'There has come over native writers', he wrote, 'an increasing desire to comment on contemporary life as well as to reflect it' (quoted in Downer, 1965: 21).

However, for a truly original drama to be born, it was also necessary for there to be professional involvement and this was achieved most notably in 1915 by the founding of the Provincetown Players, who set up on Cape Cod in Massachusetts, and the Washington Square Players in New York, who eventually became the Theatre Guild.

A very significant play from this period is the one-act piece *Trifles* (1916) by Susan Glaspell who, with her husband George Cram Cook, was one of the founders of the Provincetown Playhouse. Although this theatre is best known for having established the career of Eugene O'Neill, *Trifles* shows a very original talent exploring the idea of the impact of society on individuals through using the techniques of Naturalism. This can be clearly demonstrated by examining the playwright's stage directions for this play, which is based on a real-life situation of a woman accused of her husband's murder. In the opening moments Glaspell specifies that the scene is:

> The kitchen in the now abandoned farmhouse of John Wright, a gloomy kitchen and left without having been put in order – unwashed pans under the sink, a loaf of bread outside the bread box, a dish towel on the table – other signs of uncompleted work

Thus, by insisting on the quality of light and the detail of the domestic setting, the playwright has already enabled the audience to enter the world of the play. When the characters who are to inhabit this environment enter from 'an outer door at the rear', both their personal appearances and the mode of their entry is also clearly indicated: the Sheriff and Hale, we are told, are men in '*middle life*' and the County Attorney is a '*young man*'. They are all '*bundled up and go at once to the stove*'. The two women, the Sheriff's wife and Mrs Hale follow them in, but come '*slowly*' and '*stand close together near the door*'. The playwright enhances the sense of hesitancy and the difference between the confidence of the men and that of the women by explaining that the Sheriff's wife is a '*slight, wiry woman, a thin nervous face*' and that Mrs Hale is '*larger and would be called more comfortable looking, but she is disturbed now and looks fearfully about as she enters*'. These details have all the hallmarks of Naturalism and, before a word has been spoken, the communication of information has been intense. Glaspell also clearly envisages a 'fourth wall' in her stage setting (see Antoine), because the opening line is spoken by the Attorney '*rubbing his hands*' and suggesting 'Come up to the fire ladies'. We have already seen that the playwright has established the chill in the atmosphere and now the characters gather round a stove, which is obviously envisaged to be in the downstage 'fourth wall' as they face the audience for their dialogue.

A more intense item of naturalistic detail is contained in the stage directions that occur in the closing moments of this short play. Whilst the three men have been discussing and attempting to investigate the cause of John Wright's murder, the women have arrived at a solution by a combination of intuition and careful thinking. The key moment has been when in the women's conversations, it has emerged that Wright had killed his wife's beloved caged bird: an action that has prompted his wife to seek revenge. The killing of the bird is, perhaps, reminiscent of the use of birds as images of freedom in such plays as *The Wild Duck* (Ibsen) or *The Seagull* (Chekhov) or the killing of the bird in Strindberg's *Miss Julie*. It is an act of cruelty and provocation that appears to have precipitated the murder of a husband by his wife. Somewhat incongruously, however, the normal activity of Wright's wife has been quilting. The following stage directions describe what happens at in the final moments of the play's action:

> (HALE *goes outside. The* SHERIFF *follows the* COUNTY ATTORNEY *into the other room. Then* MRS HALE *rises, hands tight together looking intensely at* MRS PETERS, *whose eyes make a slow turn, finally meeting* MRS HALE'S. *A moment* MRS HALE *holds her, then her own eyes point the way to where the box is concealed. Suddenly* MRS PETERS *throws back quilt pieces and tries to put the box in the bag she is wearing. It is too big. She opens box, starts to take bird out, cannot touch it, goes to pieces, stands there helpless. Sound of knob turning in the other room.* MRS HALE *snatches the box and puts it in the pocket of her big coat. Enter* COUNTY ATTORNEY *and* SHERIFF.)

In important respects, Eugene O'Neill, who was to emerge as the first truly international 'great dramatist' from America followed the lead of these early plays.

Like Shaw, he provided extensive notes on the characters in his plays, sharing, perhaps, a determination that the performances would capture precisely what he envisaged rather than leave anything to the whim of producers (or directors as we would now call them) and dictating in far more detail than Ibsen or Strindberg the precise characteristics of each individual as they made their first entrance.

Shaw and O'Neill were also influenced by the writings of Darwin and of Nietzsche (see p. 55), although Bogard suggests that O'Neill's reading of Nietzsche was somewhat selective and focuses more on the emotional than the philosophical (Bogard, Moody and Meserve, 1977). For Bogard, the distinction made by Nietzsche between the 'Apollonian' and Dionysian' in his *The Birth of Tragedy* marked a fascinating connection and difference between Shaw and O'Neill. Shaw, he maintains, presents characters who strive towards a 'higher and more conscious plane of being' through education and this is an 'Apollonian motion', and for O'Neill 'the movement is Dionysian – towards the rapturous immersion of the conscious self into a centre of life-energy that is unchanging' (75).

He continues: 'Shaw is movement; O'Neill is stasis. Shaw is consciousness; O'Neill forgetfulness; Shaw is thought; O'Neill is memory. Shaw is ascetic; O'Neill is drunken. Shaw is visionary; O'Neill dreams. Shaw seeks life and O'Neill loses it' (Bogard, Moody and Meserve, 1977: 75). The same driving, creative life-force inspired Shaw to write plays of immense length and topical relevance for the growing number of Little Theatres in England.

Not everyone in America was enthusiastic about the plays from Europe which provided an impetus for the writing of psychological and naturalistic drama. Surveying the plays being presented in New York during the 1920s, for example, the critic George Nathan argued that they uniformly conveyed a depressing and negative view of life and he singled out three plays by Ibsen:

> Thus further, Ibsen's *Little Eyolf,* aiming to be a sermon against selfishness, actually makes mankind bitterly despairing with its demonstration that egoism, which is mortal man's one pragmatic religion and his one potential victorious battle cry, is the faith of the humiliated and defeated; *Hedda Gabler* instils a sense of utter futility of life by showing that the bad angel of man's destiny holds ever the whip hand: and *John Gabriel Borkman* puts hope and trust to rout with its doctrine of the eternal cruel indifference of one's offspring and with its categorical enunciation of age's chagrin and suffering. (quoted in Downer, 1965: 88)

However, a growing number of playwrights embraced the influences from Europe, and we might ask where this new generation of playwrights hoped to find actors capable of responding to the level of psychological realism envisaged in their plays when so many had been accustomed to performing in popular melodrama. To give one concrete example, how might such performers respond to Glaspell's suggestion that they 'go to pieces'?

Increasingly, it would seem American naturalistic plays would require naturalistic acting and this need was to be developed in the United States by the arrival of two members of Stanislavsky's Moscow Art Theatre company: Richard Boleslavsky and Maria Ouspenskaya. On arrival in the United States they immediately began to teach the system of approaches to acting pioneered by Stanislavsky, and in 1923 Boleslavsky founded the American Laboratory Theatre. Among his students were Lee Strasberg, Stella Adler and Harold Clurman, all of whom were founder members of the influential Group Theatre which, between the years 1931 and 1940 was the first American company to employ the adapted techniques of Stanislavsky that, particularly following Strasberg's teaching, comprised what became known as 'Method' acting.

What emerged from the Group Theatre ensemble was a generation of actors who brought new levels of truth to their appearances in plays and films. Under the influence of Strasberg, such actors avoided the sense of performance, and direct contact with audiences so common in actors of that time. They eschewed the notion that they should be admired or adulated for themselves, preferring to bring aspects of their own lives to enrich their deep understanding of the characters they sought to portray. They engaged in profound personal analysis and in detailed analysis of the text: discovering in the playwrights' works small units and 'beats' to which they could give shape and in which they could discover motivations and relationships. Employing deep levels of concentration, the 'Method' actors were able to bring a new level of psychological realism to their parts and an equally profound degree of detail that was especially effective on film and, eventually, on television. To some extent, the difference between the 'Method' actor and the approach which it replaced has remained as a division between American and English acting, for, as the critic and translator of Brecht, Eric Bentley, put it in 1954:

> a new type of American actor has evolved [...] it is a deliberate American alternative to the elocutionary 'style acting' that we import from England.
> (quoted in Downer, 1965: 194)

Responding to the arrival of this 'new type of actor', playwrights like Eugene O'Neill and Arthur Miller made increasing demands for authenticity in precise actions and expressions in their plays. O'Neill's play *Dynamo*, for instance, contains over 400 stage directions for the actors in the first act alone!

Arthur Miller and Tennessee Williams were to emerge as the leading playwrights in America in the years following the Second World War. The debt that Miller owed to Ibsen with his concern for 'ideas, with the practical function of society, with people's failings and aspirations' (Harwood, 1984: 276), is clear to see. When, therefore, Miller was caught up in the anti-communist hysteria that led to the McCarthy hearings for 'un-American activities' Miller responded by making an adaptation of Ibsen's *An Enemy of the People*, which focuses on a protagonist who stands firm against the ignorant masses. The play opened in New York in December 1950 and was subsequently presented in both television and film versions.

By contrast, Tennessee Williams, the other major American dramatist to emerge in the immediate post-war years, appears to owe much of his inspiration to Strindberg and Chekhov. His plays are peopled by the neurotic, the sexually repressed and the socially inadequate. Frequently aimless and directionless, the characters seem to inhabit a dreamy, intangible world, often dense with what we would now see as Freudian symbolism. His perception of human beings appears to be based, like Strindberg's and Chekhov's, on an understanding of the tortured self and the feeling of helplessness that emanates from it. Fortunately for the playwright, actors schooled in the profound psychological insights provided by the 'Method' brought their naturalistic skills to his plays and, in performing such roles as Blanche Du Bois and Stanley Kowalski in *A Streetcar Named Desire*, created some of the iconic characters of twentieth-century drama. Williams's plays, were not, like Miller's 'issue' or 'problem' plays and had no element of the didactic about them, they were frequently accurate studies of the disintegration of personalities, almost in the manner of Zola.

Critics and commentators on the development of American drama in the twentieth century have invariably drawn attention to the debt owed by its playwrights to the great Naturalist writers of Europe without implying that they had not developed distinct and powerful individual voices of their own. This is certainly the case with two major television series and their accompanying publications: Ronald Harwood's *All the World's a Stage* (1984) and Richard Eyre and Nicholas Wright's *Changing Stages* (2000). This latter offers a typical comparison between Arthur Miller and Tennessee Williams:

> And of course you can say that Tennessee Williams traced his lineage from Chekhov as Arthur Miller did from Ibsen – the one colonizing the territory of the personal, the other the political, the rackety, forgiving poet of the heart and the assured and assertive poet of the conscience. (182)

Eyre and Wright also go so far as to suggest that the now neglected Clifford Odets, who came into prominence through the same Group Theatre that spawned the 'Method', had Chekhov as his model, even though he was not aware of it at the time! He shared Chekhov's realism about life's compromises, his cool draughtsman's eye, his forgiving heart, and his reluctance to have plot rather than character drive the action. He also shared Chekhov's politics: things should be better, and you must live your life better my friend. But Odets was an American, and as such half in love with the dreams that he deplored (158).

CHAPTER SUMMARY

- The principles and practices of Naturalism were largely introduced to Britain and the United States through the works of Ibsen.
- Ibsen's play *Ghosts* was frequently the vehicle for the spread of Naturalism.
- In both Britain and America naturalistic plays were promoted through small-scale, private theatres that took their inspiration from Antoine's Théâtre Libre and Brahm's Freie Bühne
- George Bernard Shaw in Britain and James Herne in the United States were key figures in the promotion of Ibsen's work.
- Grein's 'Independent Theatre' and subsequently, the Court Theatre in London were major centres for promoting new writing in the naturalistic mode and this extended to Manchester through the initiative of Annie Horniman.
- The Abbey Theatre in Dublin opened on 17 December 1904. The objective was to encourage Irish playwrights to produce 'native' drama. J. M. Synge and Sean O'Casey are key dramatists associated with The Abbey.

- Amateur theatre societies played an important role in providing opportunities for new emerging playwrights in the early decades of the twentieth century. The work of Scottish playwright and poet Joe Corrie is one example. His play *In Time O'Strife* was produced by his local amateur group The Bowhill Players.
- D. H. Lawrence's drama was rediscovered in the 1960s.
- One of the most familiar features of the 'new drama' was its promotion of the 'new woman'.
- Naturalism established itself on both sides of the Atlantic as the dominant mode for modern drama: America's greatest playwrights embraced its ideas and forms.
- In order to present naturalistic plays in the United States, the 'Method' approach to acting was developed. It is characterized by deep, psychological insights and a thorough exploration of motivation, and was created by followers of Stanislavsky.
- Although apparently opposing ideas of Naturalism, the plays and productions of Bertolt Brecht drew on and developed many of its features.

SEMINAR AND WORKSHOP TOPICS

1 Identify and compare a number of plays that take 'young women in service' as a major theme. Research the conditions of 'service' and find out if any of your ancestors had these experiences.

2 What were the issues that motivated: (a) Shaw, (b) Annie Horniman, and (c) Susan Glaspell?

3 Identify the various 'small' theatres described in this chapter. Why did so many developments in naturalistic drama depend on these theatres?

4 Work on scenes from some the 'Manchester' plays that explore the generation gap.

5 Explore the way in which the characters' behaviour is determined by the environment in one of the plays which make up *The Three Dublin Plays*.

6 Compare Joe Corrie's *In Time O'Strife* with one of D. H. Lawrence's mining plays.

7 What were the characteristics of the 'New Woman'? Present a workshop performance of speeches by such women taken from the plays identified in this chapter

8 Compare D. H. Lawrence's mining plays with Galsworthy's *Strife*.

9 Work on a scene from an American, naturalistic play using what you consider to be the approach developed as the 'Method'. Identify movies and productions where you have seen this approach. How does it differ from what Stanislavsky was aiming for?

10 Discuss and reproduce the arguments about the differences between Naturalism and Realism as put forward in the *Messingkauf Dialogues*.

FURTHER READING

Ayling, R., ed. (1985) *O'Casey: The Dublin Trilogy – A Selection of Critical Essays*, Basingstoke and London: Macmillan. This provides some extremely useful contributions to our understanding of O'Casey's Dublin plays.

Bogard, T., Moody, R. and Meserve, W. J., eds (1977) *The Revels History of Drama in English*, Vol. VII: *American Drama*, London: Methuen. Gives a most comprehensive overview of the impact of European Naturalism on the United States

Downer, A., ed. (1965) *American Drama and Its Critics*, Chicago, IL: University of Chicago Press. Remains an invaluable collection of essays on the American aspects of this chapter.

Eyre, R. and Wright, N. (2000) *Changing Stages*, London: Bloomsbury. A lively and provocative account of English-speaking theatre in the twentieth century, including the impact of Brecht.

Glaspell, S. (1916) *Trifles*, in W. B. Worthen, ed., *The Wadsworth Anthology of Drama*, Fourth Edition, London: Cengage Learning, 2004. This anthology is available in many editions and each contains the texts of, and helpful guidance on, many of the plays from Europe and the United States that we have discussed.

Goodie, S. (1990) *Annie Horniman: A Pioneer in the Theatre*, London: Methuen. A valuable source of information on the Manchester School.

Nicoll, A. (1978) *British Drama*, London: Harrap. J. C. Trewin's 'Revised Edition' of this now neglected text provides some fascinating opinions on early twentieth-century drama.

Pogson, R. (1952) *Miss Horniman and the Gaiety Theatre Manchester*, London: Rockliff. A colourful evocation of the career of this extraordinary woman.

Sklar, S. (1975) *The Plays of D. H. Lawrence: A Biographical and Critical Study*, New York: Barnes & Noble. A detailed study of Lawrence's plays.

CHAPTER 10

The Royal Court Again

It is interesting to note that many accounts of mainstream theatre in London in the early 1950s are uncannily similar to those describing the theatre at the beginning of the nineteenth century. We get the impression of a theatre dominated by a small 'group' of financially astute theatre managers concerned with profit and largely producing entertainment which was guaranteed to appeal to the middle-class theatre-going public. Bound as they were by financial considerations, the producers were reluctant to produce new plays, relying instead on the 'long run' of popular plays drawing audiences with the 'star' actor. It was, it seems, very much an 'actors theatre' and there was little to encourage the emergence of new dramatists. What we tend to find on stage at this point are the plays of J. B. Priestley, Noel Coward, the middle-class 'drawing room' plays of Rattigan, and the poetic work of Fry and Eliot. Of course, this is not the whole picture but rather a reductive assessment of the situation, as Dan Rebellato quite brilliantly critiques in his introduction to *1956 And All That* (1999), arguing: 'the theatre of the forties and early fifties was quite unlike the theatre we have been told it was' (1999: 8).

Of course, there had been enormous changes brought about by the 'new' dramatists and directors at the turn of the century, the legacy of which had been the repertory theatre movement, numerous experimental independent theatre societies and amateur theatre companies operating throughout the United Kingdom which continued to offer opportunities for more experimental theatre. The two world wars had subsequently made an impact on the make-up of the theatre-going audience, the development of theatre and organization of theatre and, importantly, the organization of the arts. In 1934, ENSA (Entertainments National Service Association) was established and subsequently CEMA (Council for the Encouragement of Music and the Arts) which evolved into the Arts Council. We discover that the Scottish dramatists, dealt with elsewhere in this book, had been producing social realism before the 'new wave' dramatists took to the stage. Overall, however, it seems the intervening period which had seen two world wars had significantly interrupted any real development. In much the same way as the leading figures of 'new drama' some 50 years earlier had sought to bring about an experimental theatre to encourage new playwrights along the lines of the European model, we find now a new group of individuals who, in many respects, take up the project once again. Whilst the history of The Royal Court theatre has been well documented it is worth considering in some detail the origins of the English Stage Company at the Royal

Court, the theatre in Sloane Square which had been so instrumental in providing the venue for the Vedrenne Barker season from 1904 to 1907, and which was, once again, to play an important role in the development of British theatre.

The English Stage Company

The life of this small theatre had been curtailed in 1932 when it closed. It was later sold and reopened as a cinema only to be closed again during the blitz. It began 'its new lease of life' in 1952, when Alfred Esdaile bought it with a view to turning it into 'a theatre club' after undertaking the necessary repairs which had resulted from war damage. While Esdaile was occupied in Sloane Square with his new project, elsewhere two other quite separate groups of individuals were similarly developing plans for their own respective theatre projects.

In Devon, the seeds of what would become the English Stage Company were being cultivated by the founding members of the Taw and Torridge Festival. Having established the festival in 1953, the group were increasingly concerned about the unpromising quality of drama being programmed into the festival. Unable to attract professional companies to contribute, the members began to develop their own ideas to form a production company, with the aim of initially producing work for the festival and later extending this to other festivals and theatres. For Ronald Duncan, one of the founder members and a playwright himself, this would provide an opportunity to ensure the production of his own plays. When in 1954 he was attempting to do exactly that, he drew on the skills of Oscar Lewenstein, the then General Manager at the Royal Court and part-time 'impresario', to negotiate with theatre venues for the production of two of his plays. As a result of these negotiations Lewenstein became drawn into the development of the production company which by the end of the year had become formalized: the English Stage Company was now established. The committee of eight members now included Lewenstein and, at his suggestion, Alfred Esdaile, owner of the Royal Court, who allowed the company use of the Royal Court offices to conduct their affairs. By the time the company has been formally registered, their ambitions had extended to the rental of a London theatre in which they could actually produce work. Esdaile, owner of another theatre, offered to lease them the Kingsway which, badly damaged during the war, had remained closed. All efforts now went into securing funding for the renovation of Kingsway.

Meanwhile, some years earlier George Devine, together with Michel Saint-Denis and Glen Byam Shaw, had been involved in the Old Vic Theatre Centre initiative which had been established in 1946. The centre was in many respects a continuation of the London Theatre Studio, which Devine had assisted Michel Saint-Denis in successfully running from 1936 until the outbreak of war forced its closure in 1939. The Old Vic Theatre Centre comprised a theatre training school running alongside the Young Vic company to showcase the actors' talents. The hope was to eventually create a purpose built environment for the venture (Browne, 1975: 5). By 1951 the Centre was in crisis, 'the three boys' who had been so instrumental in the early stages were now largely excluded from the running of the scheme, with the result that Devine and his colleagues resigned and the Centre subsequently closed in 1952. Devine continued to work as a director, but all the while remained committed to finding an alternative means to develop the project further, that is until he met Tony Richardson, then working for the BBC. Phillip Roberts draws attention to the potent combination of: 'Devine's theatrical pedigree and Richardson's unfettered energy' which was now directed; 'towards the idea of new theatre work'. Citing the words of Jocelyn Herbert, whom he had interviewed: 'It was a complete break. His only interest was to have a theatre to encourage new writers' (Roberts, 1999: 6).

Driven by this new impetus, it seemed fitting that he should have considered as his base the very theatre where his predecessors, similarly in pursuit of new writers, had produced 'new drama' at the beginning of the century. He set about developing his 'Royal Court Theatre Scheme'. The opening paragraph of the draft policy, which Roberts mentions was subsequently omitted in the interest of diplomacy, might well have been that of Granville Barker: 'The policy of the Royal Court will be to encourage the living drama by providing a theatre where contemporary playwrights may express themselves more freely and frequently than is possible under commercial conditions' (Roberts, 1999: 8). Roberts makes the point that Devine's interest in new work was evident as early as 1948, citing a lecture in which he talked about the role of the producer in terms curiously reminiscent of Antoine's sentiments some 50 years earlier: 'the conductor of interpretation [is] to find the heart of the play, to represent the author, to relate the play to the audience so that the impact is real and not theatrical'. Productions: 'must be up to date – methods must change' (9). The scheme had support from the Arts Council, chiming as it did with their own initiatives. Unhappily for Devine, the Royal Court, now having acquired a public licence and being managed by Oscar Lewenstein, was experiencing a very successful period and Esdaile, not surprisingly, was not minded to let the theatre. Devine's scheme was put on hold.

The English Stage Company, now involved in their plans to establish a permanent base, needed an artistic director. Lewenstein, aware of Devine's earlier interest in the Court and his reputation, duly made contact to offer him the position of artistic director for the English Stage Company at the Kingsway. Following various meetings and discussions, Devine accepted with the proviso that Tony Richardson be offered the job of his assistant. The official launch of the English Stage Company took place in the, as yet unrenovated, 'shell' of the Kingsway Theatre in July 1955. As the ESC were to discover, the anticipated cost of refurbishment of the Kingsway would prove exorbitant and, as Alfred Esdaile was to discover, the success of one long run does not guarantee a theatre's future. The play which had earlier reinvigorated the life of the Royal Court had recently closed and the little theatre was struggling once again. Esdaile, who had in the meantime received an offer on the Kingsway Theatre, seized on an opportunity to kill two birds with one stone, by offering the ESC the lease on the Royal Court he was in a position to sell off the Kingsway.

The English Stage Company had now secured their London base and George Devine found himself in the theatre for which he had originally drawn up his scheme. Devine's tenure as artistic director was not entirely harmonious, and it became increasingly evident that the members of the ESC had not anticipated the extent to which Devine would involve himself in the running of the theatre or quite how his vision would contrast with their own.

The English Stage Company at The Royal Court Theatre

What was it about the Royal Court that made it unique? It was from the outset a writer's theatre and, as Antoine had done half a century earlier, advertisements were placed in the newspapers to encourage new writers to approach the company with their work. According to Roberts there were 675 responses, of which John Osborne's *Look Back In Anger* was one and, indeed, the only one to reach production. An artistic subcommittee was established to read new plays and make selections and Sunday-night performances without décor were introduced for the most 'promising' of these plays (1999: 33). A permanent company of actors was established, in addition to which there was a list of other actors who showed interest in contributing only occasionally. Devine drew on the talents of a number of individuals with whom he had previously worked, which resulted in different approaches to both directing and staging. The Royal Court was a small theatre and one of the features most commented upon was the 'intimacy' of the working environment and the 'workshop' atmosphere in rehearsals. This contributed enormously to the development of writing and subsequent performances and it became, as Browne (1975) notes: 'the policy that writers should be given the chance to learn the craft of playwriting by experience and to go on learning' (18). In 1958 Devine established The Writer's Group which, as Roberts notes, started out as 'a talking shop for writers' but developed into 'practically based teaching sessions' for emerging playwrights, who included among others Edward Bond and Arnold Wesker (1999: 63).

On 2 April 1956, The English Stage Company opened at the Royal Court with Angus Wilson's *The Mulberry Bush*, followed by the addition of Miller's *Crucible* on 9 April. John Osborne is, of course, the playwright most immediately associated with the Royal Court, and his play *Look Back in Anger* was introduced to the repertoire on 8 May, marking the 'new wave' of dramatists who were to redefine British theatre. The question arises as to why it should be this play that would create such a 'defining' moment in British theatre. Stephen Lacey points out that it is possible to look back and provide a different history of theatre which would centre on the innovations of Becket's work: 'Such an account would emphasis aesthetically innovatory practices, both in writing and its theatrical articulation, and would not foreground questions of realism' (1995: 2).

'New-wave' dramatists

One of the key features of Naturalism, as Zola first envisaged it, was a representation of contemporary reality and in order to appreciate the work of the 'new-wave' dramatists, we need to have some understanding of that reality.

May 1945 brought an end to the Second World War in Europe and, with it, the election of a Labour government in July of the same year. The government was responsible for implementing proposals for social reform which had been outlined in William Beveridge's report of 1942, thus the creation of the Welfare State started to emerge in the immediacy of the post-war years. In 1951, the Conservatives were elected to power where they remained until 1964. This was a period of increasing economic prosperity which had resulted in full employment, and rising standards of living which, in contrast to the austerity of the war years, now gave rise to consumer culture. Robert Lacey provides an insightful comparison of the years 1953 and 1956 to illustrate the social and political 'reality' of 1956. Lacey focuses on a number of events which symbolize the optimism of 1953: 'Bannister ran the four-minute mile, England regained the ashes, and most significantly of all the coronation of Queen Elizabeth II.' As Lacey notes, this was the first: 'modern media 'happening' (1995: 15) which the nation could follow on both radio and television: 'The new reign was presented both as a renewal of British traditions and as the dawning of a new age [...] the rising tide of affluence, full employment and all that was distinctive about contemporary social experience [...]' (15). 1956 signalled the Suez crisis and the subsequent Anglo-French invasion of the Suez Canal and the Soviet invasion of Hungary. The image of 'coherence and stability, of a nation emerging from the vicissitudes of post-war recovery' is set against one of 'dissent, instability, fracture and powerlessness' (16). It was not, as Lacey points out, that the: 'familiar landscape of the early fifties was obliterated [...] but rather that the contradictions and tensions that conservative explanations of change suppressed came to the surface' (16). So, too, the 'new wave' of dramatists surfaced at the Royal Court.

Arnold Wesker

Wesker, who saw *Look Back in Anger*: 'recognized that things *could* be done in the theatre, and immediately went home and wrote *Chicken Soup*' (*TDR*, Vol. 11, 1966). Arnold Wesker's trilogy of plays, *Chicken Soup With Barley*, *Roots* and *I'm*

Talking About Jerusalem, are those most readily associated with Naturalism and, indeed, comparisons have been made with the three mining plays of D. H. Lawrence which, similarly, are concerned with representing the lives of the working class within their own environments. Although, as Simon Trussler notes: 'Naturalism wasn't a label any of the early new-wave British dramatists would have chosen deliberately, but a shape for which they reached instinctively: it happened to meet many of the demands which they were beginning to make on the English theatre. It served as a convenient vehicle for direct social comment [...]' (*TDR*, Vol.13, No.2, 1968: 130). What we find on stage at the Royal Court then are plays which are not 'innovative' in form but rather in content, representing a contemporary social reality from the perspective of a new generation of playwrights.

Born in Stepney in the East End of London in 1932 to a Russian father and Hungarian mother, Wesker comes from Jewish working-class roots. Not unlike a number of other figures we have already come across, he was a member of an amateur theatre group and did, at some point, harbour notions of becoming an actor, attempting at some stage to get into RADA. Leaving school at 16, he found employment in a variety of jobs which, amongst others, would see him working in restaurant kitchens, as a seed sorter and farm labourer in Norfolk, where he lived with his sister. In London, he trained as a pastry cook and later, in Paris, he worked in a restaurant to facilitate a course he would later enrol on at the London School of Film Technique. Wesker's plays, as he freely acknowledges, are autobiographical, he draws on his own experience, many of the characters he represents on stage are recreated from individuals he knows whether familial or otherwise.

Wesker comes from a political background, his mother, like the character of Sarah Kahn in his play *Chicken Soup With Barley*, was a Communist and for a short time he was a member of the Young Communist League. Of his childhood in the East End, he says: 'It didn't worry me that we were poor [...] there was life in the household, a political and social life' (quoted in Hayman, 1970: 4). *Chicken Soup with Barley* concerns a Jewish East End family, the Khans, and their progressive disillusionment with Communism over a period of 20 years.

Roots was rejected by George Devine and Tony Richardson for production at the Royal Court as, indeed, was *Chicken Soup*. It premiered at the Belgrade Theatre in Coventry in May 1959 under the direction of John Dexter, transferring to the Royal Court in June, and subsequently to the Duke of York's theatre for a brief run in July. In this, the second play of the trilogy, Wesker relocates the action to rural Norfolk where he focuses on a young woman, Beatie Bryant, who returns home from London, where she lives, for a two week visit with her family at the end of which her fiancée Ronnie (a character from the earlier play) will join her. In a Note to Actors and Producers Wesker emphasizes:

> My people are not caricatures. They are real (although fiction), and if they
> are portrayed as caricatures the point of all these plays will be lost. The

picture I have drawn is a harsh one, yet my tone is not one of disgust – nor should it be in the presentation of the plays. I am at one with these people: it is only that I am annoyed, with them and myself.   (Wesker, 1964: 80)

Wesker's people are 'real', and he is 'at one' with them. Not only had Wesker lived and worked in Norfolk he also met his wife, who came from a family of farm workers, there. It is interesting to note that Dusty Wesker took Jocelyn Herbert, the designer at the Royal Court, to Norfolk to visit the rural environment in order 'to take in the setting' (Wesker, *Guardian*, 26/01/08).

The play is 'conventionally structured' in three acts and the action takes place in two domestic environments, firstly in the cluttered and ramshackle kitchen/living area of Jenny Beale's house, where Beatie arrives from London in the first act, and then in the kitchen and living area of her parents': '*tied cottage on a main road between two villages*'. In settings similar to those introduced by Lawrence in his mining plays, Wesker represents the lives of the rural working classes in the late fifties. In fact, we might draw on a number of similarities between the two plays, most obviously the working-class interior in which the action is centred around domestic work, and the introduction of regional accent in the dialogue, on which Wesker is clear in his note:

This is a play about Norfolk people; it could be a play about any country people and the moral could certainly extend to the metropolis. But as it is about Norfolk people it is important that some attempt is made to find out how they talk. A very definite accent and intonation exists and personal experience suggests that this is not difficult to know, he then proceeds to offer suggestions for pronunciation.   (Wesker, 1964: 83)

Of the Royal Court production the *Sunday Times* critic noted:

Wesker's dialogue is so natural – one suspects he must have had a tape recorder fitted in those Norfolk kitchens – that there is a danger that his characters will become as dull on the stage as they are in reality but in 'Roots' it is averted by the sympathetic and careful production of John Dexter and the playing of the company. Gwen Nelson, Patsy Byrne and Jack Rodney, in particular, give fine, studied performances, their faces telling their thoughts when words will not come.

(*Sunday Times* quoted on the Royal Court Website)

Whilst the play primarily focuses on Beatie's process as she develops from an individual reliant on Ronnie's words to one who, in the final act, finds her voice and is able to articulate her own ideas, Wesker represents a very detailed 'picture' of the Bryant family in which they go about their lives:

([...] in a routine and rural manner [...] little amazes them [...]. They talk in fits and start mainly as a sort of gossip [...]. Their sense of humour is keen and dry. They show no affection for each other – though this does not mean they would not be upset were one of them to die. The silences are important – as important as the way they speak, if we are to know them.)

(Hayman, 1970: 92)

Wesker's characters are products of their environment, both in relation to the isolated rural community which limits their experience to work and domesticity, and the wider post-war social and economic environment which limits their 'cultural' experience. These are 'people' who may not 'talk' to each other about important matters and, indeed, may not talk to each other at all but they are 'human'. Wesker provides a 'case study' albeit one in which he has a voice through the character of Ronnie, who in the end remains absent.

There have been a number of revivals of Wesker's work in London: *The Kitchen* at the Royal Court in 1994, *Chips with Everything* at the National Theatre, London in 1997, *Chicken Soup with Barley* transferring from the Nottingham Playhouse to the Tricycle in 2005. Perhaps more interestingly, two of them were revived in 2011, *Chicken Soup with Barley* at the Royal Court in June and *The Kitchen* at the National Theatre in October. Also in October, Edward Bond's *Saved* was revived at the Lyric Hammersmith.

Saved, written in 1964, presents us with an interesting play to consider in terms of its 'Naturalism'. Originally produced at the Royal Court in November 1965 under William Gaskill's direction, the play not only elicited negative reviews but it resulted in a court case for presenting an unlicensed play on stage.

In his stage directions Bond indicates:

> *The area of the play is South London*
> *The stage is as bare as possible – sometimes completely bare*   (2011: 4)

Scene 1 takes place in a room with only the minimum of furniture to indicate that it is a sitting room. The scenes in the park take place on a bare stage. What we immediately note is the absence of detail in the setting, the kind of detail which is generally associated with Naturalist staging and has hitherto been crucial to the representation of the social and physical environment.

The power of the play lies in Bond's naturalistic dialogue and the interaction between the characters. The stoning and burning of the baby in scene 6 may be shocking, but it is determined by the social circumstances in which these characters find themselves. In an interview in October 2011 Tony Selby, one of the original cast, tells Maddy Costa: 'I understood it intuitively, because I came from a working-class background. *Saved* is about ignoring young life. The baby is a sacrifice. In actual fact the baby is saved. It's saved from a non-existent life.' He goes on to talk about the bored, neglected kids in nearby Battersea Park hurling stones at squirrels: 'from there to killing the baby', he argues, takes: 'only one little leap of the imagination' (*Guardian*, 9/10/12).

In the recent revival at the Lyric Theatre in Hammersmith, London, which prompted the *Guardian* article, the play had a particular resonance with the audience who made connections to the riots in London and other British cities throughout the summer of 2011. Similar connections were made to the case of Baby P, a toddler who had suffered at the hands of his parents, and finally died of the injuries he had sustained. This was a tragic case of neglect and suffering which had dominated headlines some three years earlier.

Whilst 1956 introduced the 'new wave' of writers at the Royal Court, it also produced Brecht's play *The Good Person of Setzuan*, for which Devine had negotiated the rights directly with Brecht. The tendency in a number of quarters has been to view Brecht's concept of theatre and his respective drama as one which is in total opposition to the Naturalist form of representation. In fact, on closer inspection, we find a number of interesting similarities in terms of his attempt to explore the wider social and economic realities of contemporary life.

Bertolt Brecht

Debates concerning Naturalism occupied theatrical minds well into the twentieth century. The theatre practitioner and theorist Bertolt Brecht (1898–1956) is not usually considered as having been concerned with Naturalism: indeed, he is commonly associated with the development of a technique that appears anti-naturalistic: the 'Alienation' or 'Distancing' effect. It has often been suggested that Brecht was opposed to the illusions of reality that characterized naturalistic theatre, preferring to ensure that the audience never forgot that they were in a theatre, that they and the actors remained detached from the narrative and emotional content of the drama, and that there was no attempt to present a 'slice of life' on stage. Actors working with Brecht, it has been said, did not, as Stanislavsky would have insisted, inhabit their characters or identify with their predicaments; instead, they apparently concentrated on 'showing' what was happening and might, at any moment, break the illusion of reality by performing a song.

However, on closer investigation, it can be seen that Brecht not only built upon the legacy of Naturalism but employed some of its techniques and embraced some of its beliefs. Brecht's concept of an 'Epic' theatre, as opposed to what he called the 'Aristotelian' theatre, derived from German terminology and implied an episodic structure and an emphasis on surface detail. His theatre presented problematic situations to which he invited audiences to find solutions. Increasingly, he suggested that a Marxist world-view might provide satisfactory answers. In so far as he demonstrated the causality of attitudes and situations and subjected history and contemporary events to social scrutiny, Brecht demonstrated considerable sympathy with the Naturalist approach to drama. After all, Zola, Ibsen and Brieux had shown human beings being shaped, and sometimes destroyed, by their environments. But, to some extent, Naturalist plays were too deterministic and pessimistic for Brecht. He sought a kind of theatre that did not present human beings as existing in an unchangeable situation or as being subject to a fate that moved inevitably to its catastrophic resolution. He was particularly concerned that audiences in naturalistic theatre, absorbed in the causality of events, would be unable to discern that alternative possibilities always existed and that human beings have the freedom to change the course of events if they make informed choices.

Brecht was not only a prolific playwright and director, he also wrote constantly and engagingly on the practice of theatre. His critique of Naturalism is largely contained in a series of writings in dialogue form that began around 1939 and continued spasmodically until about 1949. In 1963 the Berliner Ensemble, which Brecht had founded in East Berlin, performed some of these 'Messingkauf Dialogues' and they were subsequently published under this name and translated into English by John Willett in 1965.

The *Messingkauf Dialogues* take place between five imaginary characters: a Philosopher; an Actor; an Actress; a Dramaturg, and an Electrician. Brecht himself is indirectly referred to as 'the Augsburger'. As they discuss the work of the theatre in the first episode 'The First Night', the Dramaturg observes that the theatre shows a vast range of human situations: 'in fact, the whole of reality as we know it' (Brecht, 1965: 12). He expands the discussion to embrace the 'representation of real life' (13) and we can see at once that we are in the territory of Naturalism. Significantly, therefore, the next fragment of the dialogue is entitled 'Naturalism'. 'Naturalistic performances', says the Dramaturg, 'gave one the *illusion* of being at a real place'. The Actor picks up his cue and responds with a reference to Chekhov: 'The Audience looked into a room and thought it could smell the cherry orchard at the back of the house' (22). This provokes a discussion about the degree to which reality can be suggested by the selection of what to show: how nature can be represented rather than reproduced by art. The Dramaturg suggests that the naturalistic playwrights: Ibsen, Hauptmann, Tolstoy or Strindberg could be accused of being 'tendentious and committed' (23): giving their own view of the natural world rather than genuinely attempting to represent it accurately. The discourse focuses on the limitations of Naturalism. It is agreed that Stanislavsky's best work came from his naturalistic period but that what obsessed him was *naturalness* and that, as a result 'everything in his theatre seemed far too natural for anyone to pause and go into it thoroughly' (23). However, the Dramaturg defends many of the achievements of Naturalism, realizing that its aims were not totally at odds with those of 'Epic' theatre. He maintains that a considerable number of social movements: opportunities for women, the challenge to hypocrisy in sexual matters, improvements in education, for example, 'have their roots in Naturalism and its works', audiences were confronted by 'a lot of conditions that couldn't be tolerated', as the Philosopher remarks 'The theatre was acting in the public interest' (23).

The general tone of this section of the dialogue, however, suggests that Naturalism had a very limited life-span and impact and we can now see how inaccurate this is. Whereas the plays of Brecht, for example, enjoyed a period of great and wide popularity in the 1960s and 1970s and his ideas continued to influence and fascinate theatre practitioners long after that, many of the plays of the Naturalist playwrights continue to be regularly produced and adapted in many countries and cultures. Quite erroneously, the Philosopher asserts that 'The subject-matter of the various plays was quickly exhausted, and often it could be shown that the theatre's representations were very superficial' (Brecht, 1965: 25). The Dramaturg then touches on problematic distinction between Naturalism and realism and provokes a remark from the actor: 'Between you and me, old chap, it's neither one thing nor the other. It's just unnatural Naturalism' (25) which is reminiscent of the opinions expressed by the celebrated contemporary director Katie Mitchell in her book *A Director's Craft* (2009).

The Dramaturg has maintained that Naturalism had a limited life because it was 'too uneventful for the politicians and too boring for the artists' (Brecht, 1965: 25) but he then goes on to assert that it then 'turned into realism' (25). The distinction lies, he says, in that 'Realism is less naturalistic than Naturalism, though Naturalism is considered fully as realistic as realism.' 'Realism', he states, 'never gives absolutely exact images of reality.' He justifies this comment by saying that realism does not attempt to reproduce dialogues of the kind 'one actually hears', but attempts to go 'deeper into reality' (25). Much of this, of course, is highly debatable. We can see, for instance that many plays by the naturalistic dramatists employ highly selective dialogue and that however exact the images of many naturalistic productions appear to be, they also are shaped and manipulated to make the statements intended by the playwright. Nevertheless, the Dramaturg concedes that 'Naturalism's images resulted in criticism of the real world' (27) and our approach has suggested that, far from being an extension of Naturalism, realism is an integral ingredient of it (see Chapter 1).

At a later stage in the dialogue Brecht's imaginary characters debate another common feature of Naturalism: the 'fourth wall'. This discussion occurs in a section entitled 'Removal of Illusion and Empathy', and centres on the idea that an audience watching the action of a play through the fourth wall are like observers looking through a key hole and the actors are behaving as if there is no audience. 'Realistic acting', the Electrician maintains, is what audiences want and actors need the concept of the fourth wall in order to achieve it. The Philosopher, however, suggests that nothing could be more damaging to the idea of reality than the process of pretending that audiences are eavesdropping on a slice of life: rather, there is the reality of sitting in a theatre: 'We want to demolish the fourth wall', he declares, 'I herewith announce our joint operation' (Brecht, 1965: 52).

In his practice, Brecht went to considerable lengths to achieve this end and his techniques almost became a cliché in the hands of his imitators: the curtain never fully lowered, scene changes in full view of the audience, no attempt to mask stage lighting, direct address to the audience and frequent invasion of the audience space by the performers. However, in many respects, Brecht's work continued the innovations of the Duke of Saxe-Meiningen (see Chapter 5) and the scientific attempts to analyse performance undertaken by Delsarte and his followers (see Chapter 4). When his Berliner Ensemble visited Britain very shortly after his death in 1958, the theatre-going public was struck by the total absence of 'star' performers and by the ensemble work. They also noted the insistence on the use of 'real' properties and furniture on stage and the fact that Brecht himself had constructed a photographic documentation of the performance in *Mother Courage and her Children* by his wife, the actress Helene Weigel. This extraordinarily detailed record of a performance was undertaken to show how Weigel reacted to key moments in the action by creating what Brecht called a 'gestus': a movement, word or facial expression that captured the 'gist' of the scene. It was, indeed, the faithfulness of this performance to Nature that made it so memorable and remarkable and its emotional intensity was far from 'distant'. What Brecht achieved was to inject new rigour, life and discipline into the theatre and Naturalism was its beneficiary.

CHAPTER SUMMARY

- In much the same way as the leading figures of 'new drama' some 50 years earlier had sought to bring about an experimental theatre following the European model in order to encourage new playwrights, we find now a new group of individuals who, in many respects, take up the project once again.
- The English Stage Company secured their London base at the Royal Court and George Devine, its director, found himself in the theatre for which he had originally drawn up a scheme
- On 2 April 1956, The English Stage Company opened at the Royal Court with Angus Wilson's *The Mulberry Bush*. John Osborne is, of course, the playwright most immediately associated with the Royal Court, his play *Look Back in Anger* marking the 'new wave' of dramatists who were to redefine British theatre.
- Arnold Wesker's trilogy of plays *Chicken Soup With Barley, Roots* and *I'm Talking About Jerusalem* are those most readily associated with Naturalism.
- 'Naturalism wasn't a label any of the early new-wave British dramatists would have chosen deliberately, but a shape for which they reached instinctively' (Trussler, *TDR*, Vol.13, No. 2, 1968: 130).

SEMINAR AND WORKSHOP TOPICS

1 Why do you think that the 1950s produced a period of renewed creativity in British theatre?
2 Discus Devine's principles for his new project. How do they compare with those of, say, Brahm?
3 What qualities of Naturalism do Wesker's plays demonstrate?
4 Imagine you are the character of Beatie in Wesker's *Roots*. How do you persuade reluctant members of your family to take your ideas seriously?
5 Can you justify the violence shown in Bond's *Saved*?
6 Which of Wesker's plays do you think deserve reviving?
7 How would you apply Stanislavsky's methods to a play by Wesker? Find scenes to work on in which you can identify sub-text and a through line.

FURTHER READING

Eyre, R. and Wright, N. (2000) *Changing Stages*, London: Routledge. As with Brecht, this provides a balanced and entertaining view of the drama of the 1950s and 1960s.
Little, R. and McLaughlin, E. (2007) *The Royal Court Theatre Inside Out*, London: Oberon Books. This is an invaluable book which provides an extremely insightful overview of the Royal Court Theatre from its origins through to 2006.
Taylor, J. R. (1962) *Anger and After*, Harmondsworth: Penguin. Remains the most comprehensive account of the new drama of the 1950s
Wesker, A. (1994) *As Much as I Dare*, London: Century. Wesker's intriguing autobiography.

CHAPTER 11
Verbatim Theatre

Throughout our exploration of Naturalism as a form of theatre representation, we have discovered a number of playwrights who have drawn on or included documentary evidence in their respective drama. As early as 1835 Büchner included 'verbatim extracts' from revolutionary speeches in his play *Danton's Death* and based *Woyczek* on medical reports. Hennique's play of 1888 *The Death of the Duke of Enghien*, originally presented at the Théâtre Libre in Paris, incorporated 'transcript material' from the actual trial which, as Jean Chothia points out: 'confronted its audience with the thrill of knowing that the dialogue had once really been spoken [...]' (1991: 62). Brieux drew on the writing of Doctor Alfred Fournier in his play *Damaged Goods* and Gerhart Hauptmann based *The Weavers* on historical accounts which contained witness evidence and descriptions of the original weavers uprising in the 1840s. These plays anticipate the documentary drama with which we have become so familiar in recent years. Indeed, we might also argue that verbatim theatre, which, increasingly, has become one of the most popular theatre forms in Britain, is a legacy of Naturalism.

Peter Cheeseman and the origins of verbatim theatre

The origins of verbatim theatre can be traced back to the early 1960s and very specifically to the work of one individual, Peter Cheeseman, the artistic director of the Victoria Theatre in Stoke-on-Trent. Cheeseman, who died in April 2010, has been described as both 'visionary' and 'pioneering', his musical documentary productions at Stoke had an immediate influence on the work of other regional theatres, and what came to be known as the 'Stoke method' was to provide inspiration for later playwrights.

Cheeseman inherited the role of artistic director of the small regional theatre in 1962 when Stephen Joseph took the decision to leave to take up a lectureship at Manchester University. Joseph, noted for introducing productions of theatre-in-the-round to Britain and for encouraging new playwrights to produce work for his touring company, had acquired the former cinema with a view to providing a permanent base for his touring company of which Cheeseman was a member. The company had, up until this point, worked in Scarborough during the summer months, where Joseph produced his plays in-the-round on a constructed stage in the main library space. During the winter the company toured, trucking the staging paraphernalia with them, setting up in halls and suitably large spaces.

In 1962, Cheeseman found himself responsible for the newly converted theatre, incorporating as it did an arena stage to accommodate Joseph's particular style of production, an ensemble of actors on contract, and a responsibility to uphold Joseph's policy of encouraging new playwrights, something to which he was equally committed.

Cheeseman evidently saw special 'qualities' in Stoke as Robin Thornber alludes to in Cheeseman's obituary, citing Alan Ayckbourn who recalled arriving at the new theatre with Peter and the pioneering troupe: 'Everyone except Peter booked digs for three weeks. We were all looking for our return tickets. Peter bought a house' (*Guardian*.co.uk, 29 April 2010). Cheeseman clearly felt an affinity with the community and his goal from the outset was as Elvgren Jr. notes: 'to break away from theatre as a "cultured" phenomenon. He wants to find a means to destroy the barriers which so often grow up between the creative artist and the most ordinary people' (1974: 88). To this end he introduced the concept of a 'resident' writer whose familiarity with the company of actors, the theatre staging and, more importantly, a strong connection with the local community would be fundamental to the work they produced. Cheeseman was keen to build audiences, he: 'wanted to explore a relationship with one coherent community to make the theatre at home there in its battered landscape. The theatre documentaries owe their origin as well as their particular style and choice of subject matter to these circumstances' (Cheeseman quoted in Soans, *Talking To Terrorists*, 2005: 104).

It was in these 'circumstances', then, that in 1964 Cheeseman developed the new documentary form that would find a place in theatre history. *The Jolly Potters* was the first of seven such 'documentary' performances, which derived their content from the history and stories of the local community and were performed for that same community. Romy Saunders, Cheeseman's widow, spoke of this first production in a BBC radio programme, *Word for Word*, presented by Paul Allen. According to Saunders, the play was inspired by the landlord of the local pub, *The Jolly Potters*, where the actors often socialized and who, jokingly, announced their entrance one evening with: 'and the next title of your next play is going to be the Jolly Potters'. For Cheeseman this wasn't a joke, but rather the seed of an idea which had merit. He took the decision that the whole group would create a play about the history of the pottery industry which, of course, was still thriving at that time: 'He took himself off to the local library and discovered masses of material and one of the key things that had happened was the potteries riots in the 1840s and they were documented because people had been put on trial' (Saunders, *Word for Word*, Radio 4, 5/4/2012).

The use of documentary material would continue to become part of an established methodology, the content of the plays would be drawn from a range of research material including newspapers, historical documentation, letters, diaries and interviews conducted with members of the community who had some kind of connection with, or memories of, the particular topic being explored and which all members of the company were tasked with finding. One of the key principles that informed the process was that of objectivity. Cheeseman insisted that no single individual should have responsibility for 'interpreting' the material. Keen to avoid the dangers of manipulation or a biased interpretation, the process relied on input at various stages from the whole company (Elvgren, 1974: 90). Actor Robert Powell, in the same BBC interview, recalled that the found material would be recited 'word for word' to Cheeseman, who would then edit it into a performable text (*Word for Word*, 5/4/2012)

Of course, Cheeseman's practice developed over time and as he says: 'By the time of the third play I had learned enough to plan the whole process and identify the style that was emerging' (Cheeseman cited in Soans, 2005: 106). In the earliest productions, as Cheeseman acknowledges, some of the scenes developed out of the actors' improvisation or devising, but this was 'phased out' as he became increasingly focused on the 'authority of a narrative composed of the actual records' (Cheeseman cited in Soans, 2005), an approach which earned him the label of 'purist'. In a previously recorded interview reproduced in Paul Allen's radio programme, he says: 'Actuality in our terms is either actual utterance in documentary form, in written form or reported form by participants or eye witnesses of actual events or recorded material collected by us by means of the tape recorder, it is that material edited together and turned into a play, nothing must be made up' (Cheeseman, *Word for Word*, 5/4/2012).

Gilbert Elvgren Jr., in an article written in 1974, following a series of interviews with Cheeseman, draws further attention to the 'purity of the representation of the factual material'. Cheeseman's view is that: 'The sensation of watching a documentary is the sensation of watching a fact. You can't write a documentary – it's a contradiction in terms. You can only edit documentary material' (quoted in Elvgren, 1974: 91). Cheeseman's role is not that of a propagandist, but rather to awaken the audience: 'We have to find a way of asking disturbing questions which do not take a single viewpoint or single political alignment' (91–2).

Cheeseman acknowledged the inspiration he had drawn from the Theatre Workshop production of *Oh What A Lovely War* and, equally, the influence radio documentary had on the development of his work. In particular, the BBC Radio Ballads by Charles Parker and Ewan McColl which had first been produced in 1958 and continued through to the early 1960s. The ballads were 'revolutionary' at the time, incorporating the edited recorded voices into the script rather than the voices of actors. The plays were accompanied by songs inspired by the stories of the interviewees and performed by McColl. This influence is evident in Cheeseman's third play, *The Knotty* (1966), when dialogue compiled from tape-recorded interviews was used for the first time and, in 1971, recorded interviews were also incorporated into the performance of *Hands Up – For You the War Is Ended!*

For Elvgren the most striking thing about Cheeseman's approach to directing was its simplicity: 'The productions at the Victoria Theatre are notable for being uncluttered, straightforward, and devoid of theatrical gimmicks' (1974: 93). This was due in part to the arena stage which to some degree dictated the 'unstagey reality'. As Elvgren points out: 'the actor has to be the primary instrument of documentation', which necessarily required a more objective approach to acting. For Cheeseman: 'The most interesting feature of the kind of documentary theatre we developed was that adhering to the primary source rule compelled us to develop all kinds of stylistic solutions to include essential, but seemingly unperformable, elements in the story when we have no suitable contemporary accounts' (Cheeseman quoted in Soans, 2005: 107). The stylistic solutions included, as Elvgren lists: 'songs and music, various types of narration, dialogue expressed in the past, sound effects, mime'. Whilst we might regard these as 'analogous' to Brecht's theories, they were clearly evolved 'in his dedication to presenting historical material objectively' (Elvgren, 1974: 94).

Derek Paget in an article written for *New Theatre Quarterly* suggests that: 'Although they were not called verbatim plays, the Stoke documentaries *Hands Up – For You the War Is Ended* (1971) and *Fight for Shelton Bar* (1974) could claim to have been the first in the field' (1987: 318). Of the second documentary, which focused on the contemporary issue of British Steel's proposal to close the North Staffordshire steel works, Paget cites Rony Robinson: 'Peter really hit the method in order to report a complex industrial dispute – he found that was the way to get at it' (318).

Alecky Blythe

It is perhaps fitting that Alecky Blythe's 'verbatim' play *Where have I been all my life?*, produced at the New Vic Theatre in April 2012, should have been commissioned by Theresa Heskins, the artistic director. It is, as she says, the first documentary production at the theatre in the twenty-first century. Blythe, whose first play, *Come Out Eli* (2003), was a success, is a dramatist whose work is rooted in the 'verbatim' form. In 2011 she achieved widespread success with *London Road*, a verbatim piece with music and singing, at the National Theatre, London, revived in July 2012. Blythe works in a very particular way which has been well-documented, the process can be lengthy, her recordings are not just one-off interviews, she tends to spend a great deal of time with the interviewees, accumulating an enormous amount of recorded material which she then edits but, importantly, does not transcribe. In rehearsals and, more interestingly, in performance, the actors wear headphones and repeat the original words copying the speech patterns in a technique learned at the Actors Centre, but originating from Anna Deavere Smith. The actors remain under instructions from Blythe not to learn the text: 'Unlike a traditional playwright who has complete control of the plot and characters, a verbatim writer has little control over where the story might go, and this is what is so exciting and enlightening about the form' (Blythe quoted in Soans, 2005: 101).

Nicolas Kent and the Tricycle Theatre

The Tricycle Theatre in North London has acquired a reputation under the artistic directorship of Nicolas Kent for producing 'political' theatre. Under this banner the 'tribunal' plays with which he is most associated naturally fall. In an interview with the *Guardian*'s Stuart Jeffries, Kent is clear that the plays are not 'dreary agit-prop': 'I want people to be challenged and make up their minds. Once I've chosen the subject, I do it without bias. My bias comes in the choice of subject – that shows where I stand' (*Guardian* 18/2/12). The 'tribunal' plays, the first of which was produced in 1994, dramatize the evidence produced at an official public inquiry or hearing, the edited transcripts form the content of the play. Journalist Richard Norton-Taylor is the person with whom Kent has worked most closely on these plays, Norton-Taylor taking responsibility for the editing and shaping the play text. The aim and, indeed, the effect is for the audience to inhabit the role of a member of the inquiry, listen to the evidence and make up their own mind.

The documentary theatre produced at the Tricycle is not limited to the 'tribunal' plays. In 2004 the Tricycle produced *Guantanamo 'Honour Bound to Defend Freedom'*, which later transferred to the West End and then New York. The text, compiled by Gillian Slovo and Victoria Brittain from edited interviews, correspondence and public statements, presents oral and written testimony from released and detained prisoners, relatives, which include an Englishman whose sister had been a victim of 9/11, and solicitors (www.tricycle.co.uk). Slovo was again commissioned by Kent to produce a 'verbatim' play exploring the riots that took place in London and other cities in Britain during August 2011. In little over three months, Slovo had conducted interviews with politicians, police, witnesses, victims and rioters. She also drew on correspondence with Chelsea Ives, the teenager who was arrested after being seen on television by her mother, and who subsequently received a custodial sentence. Slovo edited the transcripts and produced a play, *The Riots*, which presents a range of viewpoints supported by filmed footage of the events and factual information.

Documentary theatre and authenticity

The effect of documentary theatre, whatever the technique, verbatim or otherwise, is one of authenticity and something Carol Martin in her article for *The Drama Review* challenges. Using the term 'archive' to refer to the range of material upon which the form depends, interviews, correspondence, transcripts of hearings and so on, she asks: 'What is the basis for the selection, order, and manner of presentation of materials from the archive? The process of selection, editing, organization, and presentation is where the creative work of documentary theatre gets done' (Carol Martin, 2006: 9).

Robin Soans, who produced *Talking to Terrorists* for the Royal Court Theatre, asks: 'How is this any different from a well-written and well-constructed imagined play? The answer is: it isn't. The categorization is irksome. Verbatim plays are far more like conventional plays than is generally acknowledged' (Soans quoted in Hammond and Steward, 2008: 18). As Soans indicates, 'documentary' drama, whichever form it takes, needs a shape and this is no different to the structure of conventional play texts, here the editor is the one responsible for deciding what is or is not included, and at each stage of the process: 'transformations, interpretations and inevitable distortions occur' (Martin, 2006: 10).

In what ways might we view documentary theatre as a legacy of Naturalism? If we return to some of the original ideas articulated by Zola and the subsequent attempts by dramatists to represent contemporary reality at the end of the nineteenth century: 'Take our present environment, then, and try to make men live in it: you will write great works' (Zola, 1893: 364), we might consider the 'documentary' form as one which, similarly, is an attempt to represent contemporary reality as authentically as possible. In *The Experimental Novel* and, indeed, in his other writings Zola calls for a new methodology, one with a degree of objectivity and one which presents characters and their behaviour in the light of their environment, heredity and circumstances. Documentary theatre draws on a number of different techniques and focuses on a range of different subjects but at the core of the work is an attempt to represent events objectively for the audience. As Martin notes: 'at its best, it offers us a way to think about disturbing contexts and complicated subject matter while revealing the virtues and flaws of its sources' (2006: 9). Whilst the determinist 'world-view' of the early Naturalists provided the 'context' for the late nineteenth century dramatists, we still remain concerned with the 'disturbing contexts' that determine the actions of the human subject in the twenty-first century. Dramatists now deal with the simplicity of: 'the exact word spoken without emphasis, quite naturally'. The 'real' word, recorded or documented, forms the content of the play. We no longer depend on the reproduction of naturalist settings to create the environment, technology has provided this for us in advance of the performance by virtue of television coverage. Writing in the mid-1980s, Raymond Williams notes: 'It is clear, on the one hand, that the great majority of plays now produced, in all media, are technically naturalist, and, on the other hand, that many "non-naturalist" plays are evidently based on a naturalist philosophy' (1987b: 15).

CHAPTER SUMMARY

- The origins of verbatim theatre which, increasingly, has become one of the most popular theatre forms in Britain can be traced back to the early 1960s and specifically to the work of Peter Cheeseman, then the artistic director of the Victoria Theatre in Stoke-on-Trent.

- Cheeseman inherited the role of artistic director in 1962 when Stephen Joseph, known for his advocacy of theatre-in-the-round, took the decision to leave to take up a lectureship at Manchester University.

- Cheeseman clearly felt an affinity with the community and his goal was 'to break away' from theatre as a 'cultured' phenomenon.

- He developed in 1964 the new documentary form that would find a place in theatre history. *The Jolly Potters* was the first of seven such 'documentary' performances which derived their content from the history and stories of the local community and were performed for that same community.

- The use of documentary material would continue to become part of an established methodology, the content of the plays would be drawn from a range of research material.

- In the third play *The Knotty* (1966) dialogue compiled from tape-recorded interviews was used for the first time and in 1971 recorded interviews were also incorporated into the performance of *Hands Up – For You the War Is Ended*

- Cheeseman acknowledged the inspiration he had drawn from the Theatre Workshop production of *Oh What A Lovely War* and, equally, the influence of radio documentary.

- Although they were not called verbatim plays, the Stoke documentaries *Hands Up – For You the War Is Ended* (1971) and *Fight for Shelton Bar* (1974) could claim to have been the first in the field.

- The documentary theatre produced more recently at the Tricycle in London is not limited to the 'tribunal' plays. In 2004 the Tricycle produced *Guantanamo* which later transferred to the West End and then New York

- Alecky Blythe, now one of the leading exponents of verbatim theatre, says: 'Unlike a traditional playwright who has complete control of the plot and characters, a verbatim writer has little control over where the story might go' (Blythe quoted in Soans, 2005: 101).

- If we return to some of the original ideas of Zola, we might consider the verbatim form as one which similarly is attempting to represent an authentic reality.

SEMINAR AND WORKSHOP TOPICS

1 Take a number of diary entries and discuss the possibility of turning them into a play.
2 Identify a local issue that might form the basis of a piece of documentary or verbatim theatre.
3 How would you use the words of songs to contribute to a verbatim play?
4 How do Zola's scientific principles apply to verbatim theatre?
5 How did the theatre practice of Brecht help to shape the emergence of verbatim theatre?
6 Why does theatre-in-the-round provide such immediacy in performance?
7 Explore some of the verbatim plays of David Hare and discuss what he is trying to achieve by using this form.
8 Is verbatim theatre a form of Naturalism?

FURTHER READING

BBC Radio 4 (2012) 'Word for Word', presented by Paul Allen (6 April).

Elvgren Jr., G. A. (1974) 'Documentary Theatre at Stoke-on-Trent', *Education Theatre Journal*, 26:1 (March).

Hammond, W., and Steward, D., ed. (2008) *Verbatim Verbatim: Contemporary Documentary Theatre*, London: Oberon Books. This is an extremely useful source which provides contributions from a number of key figures associated with documentary and verbatim theatre.

Martin, C. (2006) 'Bodies of Evidence', *The Drama Review*, 50:3, 9–15.

Paget, D. (1987) '"Verbatim Theatre": Oral History and Documentary Techniques', *New Theatre Quarterly*, III:12 (November).

Bibliography

Plays and sourcebooks of plays

Baker, E. (1991) *Chains*, in L. Fitzsimmons and V. Gardner, eds, *New Woman Plays*, London: Methuen.

Barrie, J. M. (2003) *The Twelve Pound Look and Other Plays*, Amsterdam: Fredonia Books.

Bond, E. (2011) *Saved*, London: Methuen Drama.

Brieux, E. (1901) *Damaged Goods*, London: eBookTakeaway.

Brighouse, H. (1992) *Hobson's Choice* and *The Game*, London: Heinemann

Brittain, V. and Slovo, G. (2004) *Guantanamo 'Honour Bound to Defend Freedom'*, London: Oberon Books.

Chekhov, A. (1951/1954) *Anton Chekhov Plays*, trans. E. Fen, Harmondsworth: Penguin.

Chekhov, A. (1977/2008) *Five Plays*, ed. R. Hingley, Oxford: Oxford University Press.

Corrie, J. (1982) *In Time O'Strife*, Edinburgh: 7:84 Theatre Company. (Reprinted from original publication by The Forward Publishing Co.)

Corrie, J. (1985) *Plays, Poems and Theatre Writings*, Introduction by L. Mackenney, Edinburgh: 7:84 Publications.

Gale, M. and Deeney, J. F. (2010) *The Routledge Drama Anthology and Sourcebook – From Modernism to Contemporary Performance*, London: Routledge.

Galsworthy, J. (2006) *The Silver Box* [etc.], in *Plays: First Series*, London: BiblioBazaar (available to download).

Ganguli, U. (2005) *The Journey Within*, in T. Mukherjee, ed., *Staging Resistance: Plays by Women in Translation*: New Delhi: Oxford University Press.

Glaspell, S. (1916) *Trifles*, in W. B. Worthen, ed., *The Wadsworth Anthology of Drama*, 4th edn, London: Cengage Learning, 2004.

Grundy, S. (2001) *The New Woman*, in J. Chothia, ed., *The New Woman and Other Emancipated Woman Plays*, New York: Oxford University Press.

Hankin, St J. (1907) *The Return of the Prodigal*, New York: Library of Congress.

Hapgood. E. (1968) *Stanislavsky's Legacy*, London: Eyre Methuen.

Hauptmann, G. (1961) *Five Plays by Gerhart Hauptmann*, trans. T. H. Lustig, New York: Bantam Books.

Hauptmann, G. (1978) in *Joyce and Hauptmann Before Sunrise*, trans. James Joyce, California: PSP Graphics.

Hauptmann, G. (1980) *The Weavers*, trans. F. Marcus, London: Methuen.

Herne, J. (1996) *Margaret Fleming*, Michigan: Feedback and Prospero Press.

Houghton, S. (2010) *Hindle Wakes*, London: BiblioBazaar (available to download).

Ibsen, H. (1980a) *Ghosts, The Wild Duck, The Master Builder*, in *Plays: One*, trans. M. Meyer, London: Methuen.

Ibsen, H. (1980b) *A Doll's House, An Enemy of the People, Hedda Gabler*, in *Plays Two*, trans. M. Meyer, London: Methuen.

Ibsen, H. (1980c) *Rosmersholm, The Lady From the Sea* and *Little Eyolf*, in *Plays Three*, trans. M. Meyer, London: Methuen.

Ibsen, H. (1980d) *The Pillars of Society, John Gabriel Borkman, When we Dead Awaken*, in *Plays Four*, trans. M. Meyer, London: Methuen.

Lamont Stewart, E. (1983) *Men Should Weep*, London: Samuel French.

Lawrence, D. H. (2001) *D. H. Lawrence, The Widowing of Mrs. Holroyd* and *Other Plays*, ed. S. Trussler, Oxford: Oxford University Press.

Lewis, L. (1972) *The Bells*, in G. Rowell, ed., *Nineteenth-Century Plays*, Oxford: Oxford University Press.

Megson, C., ed. (2010) *The Methuen Drama Book of Naturalist Plays*, London: Methuen.

Miller, A. (1977) *An Enemy of the People*, Harmondsworth: Penguin.

Monkhouse, A. (2010) *Mary Broome* and *The Conquering Hero*, Michigan: University of Michigan Press (available to download).

O'Casey, S. (1998) *Three Dublin Plays – The Shadow of a Gunman, Juno and the Paycock, The Plough and the Stars*, London: Faber & Faber.

O'Neill, E. (1956) *Long Day's Journey into Night*, London: Jonathan Cape.

Robertson, T. (1972) *Caste*, in G. Rowell, ed., *Nineteenth Century Plays*, Oxford: Oxford University Press

Robins, E. [1907] (2009) *Votes for Women*, in S. Croft, ed., *Votes for Women and other Plays*, New York: Aurora Metro Publications.

Scribe, E. (2004) *Believe It or Not*, trans. R. Bolt, Introduction by N. Dromgoole, London: Oberon

Shaw, G. B. (1965) *The Complete Plays*, London: Paul Hamlyn

Soans, R. (2005) *Talking To Terrorists*, London: Oberon Books.

Strindberg, A. (1962) *The Chamber Plays*, trans. E. Sprinchorn and S. Quinn, New York: Dutton.

Strindberg, A. (1976) *Miss Julie* and *Preface, The Father*, trans. M. Meyer, London: Eyre Methuen.

Strindberg, A. (1992) *Miss Julie and Preface*, trans P. Hogg, adapt. H. Cooper, London: Methuen.

Wesker, A. (1964) *The Wesker Trilogy*, Harmondsworth, Penguin.

Williams, T. (1962) *A Streetcar Named Desire and Other Plays*, Harmondsworth: Penguin.

Zola, E. (1989) *Thérèse Raquin*, trans. P. Broughton, Bath: Absolute Press.

Books and Articles

Antoine, A. [1964] (1977) *Memories of the Théâtre Libre*, trans. M. Carlson, Miami, FL: University of Miami Press.

Ayling, R., ed. (1985) *O'Casey: The Dublin Trilogy – A Selection of Critical Essays*, Basingstoke and London: Macmillan.

BBC Radio 4 (2012) 'Word for Word', presented by Paul Allen (6 April).

Baugh, C. (2005) *Theatre Performance and Technology*, Basingstoke: Palgrave Macmillan.

Bentley, E., ed. (1968) *The Theory of the Modern Stage*, Harmondsworth: Penguin Books.

Bogard, T., Moody, R. and Meserve, W. J., eds (1977) *The Revels: History of Drama in English*, Vol. VII: *American Drama*, London: Methuen.

Booth, M. R. and Kaplan, J. H., eds (1996) *The Edwardian Theatre*, Cambridge: Cambridge University Press

Boulton, J. T., ed. (1979) *The Letters of D. H. Lawrence,* Volume I: *September 1901–May 1913*, Cambridge: Cambridge Unversity Press.

Boyle, N. (2008) *German Literature, A Very Short Introduction*, Oxford: Oxford University Press.

Braun, E. (1982) *The Director and the Stage, From Naturalism to Grotowski*, London: Methuen.

Brecht. B. (1965/74) *The Messingkauf Dialogues*, trans. J. Willet, London: Methuen.

Brereton, A. (1908) *The Life of Henry Irving*, London: Longmans Green.

Browne, T. (1975) *Playwrights' Theatre: The English Stage Company at the Royal Court Theatre*, London: Pitman Publishing.

Brockett, O. (1995) *History of the Theatre*, 7th edn, Boston, MA, and London: Allyn & Bacon.

Cardwell, D. (1983) 'The Well-Made Play of Eugene Scribe', *The French Review*, 56:6 (May), 876–84.

Chambers, J. (1935) *D. H. Lawrence – A Personal Record*, London, Jonathan Cape.

Chothia, J. (1991) *André Antoine*, Cambridge: Cambridge University Press.

Chothia, J. (1996) *English Drama of the Early Modern Period 1890–1940*, London and New York: Longman.

Clarke, I. (1989) *Edwardian Drama*, London: Faber & Faber.

Cole, T. and Chinoy, H. [1953] (1970) *Directors on Directing*, New York: Crown.

Cole, T., ed. (1961) *Playwrights on Playwriting*, New York: Hill & Wang.

Delsarte, F. (1893) *Delsarte System of Oratory*, New York: Edgar S. Werner.

Desmond, A. and Moore, J. (1992) *Darwin*, Harmondsworth: Penguin.

Downer, A., ed. (1965) *American Drama and its Critics*, Chicago, IL: University of Chicago Press.

Dukes, A. (1926) *Drama*, London: Thornton Butterworth.

Elvgren Jr., G. A. (1974) 'Documentary Theatre at Stock-on-Trent', *Education Theatre Journal*, 26:1 (March).

Eyre, R and Wright, N. (2000) *Changing Stages*, London: Bloomsbury.

Fjelde, R. (1978) *The Makers of Modern Drama*, New York: Bantam.

Furst, L. R. and Skrine, P. N. (1971) *Naturalism: The Critical Idiom*, London: Methuen.

Gaskell, R. (1972) *Drama and Reality: The European Theatre since Ibsen*, London: Routledge & Kegan Paul.

Gaskill, W. (1988) *A Sense of Direction, Life at the Royal Court*, London: Faber & Faber.

Goodie, S. (1990) *Annie Horniman: A Pioneer in the Theatre*, London: Methuen.

Gottlieb, V. and Allain, P., eds (2002) *The Cambridge Companion to Chekhov*, Cambridge: Cambridge University Press.

Hammond W. and Steward, D., ed. (2008) *Verbatim Verbatim Contemporary Documentary Theatre,* London: Oberon Books.

Hartnoll, P. (1957) *The Oxford Companion to the Theatre*, Oxford: Oxford University Press.

Harvie, C., Martin, G. and Scharf, A. (1970) *Industrialisation and Culture 1830–1914*, London: Macmillan for the Open University.

Harwood, R. (1984) *All the World's a Stage*, London: Methuen.

Hayman, R. (1970) *Arnold Wesker*, London: Heinemann.

Hayman, R., ed. (1975) *The German Theatre*, London and New York: Oswald Wolff and Harper & Row.

Hammond W. and Steward, D., ed. (2008) *Verbatim Verbatim Contemporary Documentary Theatre*, London: George G. Harrap.

Herne, J. A. (1897) 'Art for Truth's Sake in the Drama', *Arena*, 17 (February), 361–70.

Hodgson. T. (1988) *The Batsford Dictionary of Drama*, London: Batsford.

Holdsworth, N. (2004), 'Case study: Ena Lamont Stewart's *Men Should Weep, 1947*, in B. Kershaw, ed., *The Cambridge History of British Theatre*, Volume 3, Cambridge: Cambridge University Press, 228–41.

Holmes, R. (1985) *Footsteps: Adventures of a Romantic Biographer*, London: Hodder & Stoughton.

Holmes, R. (2000) *Sidetracks – Explorations of a Romantic Biographer*, London: HarperCollins.

Holroyd, M. (2008) *A Strange Eventful History*, London: Chatto & Windus.

Innes, C., ed. (2000) *A Sourcebook on Naturalist Theatre*, London and New York: Routledge.

Jones, N., compiler (1986) *File on O'Casey*, London and New York: Methuen.

Kershaw, B. (2004) *The Cambridge History of British Theatre*, Volume 3: *Since 1895*, Cambridge: Cambridge University Press.

Koller, A. M. (1984) *The Theatre Duke: Georg II of Saxe-Meiningen and the German Stage*, Stanford, CA: Stanford University Press.

Koller, A. M. (1965) 'Ibsen and the Meininger', *Educational Theatre Journal*, 17.

Koon, H. and Switzer, R. (1980) *Eugene Scribe*, Boston, MA: Twayne Publishers.

Lacey, S. (1995) *British Realist Theatre – The New Wave in its Context 1956–1965*, London and New York: Routledge.

Latham. A., ed. (2011) *The Oxford Companion to Music*, Oxford: Oxford University Press.

Lidtke, V. L. (1974) 'Naturalism and Socialism in Germany', *American Historical Review*, 79, 14–37.

Little, R. and McLaughlin, E., (2007) *The Royal Court theatre Inside Out*, London: Oberon Books.

Löb, L. (1975) 'Domestic Tragedy – Realism and the Middle Classes', in R. Hayman, ed., *The German Theatre*, London: Oswald Wolff.

Lyman, J., ed. (1976) *Perspectives on Plays*, London: Routledge & Kegan Paul.

Magarshack, D. (1950) *Stanislavsky, A Life*, London: Macgibbon & Key.

Magarshack, D. (1953/1980) *Chekhov, A Life*, Westport, CT: Greenwood Press.

Magarshack, D. (1980) *Chekhov the Dramatist*, London and New York: Eyre Methuen.

Mander, G. (1975) 'Lessing and His Heritage', in R. Hayman, ed., *The German Theatre*, London: Oswald Wolff.

Martin, C. (2006) 'Bodies of Evidence', *The Drama Review*, 50:3.

Marowitz, C., Milne, T. and Halle O., eds (1965) *The Encore Reader, A Chronicle of the New Drama*, London: Methuen.

McDonald, J. (2004) 'Towards national identities: Theatre in Scotland', in B. Kershaw, ed., *The Cambridge History of British Theatre*, Volume 3, Cambridge: Cambridge University Press, 195–227.

Mehring, F. (1893) 'On Hauptmann's "The Weavers"', reproduced in *New Theatre Quarterly*, 11:42 (1995), 184–9.

Miller, A. (1931) *The Independent Theatre in Europe*, New York: Benjamin Blom.

Nemirovitch-Dantchenko, V. (1936) *My Life in the Russian Theatre*, trans. John Cournos, New York: Theatre Art Books.

Neville, H. et al. (1897) *Voice, Speech and Gesture*, London: Charles Deacon.

Nicoll, A. (1978) *British Drama*, London: Harrap.

Nietzsche, F. (1999) *The Birth of Tragedy*: Cambridge: Cambridge University Press.

Orme, M. (1936) *J. T. Grein, The Story of a Pioneer 1862–1935*, London: John Murray.

Osborne, J. (1975) 'From Political to Cultural Despotism: The making of the Saxe-Meiningen Aesthetic', *Theatre Quarterly*, 5:17.

Osborne, J. (1998) *Gerhart Hauptmann and the Naturalist Drama*, rev. edn, London: Routledge.

Paget, D. (1987) 'Verbatim Theatre: Oral History and Documentary Techniques', *New Theatre Quarterly*, III:12 (November).

Paxman, J. (2009) *The Victorians*, London: BBC Books.

Pickering, K. (2005) *Key Concepts in Drama and Performance*, Basingstoke: Palgrave Macmillan.

Pickering, K and Woolgar, M. (2009) *Theatre Studies*, Basingstoke: Palgrave Macmillan.

Pogson, R. (1952) *Miss Horniman and the Gaiety Theatre Manchester*, London: Rockliff.

Rebellato, D. (1999) *1956 And All That: The Making of Modern British Drama*, London and New York: Routledge.

Roberts, J. M. (1997) *The Penguin History of Europe*, Harmondsworth: Penguin Books.

Roberts, P. (1999) *The Royal Court Theatre and the Modern Stage*, Cambridge: Cambridge University Press.

Robinson, M., ed. (2009) *The Cambridge Companion to August Strindberg*, Cambridge: Cambridge University Press.

Rowell, G. and Jackson, A. (1984) *The Repertory Movement: A History of Regional Theatre in Britain*, Cambridge: Cambridge University Press.

Russell Taylor, J. (1962) *Anger & After: A Guide to the New British Theatre*, London: Methuen.

Russell Taylor, J. (1967) *The Rise and Fall of the Well-Made Play*, London: Methuen.

Sagar, K. (1985) *D. H. Lawrence: Life into Art*, Harmondsworth: Penguin Books.

Schumacher, C. (1990) *Zola, Thérèse Raquin*, Glasgow: University of Glasgow French and German Publications.

Schumacher, C. ed. (1996) *Naturalism and Symbolism in European Theatre: 1850–1918*, Cambridge: Cambridge University Press.

Shaw, G. B. (1913) *The Quintessence of Ibsenism*, London: Constable.

Shaughnessy, R. (1992), *Three Socialist Plays: Lear, Roots, Serjeant Musgrave's Dance*, Buckingham: Open University Press.

Shideler, R. (2009) '*Miss Julie*: Naturalism, "The Battle of the Brains" and sexual desire', in M. Robinson, ed., *The Cambridge Companion to August Strindberg*, Cambridge: Cambridge University Press.

Sklar, S. (1975) *The Plays of D. H. Lawrence: A Biographical and Critical Study*, New York: Barnes & Noble.

Skrine, P. (1989) *Hauptmann, Wedekind and Schnitzler*, London: Macmillan Education.

Smedmark, C.R. ed. (1966) *Essays on Strindberg*, Stockholm: Beckmans.

Sprinchorn, E. (1968) 'Strindberg and the Greater Naturalism', *The Drama Review*, 13:2, 119–29.

Stanislavsky, K. (1950/67) *On the Art of the Stage*, trans. D. Magarshack, London: Faber & Faber.

Stanislavski, K. (1980) *An Actor Prepares*, London: Methuen.

Stanislavsky, K (2008) Trs. Benedetti, J. *An Actor's Work*: containing *Building a Character*; *Creating a Role*, London: Routledge.

Stanislavsky, K. (2008) *My Life in Art*, trans. and ed. J. Benedetti, London and New York: Routledge.

Stokes, J. (1972) *Resistible Theatres: Enterprise and Experiment in the Late Nineteenth Century*, London: Paul Elek.

Storr, A. (2010) *Freud: A Very Short Introduction*, Oxford: Oxford University Press.

Strindberg, A. (1968) 'Psychic Murder (Apropos "Romersholm")', *The Drama Review*, 13:2.

Styan, J. L. (1981) *Modern Drama in Theory and Practice: Realism and Naturalism*, Cambridge: Cambridge University Press.

Symons, A. (1909) *Plays, Acting and Music – A Book of Theory*, London: Constable.

Turner, M., ed. (1972) *The Parlour Song Book*, London: Pan Books.

Walker, P. D. (1968) *Emile Zola*, London: Routledge & Kegan Paul.

Wardle, I. (1978) *The Theatres of George Devine*, London: Eyre Methuen.

WD. (1925) 'Two Plays, *Juno and the Paycock* and *The Shadow of a Gunman*. By Sean O'Casey, *Studies: An Irish Quarterly Review*, 14:55 (September), 493–5.

Wesker, A. (1994) *As Much as I Dare*, London: Century.

West, E. J. (1942) 'From a Players' to a Playwrights' Theatre', *The Quarterly Journal of Speech*, XXVII.

Williams R. (1976) *Keywords: A Vocabulary of Culture and Society*, London: Fontana.

Williams, R. (1980) 'Social Environment and Theatrical Environment – The Case of English Naturalism', in R. Williams, *Problems in Materialism and Culture: Selected Essays*, London: Verso.

Williams, R. (1987), *Drama from Ibsen to Brecht*, London: Hogarth Press.

Williams, R. (1989) *The Politics of Modernism : Against the New Conformists*, London: Verso.

Woodworth, R. (1931) *Contemporary Schools of Psychology*, London: Methuen.

Worthen, J. (1991) *D. H. Lawrence The Early Years 1885–1911*, Cambridge: Cambridge University Press.

Worthen, J. (2001) 'Lawrence as Dramatist', in A. Fernihough, ed., *The Cambridge Companion to D. H. Lawrence*, Cambridge: Cambridge University Press.

Worthen, W. B., ed. (2004) *The Wadsworth Anthology of Drama*, 4th edn, London: Cengage Learning.

Zola, E. (1893) *The Experimental Novel and Other Essays*, trans. B. M. Sherman, Cassell Publishing (reprint Forgotten Books and available online).

Zola, E. (1962) *Thérèse Raquin*, trans L. Tancock, Harmondsworth: Penguin Books.

Zola, E. (1969) *Oeuvres Complètes*: Vol. 15, *Théâtre et Poèms* (Preface trans. R.W. Strang).

Zola, E. (1992) *Thérèse Raquin*, trans. A. Rothwell, Oxford: Oxford University Press.

Index